Rethinking Peripheral Modernisms

Katia Pizzi · Roberta Gefter Wondrich
Editors

Rethinking Peripheral Modernisms

Editors
Katia Pizzi
Institute of Languages, Cultures
and Societies
University of London
London, UK

Roberta Gefter Wondrich ⓘ
Department of Humanities
University of Trieste
Trieste, Italy

ISBN 978-3-031-35545-5   ISBN 978-3-031-35546-2   (eBook)
https://doi.org/10.1007/978-3-031-35546-2

© The Editor(s) (if applicable) and The Author(s), under exclusive license to Springer Nature Switzerland AG 2024

This work is subject to copyright. All rights are solely and exclusively licensed by the Publisher, whether the whole or part of the material is concerned, specifically the rights of translation, reprinting, reuse of illustrations, recitation, broadcasting, reproduction on microfilms or in any other physical way, and transmission or information storage and retrieval, electronic adaptation, computer software, or by similar or dissimilar methodology now known or hereafter developed.
The use of general descriptive names, registered names, trademarks, service marks, etc. in this publication does not imply, even in the absence of a specific statement, that such names are exempt from the relevant protective laws and regulations and therefore free for general use.
The publisher, the authors, and the editors are safe to assume that the advice and information in this book are believed to be true and accurate at the date of publication. Neither the publisher nor the authors or the editors give a warranty, expressed or implied, with respect to the material contained herein or for any errors or omissions that may have been made. The publisher remains neutral with regard to jurisdictional claims in published maps and institutional affiliations.

Cover credit: Fox Photos/Stringer

This Palgrave Macmillan imprint is published by the registered company Springer Nature Switzerland AG
The registered company address is: Gewerbestrasse 11, 6330 Cham, Switzerland

Paper in this product is recyclable.

PREFACE

In 2008, Douglas Mao and Rebecca Walkowics charted a 'transnational turn' in modernist studies as a development which had produced "at least three kinds of new work in the field: scholarship that widens the Modernist archive by arguing for the inclusion of a variety of alternative traditions [...] scholarship that argues for the centrality of transnational circulation and translation in the production of modernist art and scholarship that examines how Modernists responded to Imperialism, engaged in projects of anticolonialism, and designed new models of transnational community".[1] It is within this widened prospect, which came to question the persistent Eurocentrism of earlier modernist studies, that all the contributors of this volume take stance, and variously stress the place of modernist studies in a 'global' *and* plural perspective, which captures the distinctive trajectories of specific economic, political, and historic predicaments across the world. Multiplicity, plurality, and porousness are very recurrent concepts in critical reflections on literary and cultural modernity which can at times turn into buzzwords, but the essays of this volume actually invigorate them by probing into their centrality to a contemporary examination of the nature of Modernisms.

[1] Douglas Mao and Rebecca L. Walkowitz, 'The New Modernist Studies', *PMLA* 123/3 (2008): 737–749, 737; 739.

vi   PREFACE

Rethinking Peripheral Modernisms thus implies a critical reappraisal of different centres as they interact with each other in a plural and disseminated Modernism conceived as a transnational, transcultural, and translational phenomenon. This focus sheds light on the progressive enlargement of the centre/periphery binary into a plurality of centres, and could be seen as in keeping with the concepts of 'travelling culture'(Clifford), and of Edouard Glissant's poetics of relation, which have been distinctive of the postcolonial.

In her opening pages, Katia Pizzi offers a wide-ranging introduction, as she examines the complexity of any definition of peripherality in relation to Modernism/s by reconstructing some crucial theoretical clusters, and firmly posits it as a constituent of Modernism's history and agenda. She mentions the most significant reconceptualisations in the field of modernist studies which expanded the critical perspectives in a transdisciplinary and transnational/global direction reaching beyond both geographical determinism and capitalism as determinants, and considered postcolonialism. Pizzi points to the crucial question that British modernism imported the most advanced form of revolutionary Modernism, namely Futurism, from a country in the semi-periphery of industrialization such as Italy. Her analysis, which starts with a reference to Trotsky's notion of 'geographical differential', highlights the debated prominence of relatively backward countries in the development of the most advanced and innovative expressions of modernism as related to "the coexistence of incipient capitalist and pre-capitalist modes of production". Backwardness thus proves to be a kind of hermeneutic privilege in interpreting the evolving historical realities of the twentieth century, as in the case of Italy's Futurism. Pizzi knowingly elaborates the term (semi)'peripheral', inaugurating a shared concern of the volume, as all the chapters explore and question the very definition of a peripheral status, not so much in relation to geo-historical and cultural conditions, as, first and foremost, to the very notion of modernity in its inextricably cultural determination.

The relevance of peripheries and semi-peripheries created by the global spread of capitalism, diagnosed by the late Benita Parry, whose essay represents an invaluable staple to the present volume, is also duly referred to by Pizzi as she considers the literary representations of these peripheral cultures. Her statement of purpose in the introduction posits her "primary intent in this volume" as "to bring to the fore the comparative and international vocation of Modernism and, with it, the transcultural and translational project underpinning its multiple forms", as is testified by Modernisms in countries like Australia and Iran, examined in two chapters by, respectively, Marilena Parlati and Nigel Westbrook and Ali Mozaffari. This points to the necessity of a plural notion of Modernism as Modernisms, which the title of this volume proclaims.

The different critical approaches adopted by the contributors thus encompass questions, practices, and perspectives of postcoloniality and post-modernism, globalism and localism, binarisms and de-centredness, diasporic movements, contaminations and interrogations of 'tradition', and straddle different cultural languages and media, from literature—its primary medium—to cinema, photography, art, and architecture.

Rethinking Peripheral Modernisms is structured in three parts which are dialogically connected: the first, **"Modernism and Peripherality: Theoretical Considerations"**, engages with the paradigms of peripherality and modernity in two chapters by Maria-Irene Ramalho-Santos and the late Benita Parry which discuss, respectively, the very notion of peripherality in (peripheral) modernism and the 'stylistic irrealism' in peripheral literatures in relation to modernity.

Citing Deleuze's dictum "Il n'y a que des mots inexacts pour désigner quelque chose exactement" as epigraph, Ramalho sets forth focussing on the importance of the impossibly univocal designation of 'Modernism', as she (irresistibly) announces: "For students of Modernism, Modernism is never *exactly* Modernism". Not wishing to discard modernism as a 'period', though, Ramalho reminds that "(t)radition and resistance to tradition are two sides of the same coin. Just like center and periphery", and recalls her own *Translocal Modernism* (2008) to consider the problematic nature of 'periphery' itself as one that entails the reality of the centre and its discontent with modernisation, technological development, and infinite progress. Objecting limiting and univocal definitions, Ramalho rather stresses the continuity of modernist innovativeness, and opts for the "inexact word *Modernism* to refer to the permanent revolution in literature and the arts which, being *permanent*, has always been happening at all times and places in many different ways". Choosing poetry as her main genre, she dwells on the distance between modernity and contemporaneity as concepts, referring to Paul de Man's idea that "literature has always been essentially modern", while, according to Giorgio Agamben, the contemporary is, "untimely" and poetry is always already untimely in its resisting conceptualisation. Thus, she considers poetry's anxiety about the impossible exactitude of language and the

viii   PREFACE

impossibility of language to utter truth referring to a host of poets, from the American Hart Crane and Gertrude Stein to the Brazilian João Guimarães Rosa, the Portuguese Fernando Pessoa, and the Peruvian César Vallejo.

The closing pages of Ramalho's thought-provoking reflections on the aporias of defining Modernism delve into the instability of the language as a distinctly modernist trait, pointing to Pessoa's notion of *intervalo* as "signifying presence and absence at one and the same time (...)", the sign of the Pessoan enigma of disquietude, a space between, and mentions Kafka's baffling Odradek as a figure of Modernism's unstable, undecidable, linguistic and un/real status, but also as an enigma that amount to no less than language itself. Benita Parry's "Stylistic irrealism in Peripheral literatures as Symptom, Mediation and critique of Modernity"[2] also charts an authoritative overview of the most important recent critical reappraisals of Modernism which broadened its genealogy and temporalities, as a capitalist, non-western (mainly anglophone), pre-globalising transnational phenomenon. As a starting point, Parry stresses the importance of considering the category of periphery as "an element of capitalism's formation", rather than a matter of cultural hierarchy. She refers to the most important Marxist theorists who debated the relationship between capitalism across different socio-economic temporalities, which she identifies in "the entire zone of periphery and semi-periphery—the latter including Russia before and since the Revolution, the now disintegrated Austro-Hungarian Empire, pre-and modern China, Japan, Eastern and Southern Europe". Stressing the nature of modernity as a temporal condition, Parry refers to several critics (Harotoonian, Amir, Jameson) who consider modernity in relation to capitalism as global but "necessarily of infinite variety", and mentions attempts to uncouple modernity from Modernism and to dismantle oppositions between realism and modernism. The question of realism is then central to her theoretical elaboration: following Adorno's critique of Lukács, Parry questions the anti-realism of modernism suggesting that this and realism should be recognised as permeable modes. She borrows from Marxist critic Michael Löwy the notion of critical 'irrealism' and Timothy Brennan's 'homiletic realism' for a literature founded on the logic of that imagination, which is nonetheless alert to a critique of social reality, and offers a reading of "Xala" (1974), a novella by the Senegalese writer and filmmaker Ousmane Sembéne, as a case study which illuminates "the metamorphosis of an historical moment into aesthetic form".

The second section of the volume, **"Liminality in the 'semi-peripheries'"**, includes three essays devoted to literary articulations of urban peripheral centres of Modernism from across the globe, from the formerly settler colony of Australia (Parlati) to Dublin's modern 'peripherealities' (Gefter Wondrich) to the 'untranslatable' Trieste, a 'double periphery' which became one of the great literary cities of Europe (Pizzi).

The question of the "When, Where and How" of Australian modernism inaugurates Parlati's chapter, "Australian Modernisms strike back, or still Harping on 'Margins'", which considers two important Australian women writers, Christina Stead and Eleanor Dark, and their work dedicated to Sydney as a hub of modernist innovation. Parlati joins Pizzi and Parry in referring to Stanford Friedman's claim for a "full spatialization of modernism [which] changes the map, the canon, and the periodization of modernism dramatically", and focusses on some versions of "settler modernisms", i.e. the white Australian modernism that "both mark and depart from the centre-periphery frame", thus similarly opting for the *transformative* rather than 'peripheral' quality of the alternative modernism of Australia, New Zealand, and Canada. With the sacrifice of its young men in the Great War, Australia gained the international credit that its origins as Britain's penal colony had foreclosed, but after the end of the conflict it also underwent a nostalgic and reactionary cultural politics that turned it into a "quarantined culture" (J.F.Williams) adverse to artistic Modernism in the name of a bond with the English 'Mother Land' and its own specificity. In the interwar decades, thus, Australia was still affected by a condition of belatedness, and hovered between modern, antimodern, and modernist, with many writers expatriating to Europe and to North America. Two directions of Australian modernism are analysed in the essay: the expatriation to the British 'homeland' through the trope of the 'journey in' (as in the case of Christina Stead) or the choice to remain, as in Eleanor Dark's case. Stead and Dark's lives and work articulate both distance and proximity to modernity, set against the Australian primal scene of European settlement and the encounter with the Indigenous, through the Sidney of slums and suburban spaces as a centre of cosmopolitan modernity in *Seven Poor Men of Sydney* (1934,) and "the intricacies of colonial, national and transnational discourse" dramatised in *Waterway (1938)*.

Roberta Gefter Wondrich's "'From the Periphery of the Metropolis': on Joyce's Modern/ist Irish Peripherealities" focusses on a specific figuration of Joyce's Dublin as one of the centres (i.e. capitals) of modernist literature despite (or also thanks to) its economic and industrial peripherality. Ireland's tormented history of emancipation was to award Dublin a political prominence in (post)colonial modernity. Joyce's conception of periphery as both intrinsically dynamic and open, connected, porous, and in keeping with his "celebratory sense of urban life" (Alter) takes shape in *Ulysses* through a nexus of the modern, the peripheral, and the utopian in two fantasies: the "new Bloomusalem" in "Circe", Bloom's fantasmagoric, multicultural, and multireligious utopian Ireland, and, above all, the fancy, hypermodern suburban residence of 'Flowerville', in the seventeenth episode of *Ulysses*, "Ithaca", one of the most important of Joyce's whole work to tackle a critique of Irish modernity as a *peripheral* modernity. The architectural absurdism of this suburban utopia thus conveys a debunking of the nineteenth-century burgeois conception of the residence as an expression and container of the subject. As a fantasy aspiring to a connectedness between the margin, the core, and an imagined open world-picture, 'Flowerville' is then much more than a parenthesis in a complex chapter, but an important signifier of Joyce's inventive and provocative reflection on the modernity of Ireland as metrocolonial and peripheral.

The critical awareness of modernism as plural, both temporally, spatially, and linguistically, hence as challenging established notions of centre and periphery, is once more recalled by Katia Pizzi in her chapter on "The Literature of Trieste and the Perils of Peripherality", which opens referring to theorists like Jameson, Parry, Doyle, and Winkle, who have all argued for an understanding of Modernism in a peripheral framework. The case of northern Italy, with many Futurists who chose to expatriate after the First World War, and a number of avant-garde literati who were active in Trieste and at the extreme north-eastern borders of Italy, stands as a remarkable showcase for the restless mobility of a peripheral Modernism in which a very special outcrop of literary creativity stemmed out of the admixture of languages and cultures of this contact zone of the Habsburg Empire. As a 'double periphery', or 'the periphery of a periphery', given its peripherality both to Italy and to the imperial centre, Trieste became a crossroads of 'fractured identities' (Foot) in Joyce's and Svevo's time. There, "issues of internal colonialism, translation and inequality, predicated upon ethnicity, nationality and language, imbricated as they were with identity, were paramount", and made it both a conduit for Modernism's spread to Italy and a generator of literary innovations. By contrast, since the early 1920s' Fascist nationalistic and anti-slavic politics

PREFACE xi

restricted Trieste's multicultural vocation, shrinking it into a peripherality that was both 'central' and 'double', its artistic cultures rarely cross paths between the (prevailing) Italian majority and the Slovenian and Croatian minority groups. Pizzi's essay explores the dynamics whereby different linguistic and cultural peripheral modernisms—Slovenian and Italian—remained non-dialogical in the literary city of Trieste that saw its extraordinary potential remain, under many respects, a kind of a 'crucible manqué'(Apih) because of the prevalence of nationalist Italian politics over identitarian contaminations and proximities. The literature and history of Trieste thus represents a unique and paradoxical case of modernism in the contact zones that were also peripheral.

The third section of the volume, **"Metropolis, Technology, Cultural Transfer"**, weaves several strands which were considered in the previous chapters together, such as the metropolitan dimension, the fascination with and the impact of technology and the cultural contaminations and enforced confrontations that have invariably characterised peripheral literary cultures and artistic expressions. This is by far the most 'global' section, as it examines Russian, Brazilian, and Iranian modernisms, in this latter case analysing different forms of temporal peripherality, as in late twentieth-century Iran.

Andreas Kramer focusses on aspects of the geographical imaginations of the Russian avant-garde, before and after the 1917 Revolution, that engaged with the liminal spatial identity of the country between East and West. In these figurations the centre/periphery notion was conceived through the notion of "territorial nationality" as a "normative condition of modernity". The examples he considers—from the writer Vladimir Klebnikov, the film director Sergei Eisenstein and the writer and photographer Sergei Tret'iakov's work—all question and illuminate the centre/periphery model engaged in the "twin processes of artistic modernism and politico-economic modernization". Space is pivotal in these experimental productions: in his "transrational" poetry Khlebnikov pursues an 'active' relationship to Russian space, earth, and landscape, which strains towards a fusion of all Slavic words together, repudiating the traditional primacy of the Europeanized West over the underdeveloped South, the Asiatic East, and the great North of the country. A kind of heterotopian imagination that emphasises the "slippage between the spaces of order and disorder" which has characterised the poetics of (peripheral) literary modernisms can be identified in his poetry, and is also shared by Eisenstein's filmography, showing the Russian periphery as undergoing

xii   PREFACE

transformation but also resisting to complete (modernising) sovietization. A documentary "literature of fact" recalls the ur-question of realism in Tret'iakov's "factographic aesthetics" with regard to the visual perception and representation of the landscape. Kramer's essay thus shows how the pre- and post-revolutionary Russian modernist aesthetics used a heterotopic and non-normative geographical imagination to question the idea of the centre in relation to territorial political and ideological control.

The matrix of European modernism morphs into a transatlantic transfer in Patricia Silva's "Brazilian Modernists and the Avant-Garde: Transcultural Modernism in the Postcolonial", which considers "the re-casting and re-framing of avant-garde motifs and procedures deployed by three representative figures of Brazilian modernism" and claims a place for Brazilian modernism in the world-scale, early twentieth-century remapping of Modernisms. The nexus between Modernism and nationalism, prominent, for instance, in the European case of Ireland, is reconfigured in the postcolonial dimension of Brazil, as Silva argues that "the Brazilian modernists' aesthetic positioning, artistic practices and creative output constitute early and particularly productive instances of transcultural transposition in a postcolonial context, exhibiting exemplary traits of peripheral modernisms occurring in such contexts and anticipating subsequent theorizations in peripheral and postcolonial studies". The representation and critique of asymmetries arising from uneven modernisation and cultural (neo)colonialism in Mário de Andrade and Oswald de Andrade's poetry and Tarsila do Amaral's art are analysed "as case studies of the dynamics of aesthetic modernism in a peripheral postcolonial context", and these artists' projects as attempts to break with 'mental colonialism'. Brazilian primitivism, the "Manifesto Antropófago" and the Brazilwood Poetry Manifesto are key cultural statements of awareness and resistance which show how Brazilian modernists reconceptualised the concept of periphery in relation to modernity in the terms of hybridity and heterogeneity, authenticity, and postcoloniality.

The question of resistance and the engagement with 'tradition' that is so interestingly related to peripheral modernity, and central to Eastern and Western transatlantic expressions of Modernism, broaches a heterogeneous latitude, both geographical, cultural, and religiously connoted, as that of Iran, in the last chapter, Ali Mozaffari and Nigel Westbrook's "Degrees of Peripherality: the Rhetoric of Architecture in Late 20th Century Iran". Their contribution reinforces the centrality of spatial politics and imagination in the discourses of Modernism, and specifically of architecture itself (a role that is also hinted at in the literary analysis of the absurdism that informs Joyce's Flowerville in "Ithaca"). Mozaffari and Westbrook chart the history of Iranian modern architecture as one of engagement with Western modernity and the resistance to it through the claim for the essentialist authenticity of local tradition, which eventually lacked the true form of dialogism that is characteristic of peripheral modernisms. The authors explore the "question of peripherality as resistance within architecture", in considering two stages through which Iranian architects and theorists dealt with the question of cultural authenticity in the face of globalising Western influence, namely the discourses of cultural identity raised in the inaugural International Congress of Architects held in 1970 and the competition for the Iranian Academies, which constituted a watershed for post-Revolution Iranian architecture. The approaches considered in the chapter are marked by the attempt to attune the call of modernisation with an ideological reclamation of local Islamic tradition and heritage in search of an essentialist conception of authenticity. This, eventually, often turned to be in keeping with that Postmodernist historicism which recombined the historical and the archaic with the contemporary into a mode of anachronism, along with "elements of the centre and the periphery". Some of these attitudes would have been conceived in terms of "Critical Regionalism", a form of architectural Modernism as "self-consciously peripheral" in its most valid principles, which argued for the fruitful and conscious adaptation of foreign forms and techniques within the periphery, and which, albeit critical of modern critical legacy, is nonetheless aware of its emancipatory aspects. An adaptation which proved to be a misinterpretation, as the Academies' competitions did not produce models or projects that successfully employed Western models in the formation of a local "language", and rather opted for "mimicry or repetition". Iranian architecture was thus beset by an "intellectual failure" to recognise the global context of its condition, and rather sank into an "inward-looking and nostalgic fundamentalism" that did not valorise the potentialities of Iran's peripherality.

The last chapter thus foregrounds and confirms the political value and agency of peripherality as a condition which fostered modernist discourses across the world, as well as dialogism and resistance, in their complex, at times contradictory interplay. As Marshall Berman famously pointed out, "(a)ll forms of Modernist art and thought have a dual character: they are at once expressions and protests against the process of Modernization"[2]; this coexistence of aspiration and resistance has been variously interrogated throughout this volume, and has emerged from the different critical perspectives that were considered. Thus, while on the side of historical and spatial conditions current reflections seem to have partly updated Harootunian's definition of "peripheral" as "understood only as a relationship to the centers of capitalism before World War II",[3] it could be argued that, perhaps, the deepest significance of 'peripheral' in relation to Modernism/s as, among others, a source of resilience, can still be traced back to its ancient etymology, as περιφέρω means to carry round, but also to transfer, to refer, to shift but also to survive, to endure.[4]

Trieste, Italy

Roberta Gefter Wondrich

[2] Marshall Berman, *All that is Solid Melts into Air* (London: Penguin, 1988), 235.

[3] Harry Harootunian, *History's Disquiet. Modernity, Cultural Practice and the Question of Everyday Life.* (New York: Columbia UP: 2000, 62).

[4] Henry George Liddel & Robert Scott, *A Greek-English Lexicon.* Oxford: Oxford University Press (1843) 1996, 1392.

CONTENTS

Introduction Katia Pizzi	1

Modernism and Peripherality: Theoretical Considerations

A Departure from Modernism: Stylistic Strategies in Modern Peripheral Literatures as Symptom, Mediation and Critique of Modernity Benita Parry	15
What is Peripheral about Peripheral Modernisms? Maria-Irene Ramalho-Santos	43

Liminality in the 'Semi-peripheries'

The Literature of Trieste and the Perils of Peripherality Katia Pizzi	61
"From the Periphery of the Metropolis": On Joyce's Modern/ist Irish Peripherealities Roberta Gefter Wondrich	77
Do Australian Modernisms Strike Back? Still Harping on 'Margins' Marilena Parlati	99

xv

xvi CONTENTS

Metropolis, Technology, Cultural Transfer

**Geographies of Peripheral Modernism: The Case
of the Russian Avant-Garde (Khlebnikov, Eisenstein,
Tretyakov)**   121
Andreas Kramer

**Brazilian Modernists and the Avant-Garde: Transcultural
Modernism in the Postcolonial Periphery**   141
Patrícia Silva

**Degrees of Peripherality: The Rhetoric of Architecture
in Late Twentieth-Century Iran**   163
Nigel Westbrook and Ali Mozaffari

Index   193

Notes on Contributors

Andreas Kramer is Professor of German and Comparative Literature at Goldsmiths, University of London. He has written extensively on twentieth-century German-language literature in its international and interdisciplinary contexts, with a particular emphasis on Expressionism, Dada, the European avant-garde, literature and film, and literature and sport. Recent books include the monograph *Sport und literarischer Expressionismus* (2019) and a collection of essays, *Sport and the European Avant-Garde (1900–1945)*, co-edited with Przemysław Strożek (2022). His current research is on geographical imaginations of the European Avant-Garde.

Ali Mozaffari is Australian Research Council Fellow and Senior Research Fellow with the Alfred Deakin Institute, Deakin University, Melbourne. his most recent publications include Mozaffari, A. and Westbrook, N., 2020. *Development, architecture, and the formation of heritage in late twentieth-century Iran: A vital past.* Manchester University Press.

Marilena Parlati is Professor of British and Anglophone Literatures at the University of Padua (Italy). Her main areas of research are Anglophone and Australian literatures and cultures of the long nineteenth century, namely thing culture, commodity culture, and waste issues; she also works on contemporary fiction related to trauma, disability, environmental and postcolonial cultural issues, suspended and altered embodiment, with

xviii NOTES ON CONTRIBUTORS

a book on these issues forthcoming, and essays on Jim Crace, Hanif Kureishi, J.M. Coetzee, Eva Figes, Rosa Cappiello, and Christos Tsiolkas.

Benita Parry (1931–2020) was Emerita Professor in English and Comparative Literary Studies at the University of Warwick. One of the founding theorists of postcolonialism, Parry has written on the imperial and colonial literatures, peripheral modernisms, and postcolonial studies. Her monographs include *Delusions and Discoveries: Studies on India in the British Imagination* (Verso, 1972, 1998), *Conrad and Imperialism: Ideological Boundaries and Visionary Frontiers* (Palgrave, 1984), and *Postcolonial Studies: A Materialist* Critique (Routledge, 2004).

Katia Pizzi is Director of the Italian Cultural Institute in London and Senior Lecturer in Italian Studies at the Institute of Languages, Cultures and Societies, School of Advanced Study, University of London. Pizzi published extensively on the Italian Futurist avant-garde, especially technology and machines, the literature, history, and cultural memory of the Italian North-Eastern borders, urban cultures in modernity, and Modernist android cultures. Pizzi's recent volume-length publications include *Italian Futurism and the Machine* (Manchester University Press, 2019); *Trieste. Una frontiera letteraria* (Vita Activa, 2019); and *Pinocchio, Puppets and Modernity: The Mechanical Body* (Routledge, 2012).

Maria-Irene Ramalho-Santos is Professor Emerita of English, American Studies, and Feminist Studies at the Faculty of Letters, University of Coimbra, where she was scientific coordinator of the doctoral programs in American Studies and Feminist. From 1999 to 2019 she was visiting professor at the University of Wisconsin-Madison. She has published extensively on English language literature and culture (with a special focus on American poetry), as well as on American studies, comparative literature, poetic theory, cultural studies, and feminist studies. Her current research interests include problems of modernity and modernism, comparative poetics, poetry and philosophy, theories of American studies, and theories of feminism. Her latest publication is *Fernando Pessoa and the Lyric. Disquietude, Rumination, Interruption, Inspiration, Constellation.* Lanham, MD: Lexington Books (2022).

Patrícia Silva is research fellow at CES, Centre for Social Studies, University of Coimbra. Her research in comparative studies focusses on cultural networks and exchanges between literary and artistic movements in Brazil and in Portugal, and between these and European and Anglo-American ones. Centring on processes and contexts of reception, translation, and transcreation characteristic of Modernism understood as a transcultural phenomenon. She holds a Ph.D. in Portuguese & Brazilian Studies from King's College London (2009), was a visiting lecturer at the University of Cambridge (2010–2012) and University College London (2012–2013), and Queen Mary, University of London (2013–2018). She has published on Modernism, Lusophone Studies, Comparative Literature, Cultural History, (Inter)cultural and Interarts Studies, and Visual Cultures. In 2020 she published *Yeats and Pessoa: Parallel Poetic Styles* (Routledge).

Nigel Westbrook is Associate Professor at the University of Western Australia School of Design, Perth. Recent publications include A. Mozaffari and N. Westbrook, 2020. *Development, architecture, and the formation of heritage in late twentieth-century Iran: A vital past*, Manchester: Manchester University Press; L. Mulvin and N. Westbrook, 2019. *Late Antique Palatine Architecture: Palaces and Palace Culture: Patterns of Transculturation*, ed. L, Architectural Crossroads: Studies in the History of Architecture, vol. 5, Turnhout, Belgium: Brepols Publishers; N. Westbrook, 2019. *The Great Palace in Constantinople: An Architectural Interpretation*, Architectural Crossroads, vol. 2, Turnhout Belgium: Brepols Publishers.

Roberta Gefter Wondrich is Associate Professor in English Literature at the University of Trieste (Italy) and Editor in chief of *Prospero–A Journal of foreign literatures and cultures*. Her field of interests include the contemporary Anglophone and Irish novel, on which she has written a book and many articles, neo-Victorianism, biofiction, James Joyce, J. M. Coetzee, thing theory and culture, and sea narratives. Among her recent publications are book chapters in *Sea Narratives: Cultural Responses to the Sea, 1600-present* (Palgrave 2016), in *Neo-Victorian Biofictions* (Brill-Rodopi, 2020), and in *Cosmopolitan Italy in the Age of Nations* (Routledge, 2022), and articles in *The European Journal of English Studies* and *Between*. She is currently completing a monograph on the cultural object in contemporary English fiction.

LIST OF FIGURES

Brazilian Modernists and the Avant-Garde: Transcultural Modernism in the Postcolonial Periphery

Fig. 1 A Caipirinha (1923)   152
Fig. 2 Estrada de Ferro central do Brasil (Central Railway of Brazil 1924)   155

Introduction

Katia Pizzi

When I began to think about editing this collection, echoes of the 100th anniversary celebrations of Filippo Tommaso Marinetti's *Founding and Manifesto of Futurism* were resonating widely. Italian Futurism has frequently been taken as a point of departure to interrogate some of the issues raised in this volume. *Futurismo* provided, and, to some extent, continues to provide, barring of course geographic determinism and an equally reductive reliance on capitalism as a heuristic, useful lessons in alternative modes of development and geographical displacement which help interrogate 'peripheral' angles of the Modernist phenomenon.

In a plethora of pronouncements,[1] Marinetti had petulantly attributed to *Futurismo* the primacy over a vocal progeny: Orphism, Dadaism, Simultaneism, Purism, Zenithism, Vorticism, Surrealism, Creationism, Cubo-futurism, Expressionism, Constructivism, Suprematism, Ultraism, Imaginism, to name but a few. Although its strategic launch in Paris

---

[1] Several pronouncements are recorded in Filippo Tommaso Marinetti, *Teoria e invenzione futurista*, ed. Luciano De Maria (Milan: Mondadori, 1996), *passim.*

K. Pizzi (✉)
Institute of Languages, Cultures and Societies, School of Advanced Study, University of London, London, UK
e-mail: katia.pizzi@sas.ac.uk

© The Author(s), under exclusive license to Springer Nature Switzerland AG 2024
K. Pizzi and R. Gefter Wondrich (eds.), *Rethinking Peripheral Modernisms*, https://doi.org/10.1007/978-3-031-35546-2_1

enabled its swift diffusion across Europe, the movement enjoyed a degree of geographical specificity, thriving in specific local clusters across the regions of Italy. If, on the one hand, Marinetti's privileged access to a major centre of European artistic production and to mass means of cultural dissemination afforded Futurism the cosmopolitan status of international movement, on the other hand its national origin and regional expressions reflect the atomisation and cultural decentring which characterise other avant-garde movements in the early twentieth century. The latter phenomenon stems, to a great extent, from the ascendancy of cultural nationalisms, or what Paul Peppis calls 'the Age of Nationalism'. According to Peppis:

> many of the young artists and writers who constituted the avant-garde movements [...] shared an acute sensitivity to evidence of uneven development in the cultural sphere. The avantgardists responded to their perceptions of cultural inequality in much the same way that European governments responded to their perceived economic, industrial and military inequalities: they would bring nationalism to the aid of advanced art.[2]

The 'perceptions of cultural inequality' Peppis identifies as catalysts to the majority of early avant-garde movements reflect, in turn, more generalised inequalities apparent in the society of the time.

As early as 1924, Trotsky highlighted significant asymmetries between economic status and impact in the cultural field, arguing that 'the backward countries ... reflected in their ideology the achievements of the advanced countries more brilliantly and strongly'.[3] Providing Futurism as example, he claims the movement 'obtained its most brilliant expression, not in America and not in Germany, but in Italy and Russia'.[4]

While pertinently objecting to Trotsky's 'questionable form of geographic determinism'—evident in the terminology used, namely 'backward' and 'advanced', Martin Puchner, in appraising the pre-war

---

[2] Paul Peppis, *Literature, Politics, and the English Avant-Garde: Nation and Empire (1901–1918)* (Cambridge: Cambridge University Press, 2000), 5.

[3] Leon Trotsky, *Literature and Revolution* (1924), cit. in 'The Aftershocks of *Blast*: Manifestos, Satire, and the Rear-Guard of Modernism', in *Bad Modernisms*, ed. Douglas Mao & Rebecca Walkowitz (Durham and London: Duke UP, 2006), 44–67 (46).

[4] *Ibid.*

Modernist moment in Britain, recuperated Trotsky's notion of 'geographical differential [...] to pose the question of why British Modernism would have to import the latest and most advanced form of revolutionary Modernism, namely Futurism, from a country at the semi-periphery of industrialization such as Italy'.[5] According to Trotsky's thesis, Puchner argues, in the first decades of the twentieth century 'Russian and Italian Futurists are the most advanced artistic movements precisely because these two countries are torn between a still dominant traditional peasantry and small pockets of industrialization'.[6] What is implied, therefore, is that the dynamic, innovative quality of artistic movements emerging in regions considered to be (semi)peripheral, in terms of economic development at the time of their appearance, is causally linked to the coexistence of incipient capitalist and pre-capitalist modes of production in those regions.

Trotsky's early account of spatial and temporal asymmetries between modernity and Modernism also echoed in Fredric Jameson's 'The End of Temporality'. Here Jameson describes Modernism as a 'culture of incomplete modernization' and ascribes 'the emergence of the various Modernisms' to the 'partially industrialized and defeudalized social order' prevalent 'in most European countries until the end of World War II'.[7] According to Jameson, the first European Modernists experienced both modern and traditional realities in varying degrees depending on the level of modernisation of their country, which effectively corresponds to the geographical differential in Trotsky's account of the emergence of Futurism in Italy and Russia.

Other prior contributions to Modernist studies demonstrated that this phenomenon extends beyond Europe, reflecting the global spread of capitalism and the association between its expansive reach and modernity noted by Jameson.[8] In attempting to outline its breadth in 'Aspects of Peripheral Modernisms', the late Benita Parry argued that:

---

[5] *Ibid.*

[6] *Ibid.*

[7] F. Jameson, 'The End of Temporaility', *Critical Inquiry*, 29:4 (2003), 695–718, (699). Puchner criticises Jameson for failing to mention Trotsky in this regard. See also Jameson, *Postmodernism: or the Cultural Logic of Late Capitalism* (London: Verso, 1991), 309–310.

[8] Jameson, *A Singular Modernity: Essay on the Ontology of the Present* (New York: Verso, 2013), 5.

4   K. PIZZI

> Since capitalist penetration was and remains global, the peripheries and semi-peripheries of core capitalism extended and still extend to a larger geo-political expanse than the colonized regions, all occupying a shared position of structural underdevelopment within an uneven and unequal world system once dominated by the nation-states of North Western Europe, later overshadowed by the super-power of the USA, and now undergoing further reconfigurations.

The value of understanding these spaces as being 'the rest of the world' and including Eastern and Middle Europe, Turkey, Ireland, Scotland, Spain, Iceland, etc., is that it facilitates the search for affinities amongst the many and different peripheral modernities, and by extension the experiences of these as re-presented in literature.[9]

This notwithstanding, Parry also adds that 'any inquiry into the generic modes and stylistic mannerisms of modern peripheral literatures since the nineteenth century is inseparable from considering the distinctive experiences of *modernity* in spaces *outside* Western Europe and North America, but *within* an Imperialist world-system'.[10] In the opening essay of this volume, Parry further maintains that, if Modernism is temporally uneven, as posited by Jameson, its unevenness is more acutely felt on the fringes of the capitalist world system, since 'the "simultaneity of the non-simultaneous" was for longer structural to peripheral societies, and continues to be so'.[11] Hence, the phenomenon identified by Jameson is exacerbated in the peripheries where, claims Parry, the sustained temporal asymmetries resulting from a belated or protracted modernity account for 'the "generic discontinuities", the uncanny juxtapositions of time and space and arresting stylistic mannerisms that are distinctive in all peripheral literatures'.[12]

In accordance with the aforementioned spatial–temporal logic, which echoes Trotsky's notion of 'geographical differential', for critics like Parry and Jameson the formal complexity of the artwork appeared to increase the further the distance from the hegemonic core of the capitalist world

---

[9] Benita Parry, 'Aspects of Peripheral Modernisms', *ARIEL: A Review of International English Literature*, 40:1 (2009), 27–55 (27–28).

[10] Parry, 27.

[11] Parry's essay in this collection cites Frederic Jameson, *Postmodernism or the Cultural Logic of Late Capitalism* (London: Verso, 1991), 307.

[12] *Ibid.*

system. Similarly, the claim of belatedness, characteristic of peripheral contexts, recuperates Trotsky's arguments about the creative potential of economic 'backwardness'. Resuming this line of argument, Stefano Brugnolo claims that:

> the backwardness of the periphery allows its writers to perceive in a more intense and acute way certain phenomenologies which had become routine at the centres. Not only that, however: it would seem that the vision from afar which the great figures of the peripheries enjoyed is transformed into a vision of the impending future, 'prophecy', a Utopian or Dystopian perspective.[13]

Along similar lines and offering Russian Realist fiction and 'the subsequent Japanese, Latin-American and African novels' as examples, Brugnolo highlighted 'the privilege of backwardness' through which 'peripheral writers possessed, at least on a theoretical level, the privilege of later reconsidering and redefining those processes that elsewhere had become stabilised'.[14] His account underscores the effects of both temporal and spatial removal from centres of material production, as well as the critical insight gleaned from systemic dissonance which, in his view, endows peripheral literature (and by extension, other forms of cultural expression) with a premonitory quality, becoming a powerful means of critiquing modernity.

Renewed scholarly interest in Modernism and avant-garde studies in the last decades led to the publication of monographs like Charles Pollard's *New World Modernisms* (2004), Jahan Ramazani's *A Transnational Poetics* (2009), and Susan Stanford Friedman's *Planetary Modernisms* (2015), and of essay collections like Peter Brooker and Andrew Thacker's *Geographies of Modernism* (2005), Laura Doyle and Laura Winkiel's *Geomodernisms* (2005), Irene Ramalho Santos and António Sousa Ribeiro's *Translocal Modernisms* (2008) and Mark Wollaeger and Matt Eatough's *The Oxford Handbook of Global Modernisms* (2012). These and more recent works, including Marc Caplan's *How Strange the Change. Language, Temporality and Narrative*

---

[13] Stefano Brugnolo, 'The Pendulum Swing and the Privilege of Backwardnes', in *It started in Venice: Legacies, Passages, Horizons. Fifty Years of ICLA*, ed. P. Mildonian, C. Tinelli, A. Scarsella (Venice: Cafoscarina, 2009), 413–421 (419).

[14] *Ibid.*

Forms in Peripheral Modernisms (2011), Juliet Taylor-Batty's *Multilingualism in Modernist Fiction* (2013) and Tessa Haudswedell, Axel Körner and Ulrich Tiedau's *Remapping Centre and Periphery. Asymmetrical Encounters in European and Global Contexts* (2019), contributed to a reconceptualisation of the field of Modernist studies, avoiding the traps of geographic determinism and a limiting reliance on the role of capitalism alone as a heuristic tool. These studies refigured the spatial and temporal axes of Modernism drawing on transdisciplinary perspectives, remapping Modernism as a global phenomenon and emphasising the link between modernity and (post)colonialism.

In their 2008 survey of the New Modernist Studies, Douglas Mao and Rebecca Walkowitz argue that 'Modernist studies is undergoing a transnational turn', concluding that 'scholarly inquiry in this emerging field has increasingly extended to matters of production, dissemination, and reception'.[15] Their claim at the time that 'increasing emphasis on transnational exchange' promises to remain a radically transformative and defining tendency in this field has been corroborated by the body of work produced since then—some of which by authors contributing to this volume—which has underscored 'the centrality of transnational circulation and translation in the production of Modernist art'.[16]

The modern experience can be at once migratory and rooted, international and local, 'singular' and plural. Its roots are said to plunge into a paradigm of systemic global expansion, for, as noted by Arjun Appadurai, 'the post-Renaissance European idea of modernity [...] requires *complete global expansion for its own inner logic to be revealed and justified*'.[17] This expansive notion of modernity is encapsulated still in Fredrick Jameson's notion of a 'singular modernity'. According to this hypothesis, the global expansion of capitalism went hand in hand with imperialism and colonialism, since a 'contradiction between the urge to translate and interpret other worlds, and the urge to colonise and to convert, often by means of violence' characterised European cosmopolitan impulses until very recent times.[18] However, this expansive model is being called into question

---

[15] Douglas Mao and Rebecca L. Walkowitz, 'The New Modernist Studies,' *PMLA* 123: 3 (2008), 737–748 (738).

[16] Mao and Walkowitz, 738–739.

[17] Arjun Appadurai, *The Future as Cultural Fact. Essays on the Global Condition* (London and New York: Verso, 2013), 225. Emphasis is in the original.

[18] Appadurai, *The Future as Cultural Fact*, 225.

INTRODUCTION 7

within the ongoing debate about modernity/Modernism. As noted by Irene Small,

> [i]n recent years, scholars have invoked 'alternative', 'synchronous', and 'multiple' Modernisms in order to complicate the notion of modernity as a Western phenomenon that spreads to the so-called periphery, erasing local expressions of difference in its wake. Such frameworks have catalysed the recovery of aesthetic practices previously neglected within hegemonic matrices of artistic influence, innovation, and critique.[19]

The transnational turn in Modernist studies belies neat national, cultural and identitarian vectors, as well as history's grand narratives. This revisionist inflection challenges traditional critical frameworks, re-orienting them towards a dialectic of centre–periphery to 'construct the major through the minor.'[20] The aforesaid dialectic raises numerous questions, notably which singularity and which plurality are at play? And further, how does one define centre and periphery? A straightforward binary, as is, for example, typified in the relationship between overseas colonies and mainland Empires? An alternative model sees Empire pitted against nation, whose centre is provincial with reference to the wider nation (e.g. the case of the Hapsburg Empire).

Addressing the contradictions arising from competing national and metropolitan roles, Boaventura Sousa Santos elaborates on the 'semiperipheral condition' underpinning 'a subaltern colonialism', 'marked by a position of intermediation between the center and the periphery of the world economy', in his case study of 'the Portuguese colonial system'.[21] Conversely, with regard to the field of cultural production, Santos identifies a form of hierarchization which distances itself from rigid notions

---

[19] Irene V. Small, '*Pigment Pur* and the *Corpo da Côr*: Post-Painterly Practice and Transmodernity', *October* 152 (Spring 2015), 82–102 (82). Examples of some works that follow this line of argumentation comprise: Eisenstadt, Shmuel N., 'Multiple Modernities', *Daedalus* 129: 1 (Winter 2000); Timothy Mitchell, ed., *Questions of Modernity* (2000); Dilip Gaonkar, ed., *Alternative Modernities* (2001); Dipesh Chakrabarty, *Provincializing Europe: Postcolonial Thought and Historical Difference* (2007); Kobena Mercer, ed., *Cosmopolitan Modernisms* (2005); Nicholas Bourriaud, *Altermodern*, exh. Cat. (2009).

[20] Chana Kronfeld, *On the Margins of Modernism* (Berkeley: University of California Press, 1995), 5.

[21] Boaventura Sousa Santos, 'Between Prospero and Caliban: Colonialism, Postcolonialism, and Inter-identity' *Luso Brazilian Review* (Winter 2002), "Portuguese Cultural Studies", ed. P. de Medeiros and H. Owen, 39:2 (2022), 9–43 (9, 10).

8   K. PIZZI

of 'center, semi-periphery, and periphery' and 'distinguishes between what in the world system is produced or defined as local and what is produced or defined as global' (Santos, 2002: 10). Therefore, in examining the cultural production of Modernist movements which emerge in (semi-)peripheral contexts one need also consider their negotiation of local and cosmopolitan imperatives, and, as highlighted by Maria-Irene Ramalho-Santos and António Sousa Ribeiro, their translocal exchanges with metropolitan and non-metropolitan cultures.[22]

Susan Stanford Friedman criticises '[t]he pervasive Eurocentrism in Modernist studies', claiming that:

> [t]he centrality of colonialism and postcolonialism for the twentieth century requires a new geography of modernity and Modernism, one based on an understanding of what Edward Said has called "traveling theory", anthropologist James Clifford terms 'travelling cultures', and what the Caribbean poet and theorist Eduard Glissant names as 'poetics of relation' that produces *créolité* or "the immeasurable intermixing of cultures".[23]

While highlighting the efforts of those who are 'trying to think outside the European box of Eurocentric *diffusionism* by positing a notion of multiple or alternative modernities', she distances herself from critics like 'Dilip Parameshwar Gaonkar and others who sharply separate "societal modernization" on the one hand and a "cultural modernity [that] [...] rose in opposition" to it, on the other (*Alternative Modernities*, 2)'.[24] Instead of 'a mosaic of different Modernisms, each separated from all others by the fixed barriers of geopolitical and cultural borders around the world', she proposes that we 'regard the boundaries between multiple Modernisms as porous and permeable, fostering self-other confrontations and minglings as mutually constitutive'.[25] Endorsing Ella Shohat and Robert Stam's '"polycentric" approach that sees multiple and distinct

---

[22] Maria-Irene Ramalho-Santos, António Sousa Ribeiro (eds), *Translocal Modernisms: International Perspectives* (Bern; New York; Oxford: Peter Lang, 2008).

[23] Susan Stanford Friedman, 'One Hand Clapping: Colonialism, Postcolonialism, and the Spatio/Temporal Boundaries of Modernism', in Ramalho, Ribeiro (eds), *Translocal Modernisms*, 11–40 (15, 21).

[24] Friedman, 15, 17.

[25] Friedman, 21.

centers that interact with each other on a global landscape',[26] she concludes that in aesthetic terms, this new geography involves a radical rewriting of what critics have called Modernism's internationalism: its polylingualism and polyculturalism, its anti-nationalism, and its embrace of the non-Western Other as a means for revitalizing the various sterilities of the 'West. [...] Instead of this center/periphery model, the new geography of Modernism needs to locate many centers across the globe, focus on the cultural traffic linking them, and interpret the circuits of reciprocal influence and transformation.'[27]

The polylingual and polycultural facets of Modernism Friedman mentions in the above excerpt have also received renewed attention as a result of the transnational and translational turn in Modernist studies, which, according to Juliette Taylor-Batty, is accompanied by 'a multilingual turn'.[28] According to Taylor-Batty, '[t]he emblematically Modernist themes of exile, travel and intercultural encounter lead, inevitably, to the necessity of representing different languages', establishing a direct link between the fictional representation of linguistic difference and 'Modernism's "linguistic turn" because attempts to represent languages other than the primary language of the text inevitably draw attention to the problems of linguistic representation per se'.[29] While potentially exposing conflicting linguistic and identitarian tensions, Taylor-Batty notes that language is a key vehicle in Modernist writing to convey incommunicability and the failure of language to 'communicate in any transparent way. That tension, however, produces not textual failure, but a fascinating and compelling exploration of the ways in which the encounter with linguistic and cultural difference can become a transformative experience. (...) The interlingual encounter—and its representation—always brings distortion, problems of interlingual and intercultural communication, and a foregrounding of difference. In some Modernist texts, such distortion is (...)

---

[26] Friedman, 17. Mentions Ella Shohat and Robert Stam, *Unthinking Eurocentrism: Multiculturalism and the Media* (1994).

[27] Friedman, 22. In fact, this constitutes the main argument of her recent monograph *Planetary Modernisms: Provocations on Modernity Across Time* (New York: Columbia University Press, 2015).

[28] J. Taylor-Batty, *Multilingualism in Modernist Fiction* (Basingstoke: Palgrave Macmillan, 2013), 4.

[29] Taylor-Batty, 39.

10   K. PIZZI

highly problematic, reflecting an anxiety regarding interlingual and intercultural mixing that recalls Leavis' lament for a lost "absoluteness" that is incurred by the "mingling" of "traditions and cultures" in modernity.[30]

Taylor-Batty further suggests that this encounter can yield positive results, such as 'a rejuvenation of language', where interlingual difference can lead to 'the construction of new stylistic and expressive forms'.[31] As illustrated by her analysis, the multilingual facet of Modernist works raises key issues related to the role of language in relation to linguistic and cultural identity.

An unequivocally transnational and translational phenomenon, Modernism encompasses, in short, travelling cultures, contact zones and their overlaps, together with a corollary of diasporic, exilic, migrant and translational cultures, discourses and practices. Where neat vectors of national and cultural allegiance are being disavowed, and in the light of its diasporic vocation, Modernism becomes a paradigmatic 'travelling culture' as James Clifford has it and as already noted by Stanford Friedman. By analogy, such a model relies on the concept of 'nodal points' and on a multi-directional flow between shifting nodes of influence and dissemination, reflecting changes in the cultural role played by different regions in the transition from early to late Modernism to Postmodernism, as Lucia Boldrini persuasively underscores.[32]

Inscribing itself within this latter theoretical and methodological line of enquiry in comparative Cultural Studies, my primary intent in this volume is to bring to the fore the comparative and international vocation of Modernism and, with it, the transcultural and translational project underpinning its multiple forms, as is testified by Modernisms in Australia (see Parlati, in this volume) and Iran (see Mozaffari, in this volume), amongst others, as particularly fertile cases in question. The Modernist project is explored in this issue as an epoch-changing tide of transformation characterised by new mobilities, diasporas, migrations, multilingualism, cosmopolitanism, the rise of the new metropolis, amongst others. To encompass this tidal force, our gaze is pointed to a constellation of approaches, e.g. Postcolonial, Postmodern, the dialectic

[30] *Ibid.*

[31] *Ibid.*

[32] Boldrini, Lucia, 'Comparative Literature in the Twenty-First Century: A View from Europe and the UK', *Comparative Critical Studies* 3:1–2 (2006), 13–23.

between global and local and centre and peripheries. The broad range and multi-disciplinary scope of the contributions making up this collection are a testament to the timely reassessment of Modernism in the light of its geographical spread in tandem with its margins, hence the plural Modernisms in our title.

Modernism and Peripherality: Theoretical Considerations

A Departure from Modernism: Stylistic Strategies in Modern Peripheral Literatures as Symptom, Mediation and Critique of Modernity

Benita Parry

It is well known that although modernist studies had from the outset assimilated writings from Ireland and the Austro-Hungarian empire into the canon (Joyce, Beckett, Kafka, Musil), modernism was subsequently institutionalized as the aesthetic invention of an avant-garde from Western

---

This chapter draws on the researches and writings of the Warwick Research Collective (WReC) within the English and Comparative Literature Department at Warwick University. A publication Combined and Uneven Development: Towards a New Theory of World Literature was published by Liverpool University Press in 2015.

B. Parry (✉)
Emerita Professor English and Comparative Literary Studies, University of Warwick, Warwick, UK

© The Author(s), under exclusive license to Springer Nature Switzerland AG 2024
K. Pizzi and R. Gefter Wondrich (eds.), *Rethinking Peripheral Modernisms*, https://doi.org/10.1007/978-3-031-35546-2_2

16   B. PARRY

Europe writing during the late nineteenth and earlier decades of the twentieth century.[1] Specifying the distinctive features of modernism as a literature of the city, radically innovative in style, autotelic and self-referential, discontinuous and ironic, eminent scholars acclaimed its achievement in mapping the psychic and emotional horizons of the new metropolitan middle-class subject and devising a typology of its tormented self- and inner consciousness. As is also common knowledge, this model has been charged with canonizing a selective tradition excluding writings that in continuing the tradition of social realism devised new vocabularies and narrative strategies to transfigure the unprecedented social forms generated by modernity, and more, to construe a critique of 'the real' (Williams, 1989, 32).

Of late, critics have questioned whether modernism's metropolitan location is as exclusive, its aesthetic as individualistic, its ideology as detached from the social world and its preoccupation with stylistic departures as uniquely an expression of a new and fractured urban sensibility as has been assumed. This current interest in modernism's 'global engagements' and wider vistas has stimulated those engaged in the revision to detect a transnational genealogy, a longer temporal span and a larger geopolitical space within which a greatly enhanced corpus of writing has been produced.[2] Adam Barrows, for instance, situates modernism's

---

[1] See Joe Cleary: 'Twentieth-century modernism, as Franco Moretti writes, emerged with the greatest violence and brilliance not at the center of the modern literary world-system but on the semi-peripheries of that system (in the United States, Germany, Ireland, the Scandinavian countries, Bolshevik Russia), and it was from the semi-peripheries too (Germany, Hungary, the early USSR) that the most astonishing histories of realism were to be penned, all amid "the ruin of all space, shattered glass and toppling masonry." [...] some of the semiperipheral modernisms emerged in countries in the throes of imperial collapse (Austria, Russia, Germany, Ottoman Turkey), others in countries emerging as major new world powers (the United States, the USSR, Japan, Germany), others still in largely agrarian colonies proximate to imperial metropoles and undergoing their own revolutionary independence struggles (Ireland, Mexico), others again in radicalized ethnic enclaves within the metropolis that had links to peripheral cultures beyond the metropole (Harlem)' (Cleary, 2012, 257–8, 260–1).

[2] A glance at the discussions in the journal *Modernism/modernity* during the past five years shows the inclusion of Edward Upward and J. B. Priestley, both socially aware 'realist' British writers, as well as the avant-garde Soviet painter and architect Vladimir Tatlin and the experimental Portuguese author Fernando Pessoa. Topics range from art, sculpture, jazz, cinema, photography, cabaret and ballet, and themes from Futurism, Dada, the Harlem Renaissance, Fascism, queer and celebrity studies. The topographical expanse of articles covers China, Japan, Brazil, Mexico, Spain, Asia, Africa, the Pacific, Australia and

preoccupation with temporality in the context of the political and legislative arguments over world standard time, a contest he shows to be part of the globalization of imperial processes and policies. In examining how this stimulated writers to experiment with new ways of representing human time, Barrows cites Victorian adventure novels (Rider Haggard, Bram Stoker and Rudyard Kipling), early English-language South Asian novels as well as high modernist texts (Joyce, Woolf and Conrad), suggesting that these 'indicate an engagement with questions of paramount public concern rather than a philosophical retreat into bourgeois, private interiority' (Barrows, 2010, 4).[3]

In a wide-ranging study, *1913: The Cradle of Modernism*, Jean-Michel Rabaté has proposed that modernism be understood 'as the inception of our modern period of globalization' covering manifestations in societies beyond Western Europe, a view he goes on to contradict when itemizing its essential features as those noticeably to the fore in its metropolitan incarnations (Rabaté, 2007, 1).[4] Previously, William Everdell had also located 1913 as modernism's *annus mirabilis*, adding Vienna and

---

South Africa. In a special issue of the journal *Modern Chinese Literature and Culture*, Eric Hayot presents a two-pronged attack on the notion that modernism began in the West, arguing first that 'at the socalled origin of European modernism, the foreign has already inserted itself', and second that 'it ought to be possible to reconceive a definition of modernism itself that [...] would consider the entire global output that has occurred under the name "modernism"'. This consideration, Hayot argues, 'would permit an understanding of "modernism" from a much larger historical and cultural perspective' (2006, 131). Seeking to expand modernism's locations and challenging its 'Europeanness', Hayot's work has examined the creation of a modernist tradition in Chinese literature (cf., for example, Hayot's *The Hypothetical Mandarin: Sympathy, Modernity, and Chinese Pain* [2009]).

[3] Jed Esty, although very differently, also addresses modernism's sensibility of time when arguing that the English 'high' modernist writers and intellectuals sought, in the wake of imperial disintegration, refuge in an insular integrity, introducing 'a moment of shaped time from the resources of national culture', the narrowing of the spatial aperture of metropolitan perception leading to 'an increased focus on the national significance of time as opposed to its transformative, revolutionary potential, and marking them not as aesthetic dinosaurs, but as participants in the transition from metropolitan art to national culture' (Esty, 2004, 8, 50).

[4] Rabaté's focus is on 'literary techniques [...] the use of free indirect speech tantamount to inner monologues [...] the numerous verbal leitmotifs and ironically repeated phrases and sentences, and the playfulness of the language that often engages in jokes, puns and double entendres. Modernist too is the overarching perspectivism that makes the point of view shift all the time, multiplying while integrating modern science so as to educate the reader' (2007, 154).

18   B. PARRY

St Petersburg to the capital cities of Paris and London, and Mississippi to its geography, while also embracing art, music, film, physics, mathematics and philosophy as articulations sharing an 'assumption of ontological discontinuity' (Everdell, 1997, 347). The Russian Futurists alluded to above are also included in Peter Nicholls's study, *Modernisms: A Literary Guide*,[5] serving as a reminder that this group was a precursor to the kaleidoscopic creativity of the short-lived Soviet avant-garde, whose participants had incorporated experimentation in poetry and novels, painting, film, architecture and the design of artefacts, the whole animated by, and often aligned with, the ideas and ideals of the Revolution. The genesis, political affiliations and radical inventiveness of this movement which have been discussed in depth by Paul Wood in a brilliant and neglected essay ('The Politics of the Avant-Garde') remains to be allotted its proper place in the discussion of the modern vanguard and is central to any consideration of its manifestations in peripheral locations, as well as in the larger discussion about the ingenuity of 'committed' art.

Still more recently and in line with what they call the current tendency of 'New Modernist Studies', Douglas Mao and Rebecca Walkowitz (2008), when observing how the enlargement of the field has challenged the notion of modernism as a product of 'the West', have promoted the study of literatures beyond Europe and North America, as well as that from marginalized communities within the metropoles.[6] As editors of *Bad Modernisms* (2006), they argue for extending its borders to include novels from the Harlem Renaissance and the Philippines, together with manifestos, philosophical treatises, movie musicals, anthropological essays and advertising campaigns, their aim being to demonstrate modernism's aesthetic to be inherently socially aware and subversive. The dissident credentials of modernism have also been asserted by Vicki Mahaffey

[5] Nicholls too refuses to regard modernism as in the past.

[6] As Douglas Mao and Rebecca Walkowitz note in their essay 'The New Modernist Studies', 'There can be no doubt that modernist studies is undergoing a transnational turn. This has produced at least three kinds of new work in the field: scholarship that widens the modernist archive by arguing for the inclusion of a variety of alternative traditions [...] scholarship that argues for the centrality of transnational circulation and translation in the production of modernist art and scholarship that examines how modernists responded to imperialism, engaged in projects of anticolonialism, and designed new models of transnational community' (2008, 738). The authors cite work on Brazil, Lebanon, India, China and Taiwan as well as the townships of Dublin and Native American communities in the United States (739).

(2007), who discusses the 'high' modernists such as Eliot, Joyce, Pound and Yeats alongside women, gay writers and participants in the Harlem Renaissance. She relates the modernist impulse to broader cultural and historical crises and movements, and claims for the field a special political and ethical relevance.

In a related vein, Jessica Berman examines the articulations of modernism comparatively in Britain, the Caribbean, India, Ireland, Spain and the United States, maintaining that 'reading modernism transnationally shifts our perspective on the forms and commitments of modernism' to reveal 'the continuum of political engagement that undergirds its world-wide emergence' (2012, 9). By understanding modernism as 'a constellation of rhetorical actions, attitudes, or aesthetic occasions motivated by the particular and varied situations of economic, social, and cultural modernity worldwide and shaped by the ethical and political demands of those situations', she pursues a connection between the narrative ethics and the literary politics of modernism, designating modernism as a player in anti-colonial discourse and maintaining that modernist narrative acts to help us 'imagine justice' (2012, 7).

Common to the above studies is the determination to redraw modernism's landscape so as to include the peripheries and semi-peripheries, rather than to focus on how the aesthetic strategies of such writing deviated from the normative criteria allotted to the modernist project. This tendency is amplified by those critics interested in identifying the specific character of peripheral modernism, even when this is not named as such. In an 'Afterword' to *The Oxford Handbook of Global Modernisms*, Laura Doyle chides 'the notion of borrowing [that] deforms and haunts all consideration of the relation between canonical modernism and other literatures, especially postcolonial literatures', and goes on to fault this position for 'a blindness to dialectical co-formations' (2012, 671). For Doyle, two clusters of words signify the opposing tendencies discernible in the discussion, both of which she rejects: on the one hand, 'belated', 'third world', 'expropriated', 'appropriated' 'derive' and 'revise'; on the other, 'original', 'metropole', 'first world', 'generate' and 'innovate' (2012, 671), a schema that I find registers allied and not contesting stances.

Instead of relegating belatedness, borrowing and extensive assimilation as categorically negative, Doyle proposes that we acknowledge the 'coproduction of cultures' (2012, 678) as the proper source of creativity. Hence her assumption that influences from core to periphery and peripheries to core constitutes a joint venture conducted by equivalently placed participants within a global space. Since this emerges as unencumbered by a history of dispossession and violence, there are, in her account, no traces of force and aggression for the critic to find and map onto its past and contemporary topography. Indeed, this infers an arena within which the 'European' and 'non-European' cultures, cognitive traditions and literatures had interacted cordially as equals and continue to do so in amicable transnational exchanges (Doyle, 2012, 682)—an astonishingly cosmetic portrait of imperialism's historic face.

If Doyle offers the conceit of 'dialectical co-formations' as the mainspring of modernism everywhere, then Andreas Huyssen, while setting out to 'dewesternize modernism', proceeds to undermine his own rejection of a geography confined to the metropolitan cities of Europe and North America. This he does by confining the ingenuity of writing in the colonial and postcolonial countries to its 'transformative negotiation with the modern of the metropolis' (Huyssen, 2005, 6), whereby metropolitan culture was 'translated, appropriated and creatively mimicked' (9). Another critic, Susan Stanford Friedman, who protests at the 'curse of presumed derivativeness' attached to colonial and postcolonial modernisms, intends to redress the silencing of 'the creative energies of colonial and postcolonial subjects as producers of modernism', but succeeds in restoring 'Western' aesthetics as its fount and origin by ascribing this vitality to the 'indigenization' and 'cannibalism' of cultural traditions from the West, transmitted through 'contact zones' and emerging as 'alternative' modernisms (2006, 431–43).[7] These efforts to expand the extent of modernism signally fail to address that which is

---

[7] See also Timothy Mitchell's introduction to *Questions of Modernity*, where he recognizes the significance of empire and the place of the 'non-West' in the rise of modernity (2000, 23). It is refreshing to come across an essay by the eminent architectural historian Gwendolyn Wright, which if sometimes lenient in her usage of the terminology circulating in the current discussion on modernity, imperialism and globalism holds that 'modernism came into being in a world framed by colonialism [...] The politics of space involved complex, asymmetrical assertions of power: domination, resistance, incorporation, and exclusion. It was an unstable calculus, both morally and practically [...] The fears and realities of inequality, instability, and extraneous control, all of which began under colonialism, have grown apace under the pressures of today's global economy [...] definitions of modernity tend to be inflexible, denying the multiple, even conflicting layers of conventions and change that shape any place or person. Ernst Bloch's term "nonsynchronicities" underscores the simultaneous but radically divergent experiences of "Now"' (2002, 125, 126 and 129).

stylistically novel in peripheral writings, which, as I go on to propose, always exceeds a metamorphosis of extant configurations and transcends the normative modes attributed to modernist literature.

Because my concern is with writing from the peripheries of capitalism's world-system, I must emphasize that in discussions on globalization, modernity and world literature, the use of core and peripheries/semi-peripheries signifies not a civilization hierarchy or a cultural ordering, but the geopolitical locations of pre- or nascently capitalist societies co-opted or coerced into world capitalism.

As well as the colonized worlds, these include Russia before and since the Revolution, the now disintegrated Austro-Hungarian empire, pre- and modern China, Japan, Eastern and Southern Europe, and the deprived and marginalized populations within the core. This accounts for the paradoxical beginning conditions of modern cultural forms among peoples who seemed, and may still seem, to inhabit multiple histories and temporalities, to be both modern and traditional.[8] When interpreting this historic process as it had unfolded in China and pre-revolutionary Russia, Leon Trotsky proposed a theory of combined and uneven development delineating a contradictory amalgam of pre-existing local structures of social life and external sociopolitical and cultural influences. These insights into the coexistence of antiquated modes and modern social formations and institutions were derived from observing that the imperialist powers had introduced into the non-capitalist world the most advanced means of commodity production accompanied by capitalist relationships while also safeguarding the continuation of 'archaic forms of economic life' and the maintenance of feudal social arrangements: 'The most primitive beginnings and the latest European endings', modern capitalist industry in an environment of economic backwardness; 'the Belgian or American factory, and round about it settlements, villages of wood and straw, burning up every year', a proletariat 'thrown into the factory cauldron snatched directly from the plough' (Trotsky, 1965, 476).

---

[8] As Neil Larsen has remarked, 'It has now in fact become something of an intellectual commonplace to remark on the distinctly Latin American and perhaps generally "post-colonial" of being both modern and traditional, both "ahead of" and yet "behind the times" at once, as if not one but two or multiple histories were being lived out in one and the same space' (2001, 139–40).

22   B. PARRY

Whereas some critics have spoken of modernity as marking a ruthless break with preceding historical conditions, Perry Anderson has emphasized that its historic time accommodates eras discontinuous from each other and heterogeneous within themselves (1984, 101). In the same vein Fredric Jameson, echoing Trotsky, has argued that modernity uniquely corresponds 'to an uneven moment of social development' when realities from radically different moments of history coexist—'handicrafts alongside the great cartels, peasant field with the Krupp factories or the Ford plant in the distance' (1991, 307). Elsewhere, in the essay 'The End of Temporality' (2003), Jameson writes of modernity as a culture of incomplete modernization in the metropoles as well as the peripheries, because of which, he maintains, we have to explain the emergence of various modernisms in areas of only partially industrialized and partially defeudalized social orders, and where the first modernists in their own lived experience had to negotiate two socio-economic temporalities.

It is true that residual traces of archaic ideologies and customs can be found in contemporary Western Europe and North America, where the capital cities remain contemporaneous with peasant or agrarian societies—about which John Berger has written with empathy and critical distance in *Pig Earth* (1979) and which William Faulkner encrypts in fictions located in the Deep South of twentieth-century United States—even if these most commonly exist as vestiges. However in the zone of the semiperiphery, the synchronicity of disjunctive temporalities and discrepant types of social and economic organization persisted and continues to do so. Where lands were seized and colonized for their natural and labor resources, and expropriation and precipitate, selective modernization were imposed with memorable violence,[9] the survival of pre-existing forms of social life and culture interrupted/disrupted by the arrival of capitalism ensured that anomalies remained and continue to remain structural.

This does not mean that the peripheries were latecomers to or existed/exist outside of modernity, as this can be conceived as the temporal condition of people everywhere since transformation was propelled by the same

---

[9] In 1919, Antonio Gramsci had written: 'The colonies were exploited to an unprecedented degree, using inflexible and inhuman methods such as can be conceived only in periods of civilization as marvellous as that of capitalism. The indigenous peoples of the colonies were not even left their eyes for weeping; foodstuffs, raw materials, everything possible was combed from the colonies to sustain the resistance of the warring metropolitan peoples' (1988, 112).

mode of production, even if at different speeds and to varying degrees. Paradoxically, some postcolonial critics have considered major modernist concerns such as consciousness, temporality and the experience of modernity as being markedly 'Western' preoccupations, rather than coextensive with capitalism's worldwide consolidation, and as a consequence have proposed that peripheral modernities be perceived as 'translations' of, or counters to, the Eurocentric prototype.[10] A strong case against 'transmuting a temporal lag into a qualitative difference' has been made by Harry Harootunian (2000a, 23). Acknowledging that modern forms were introduced into societies outside of Europe through imperial expansion, the export of capital and colonial deterritorialization, he emphasizes its consequences in creating a world where 'all societies shared a common reference provided by global capital and its requirements' (Harootunian, 2000a, 62–3). He thus directs attention to the disparate but simultaneous experiences of change and upheaval precipitated transnationally by capitalism, these generating 'differing inflections of the modern' and promising not alternative, divergent, competing and retroactive modernities—which imply 'the existence of an "original" that was formulated in Europe followed by a series of "copies" and lesser inflections'—but 'coeval ... modernities or, better yet, peripheral modernities' (62–3).[11]

Similarly, Samir Amir (1974) maintains that conditions in the peripheries represent not an earlier stage of development, but an equally modern consequence of the continuous alterations to which these societies have been subjected by capitalism.[12] This argument implies that metropolitan and colonial populations, whatever the profound material and cultural differences between and among them, were hurled into modernity at the

---

[10] See, for example, Homi Bhabha's *The Location of Culture* (1994, 241). Some have theorized modernity as a *Western* phenomenon against which postcolonial thinking advances counter-discourses to its terms and truth-claims. See, for example, Tsenay Serequeberhan's 'The Critique of Eurocentrism' (1997, 142, 143).

[11] See also footnote 4 (2000a, 163) and Harootunian's comment that 'whatever and however a society develops', its coeval modernity 'is simply taking place as the same time as other modernities' (2000b, xv).

[12] For Enrique Dussel who rejects the developmentalist and Eurocentric position where modernity is conceptualized 'as an exclusively European phenomenon that expanded from the seventeenth century on throughout all the "backward" cultures', contending that the phenomenon should be understood as a global one within which Europe, through the discovery, conquest, colonization and integration of other spheres, attained centrality as the system's managers (Dussel, 1998, 18).

24   B. PARRY

same moment,[13] a perspective registered in Peter Osborne's designation of modernity as 'our primary secular category of historical totalization' (1995, 29)[14] and a description which brings its global reach into proper focus, serving as a reminder that modernity and modern times cannot be abstracted from the universalizing tendencies of capitalism. This concept of a singular capitalist modernity has been elaborated by Fredric Jameson: it is singular because worldwide, and because it is global, it is necessarily of infinite variety (2002).

The resituating of literary modernism within wider spatial and temporal perspectives has not been matched by a revaluation of modernism's status as the proper and only articulation of modernity. In a conjunctural model, modernity has been described as a consciousness, sensibility or time–space sensorium consistent with capitalism's economic and technological modernization, and aesthetic modernism perceived as generating a style adequate to mediating the lived experience of this historical transformation. But since modernity is one and many, is modernism its sole voice? The need to uncouple modernity from modernism so as to account for all literary forms born of modernity has been persuasively made by the editors and contributors to a special issue on 'Peripheral Realisms' in the *Modern Language Quarterly* (2002). In the introduction, Jed Esty and Colleen Lye write of an 'accustomed habit of reading against realism' which selects for canonization 'works that stylize global capitalism rather than describe its effects', thereby enabling 'North American scholars of the contemporary period to produce interconnected atlases of alternative, late, and global modernisms while ignoring a world of peripheral realisms' and consequently forgoing 'the possibility [...] of representing the world-system rather than thematizing its unrepresentability' (2012, 17).

---

[13] This scope is invoked in the opening lines of Marshall Berman's *All That Is Solid Melts into Air: The Experience of Modernity*: 'Modern environments and experiences cut across all boundaries of geography and ethnicity, of class and nationality, of religion and ideology: in this sense, modernity can be said to unite all mankind. There is a mode of vital experience—experience of space and time, of the self and others, of life's possibilities and perils—that is shared by men and women all over the world today. I will call this body of experience "modernity"' (2003, 1).

[14] Osborne has suggested that there are 'three distinct but connected approaches to the concept of modernity: modernity as a *category of historical periodization, a quality of social experience and an (incomplete) project*' (1995, 5).

However, it is an essay written by the Marxist theorist Theodor Adorno that has done much within radical circles to relegate realism. In an impassioned response to an article by Lukács—certainly one that appears as uncharacteristically inflexible—Adorno accused Lukács of projecting a dogmatic sclerosis of content, of art imitating reality, as if content is 'real' in the same sense as social reality. Claiming modernism as the singular source of a critical perspective on modernity, Adorno ascribed to it an intrinsic negative critique, whether delivered from the left or the right, directed at capitalism's intensification of dehumanization, while categorizing realism as formally anachronistic because unable to grasp, assimilate and transfigure the trauma of modernity. Lukács's indignation at the 'worldlessness of interior monologue' within modernist writing is met by Adorno's insistence that this mode is 'both the truth and the appearance of a free-floating subjectivity—it is truth, because in the universal atomistic state of the world, alienation rules over men', and it is 'appearance [...] inasmuch as, objectively, the social totality has precedence over the individual, a totality which is created and reproduces itself through alienation and through the contradictions of society' (Adorno, 1977, 160).[15] Adorno goes on to name Joyce and Kafka as exemplars of modernism, before rebuking Lukács with the reminder that Balzac and Dickens— writers Lukács held in high esteem—are 'by no means as realistic as all that', since Balzac's novels were 'an imaginative reconstruction of the alienated world, that is, of a reality no longer experienced by individual subject' (Adorno, 1977, 163). In suggesting that 'the difference between this individual subject and the modernist version is not that great', and implying the artificiality of containing realism and modernism within a rigid and exclusionary temporal framework, Adorno defuses some of the explosive rhetoric in his polemic (1977, 163). Concerning Dickens, Adorno elsewhere observed that he created characters who failed to internalize the domination of society, because of which—as the bearers and

---

[15] As Adorno also notes, 'There is no material content, no formal category of artistic creation, however mysteriously transmitted and itself unaware of the process, which did not originate the empirical reality from which it breaks free [...] it is precisely as artefacts, as products of social labour, that they [artworks] also communicate with the empirical experience they reject and from which they draw' (Adorno, 1977, 190).

26   B. PARRY

not the agents of objective factors—they remained experientially separated from the conditions determining their existence.[16]

After exposure to Adorno's scorn, it is necessary that the interested reader look at Lukács's more characteristically nuanced essay on Dostoevsky, written in 1943 and first published in 1949. He begins by observing that there is 'nothing unusual in the fact that a backward country produces powerful works', since locations deemed underdeveloped in terms of modernization were all the same the contemporaries of the metropolitan centers within the totality of world capitalism (1973, 146). In Dostoevsky he sees 'the first and greatest poet of the modern capitalist metropolis', the first to draw 'the mental deformations that are brought about as a social necessity in the life of the city' and the first to recognize and represent 'the dynamics of a future social, moral and psychological evolution from germs of something barely begun' (1961, 153). The journalist Dostoevsky, writes Lukács, spoke consolingly and as a conservative; only in his poetic writings does his social answer triumph and assert itself over political intentions: 'It is a revolt against the moral and psychic deformations of man which is caused by the evolution of capitalism', the experimentation of his character being 'a desperate attempt to break through the barriers which deform the soul and maim, distort, and dismember life' (1961, 156).

Lukács's reading disarrays any attempt to contrive a time frame for periodizing realism and modernism, since both have their source in the impulse to invent forms able to grasp and transfigure changing social and psychic landscapes.

Indeed, scholars of Japanese literature claim that the construction of bourgeois everyday life in the realist moment took place simultaneously and in conversation with its modernist moment. Following on the convincing argument made for recognizing that within the body of peripheral literatures are fictions that cannot be accommodated under modernism, including the recently expanded versions, I go on to suggest that such writing is better served by other terms. One such is 'irrealism', a literary form identified by Michael Löwy, and to which I will

---

[16] In a 1931 essay on *The Old Curiosity Shop* (1841), Adorno observes that 'the prebourgeois form of Dickens' novels becomes a means of dissolving the very bourgeois world they depict', adding that the novels of Dickens 'contain a fragment of the dispersed baroque that maintains a strange ghostly presence in the nineteenth century' (1991–1992, 2, 171, 172).

return; another is 'Homiletic Realism', proposed by Timothy Brennan, who argues that: 'Instead of reclaiming modernism for the periphery, my view is that we [...] explicitly depart from it' (2014a, 10). By grounding writings scored by linguistic polyphony and disjunctive narrative modes in the worldly conditions they also critically address, such suggestions open the way to show that the reconfiguration of what is incommensurable and absurd in institutional structures and social forms (cf. Jameson, 1986a) is not confined to theme, but is embedded in the peculiarities of its stylistic mannerisms.

There have been many attempts at identifying the characteristics of peripheral literatures, such as the overused category of the marvelous real, or magic realism,[17] before which there were definitions of Caribbean aesthetics that are arresting in their perceptions of a heritage of historical admixture and temporal and spatial unevenness. Such situations, critics argued, made for cultural métissage or creolization,[18] described by Wilson Harris as a heady mix 'bearing traces of the pre-Columbian, the rubble of the extinct Carib past, Arawak icons, vestiges of Amerindians' fable and legend, practices stemming from African vodun and limbo born on the slave ships of the Middle Passage' (1970, 30). The broken histories of the islands were also to the fore in the writings of the Martinican novelist and critic Édouard Glissant, who cited the subjugation, alienation and ultimately extermination of indigenous peoples by early colonial conquest, African slaves sold to the new world and the dehumanizing conditions endured by East Indian and Chinese indentured labor on the plantations (Glissant, 1989, 221–2, 260). Long before these observations, the Cuban novelist and musicologist Alejo Carpentier had noted the improbable coexistence of the ancestral and the contemporaneous in Latin America. Designating surrealism as the expression of the First World's subjective craving for heterogeneity and dereification, he attributed the superficially

---

[17] See in this context Gabriel Garcia Marquez's comment: 'I am a realist writer because I believe that in Latin-America, everything is possible, everything is real—We live surrounded by these fantastic and extraordinary things [...] I believe that we have to work, investigating language and the technical forms of narration so that the entire fantastic reality of Latin America might form part of our books, and so that Latin-American literature might in fact correspond to Latin-American life where the most extraordinary things happen every day [...] I believe that what we should do is to promote it as a form of reality which can give something new to universal literature' (qtd. in Harris, 1967, 24–5).

[18] See Thierry Bayle's 'Plea for Créolité' (1994) and Martin Munro's 'Chronicle of the Seven Sorrows (Review)' (2005).

28   B. PARRY

similar trend in the literature and art of Latin America in the 1920s and 1930s as springing from the fact of combined and uneven development in the object world itself, where 'stages of civilization known to humans throughout history can be witnessed in the present' (1995, 88).[19]

A different understanding of the stylistic mismatches and improbable contiguities in the formal features of the imported novel form in the peripheries is offered by the Brazilian critic Roberto Schwarz, who accounts for the fictions' 'originality' in the inappropriate affirmation of European ideas within conditions of historical backwardness (1992, 3, 29).[20] By locating the literary devices of the peripheral novel in its social ground, Schwarz finds that these, whether realist, fabulist, modernist or avant-garde, can be read as transfiguring and estranging the incommensurable material, cultural, social and existential conditions of an emergent capitalist modernity, where a system of ambiguities grows 'out of the local use of bourgeois ideas' (3, 29). Expanding on these observations in his study on the nineteenth-century novel in Brazil, Schwarz suggests that when the ideas and ideals of European liberalism were asserted in a society where social relationships were based on latifundia and the unfree labor of slaves, these reveal themselves as displaced, as not fitting the circumstances of Brazilian life. However, as he writes of Machado de Assis's *The Posthumous Memoirs of Brás Cubas* (1889), it is in 'their quality of being improper' that the ideology, through a Brechtian process of reproducing

[19] The latter part of the essay 'On the Marvellous Real' first appeared as the Preface to Carpentier's novel *The Kingdom of this World* (1949), later expanded in 1967 and more recently published in *Magical Realism: Theory, History, Community* (1995). *In Journey through the Labyrinth: Latin American Fiction in the Twentieth Century*, Gerald Martin cites the following passage: 'After having felt the undeniable enchantment of this Haitian earth, after having discerned magical warnings on the red roads of the Central Plateau, after having heard the drums of Petro and Rada, I was moved to compare the marvelous reality I'd just experienced with the tiresome attempts to arouse the marvelous that has characterized certain European literatures for last thirty years' (1989, 171). For an analytic overview of the intellectual climate in which Carpentier was writing, see Timothy Brennan: 'he was convinced that surrealism—laboriously constructed in the urban centers of Europe—already existed in the Americas [...] arguing that everything visually associated with surrealist discovery can already been found there' (2001, 18).

[20] See also Roberto Schwarz's *A Master on the Periphery of Capitalism* (2001, 27). In 'On Magic Realism in Film', Fredric Jameson refers to Cuban theoreticians of the 1980s who, instead of decrying the technological underdevelopment of Cuban film, affirmed a 'Third World aesthetic politics' whereby 'its own "imperfect cinema"', consequent on economic constraints, is transformed 'into a strength and a choice, a sign of its own distinct origins and content' (1986a, 316).

and estranging, becomes 'material and a problem for literature' (Schwarz, 2001, 47). What Schwarz finds is that the incompatibilities and improbable juxtapositions in narrative form and style—which he calls a 'Babel of literary mannerisms' (17) and a 'bazaar of classical and realist registers' (15)—correspond to an implausible society, slave-owning and bourgeois at the same time.

The question of what critical discourses authorize as exemplary, and how these instruct us to read, impinges on the classification of literary form. During the last decades, prominent tendencies in postcolonial studies had privileged writings from the once-colonized peripheries which stylistically inscribe hybridity, pastiche, irony and defamiliarization. The outcome, as Neil Lazarus contends in his book *The Postcolonial Unconscious* (2011), is that realist-associated conceptual categories such as mode of production, historical transition, nation and nationalism, class and class consciousness, land and environment are excluded (2011, 22). As to the first question about what we are directed to read, Lazarus refers us to a vast body of 'realist' writing from the peripheries that have been programmatically ignored. As to the approved reading practices, we can observe how critical commentary has determined the ways fiction is put into circulation and fixed in an allotted category. Consider Yambo Ouologuem's once notorious novel *Bound to Violence* (1968), earlier hailed by Kwame Anthony Appiah as a political novel that 'seeks to delegitimate' nationalism and the nationalist project of the postcolonial national bourgeoisie (1991, 352). Republished in 2008 as *The Duty of Violence*, its excesses could now be recuperated as a chronicle of the harrowing transition to capitalism in an African state.[21]

Or consider Sharae Deckard's 'Peripheral Realism, Millennial Capitalism' (2012) and Nicholas Lawrence's essay on Roberto Bolaño's *2666*, where against the grain of its designation as a postmodern novel, both read its narrative arc as encompassing capitalism's global system, its consciousness incorporating the ubiquitous ramifications of world imperialism and its destiny a critique of a system that engenders moral and psychological deformation. As Lawrence writes:

> The global 'lit-system' thus forms not just the context but the content of a work such as Roberto Bolaño's novel *2666*, which is concerned to

---

[21] See Yusufu Maiangwa's 'The Duty of Violence' (1979).

trace the imbrication of literary unevenness with the starkest manifestations of inequality in the social and economic realm—the 'deathworld' epitomized by the serial killings of female workers in the maquiladoras of Ciudad Juárez on the US-Mexican border. (2015, 68)

There was a time when commentators on peripheral literatures sought signs of synthesis, symbiosis and negotiation between the contradictions attendant on using a narrative form privileging the values of a liberal ideology and individual choice, when representing a tradition-bound society where life was mapped by family, community and the maintenance of social order. These glosses were intent on detecting the *marriage* of two cultures—the fables, myths and folktales of the native tradition *blended* with the traditions of the novel found in the literatures of the ruling empires (see Bahri, 2003).[22] Whereas Christopher Prendergast has generalized this mode when claiming the 'amalgamation' of different traditions as the source of cultural originality, Franco Moretti (2006) argues that this does not monopolize the process of change and suggests instead that major transformations occur when a device or genre enters a new cultural habitat.[23]

In the habitat of the peripheries, the intensity of the social and political disjunctions suggests that among the appropriate and productive designations of its literary domain is what Brennan names as 'Homiletic Realism',

[22] In proposing a postcolonial critical aesthetics, Bahri notes but without demonstrating that postcolonial literature provides glimpses of the contradictions and unevenness of global social development in the atonality of two time-schemes. Her interest is in formal innovation of traditional form that is in keeping with the preoccupation with hybridity in cultural studies where words like border-crossings abound. See also Stephen Heath's contribution to the debate on *World Literature*: 'The very idea of the study now of world literature is involved in the hybrid: reading not merely comparatively and generically, this novel from here next to that one from there, but migrationally and impurely, writings intermingled with one another, against the grain of ready—legitimate—identities. To look at genre politically is to read with just such a migrant's-eye view, which is another definition of "world literature", the newness its study makes' (2004, 74). Here the new is conflated with the hybrid and the hybrid conceals the singularities marking the literatures of the peripheries.

[23] Arguing for the correlation between space and style, Moretti refers to Ernst Mayr's theory of allopatric speciation predicting that 'all major transformations occur when the device enters a new cultural habitat', a concept which posits that 'a change in the environment encourages the spread of morphological novelties of which speciation is *the most significant* but not the only one' (2006, 78, 79).

which 'exhorts its reader first to have faith in, and second to engage with, a totality that lies *behind* appearance' (Kent and Tomski, 2017, 265).

To substantiate the methodology I have argued is adequate to disclosing the singularities of modern peripheral writing, I will propose a reading of *Xala* (1974), a novella by the Senegalese writer and film-maker Ousmane Sembéne (earlier transcribed as Sembéne Ousmane). Born in 1923, Sembéne had little schooling and was in turn fisherman, brick-layer, plumber and apprentice mechanic before being drafted into the French army during the Second World War. After moving to France, he was docker, trade union activist, member of the French Communist Party and a conscious internationalist. Without any affinity with Négri-tude, a cultural and political movement of the 1930s, in which Senegal's long-serving post-independence president Léopold Sédar Senghor was a founding member, Sembéne was critical of Senghor's policies which he accused of fostering the French connection as the agency of metropolitan capitalism's continued domination over Senegal. His commitment to Communism was further marked by his choosing to learn his skills as a film-maker in the Soviet Union during the 1950s, unlike other Fran-cophone African film-makers, especially those from Burkina Faso, who apprenticed themselves to the French.

Initially intended as a film script, *Xala* was published as a book in 1974 and two years later it was again revised for cinema. Both versions drama-tize the coercive modernization of a pre-capitalist African society and the consequent trauma of immersion in conditions of uneven development. It was Sembéne's intention that his writings and films should reach as many as possible within a largely illiterate population. Since *Xala* was written in a mixture of standard French, its vernacular form and the native Wolof (nuances that are lost in translation), its narrative is marked by unset-tling shifts in genre, and its address encompasses the accents of both oral delivery and modern narration. It is thus uncertain that his ambition was fulfilled—which may have prompted Sembéne's return to the more acces-sible medium of cinema in order to tell his story to a wider audience. Although positioning himself within the tradition of the *griot* (the bards of West Africa considered to be the keepers of folk stories and indigenous systems of knowledge), Sembéne also understood the role of the artist

32 B. PARRY

as giving voice to the 'inner screams' of the people,[24] while his admonitory intercessions on colonialism, corrupt post-independence regimes and the persistence of deleterious tradition characterize a writer who accepted a responsibility to admonish and persuade his readers. If these positions suggest, as some commentators have claimed, that Sembéne worked within a functional aesthetics,[25] his expressionist style, which others have compared to that of Brecht,[26] frustrates transparent readings of narrative content.

The improbable juxtapositions of the recognizable and the fantastic in *Xala* are generated by the absurdities and incongruities of a society adhering simultaneously to the socialities, cultural forms, cognitive traditions and ethical sensibilities of both the ancestral and the nascent, evoking a locale inhabited by holy men in scanty robes and slickly suited entrepreneurs; where the journeys of the Mercedes are thwarted by unpassable roads and the antique sounds of the *kora* are drowned by the tango and rock music; in which the villages and shanty towns lack sanitation and the African urban elite drink only imported bottled water; where both seers and psychiatrists practice their crafts; and where a French-speaking African business class anxious to be seen as belonging to the modern world seeks the ministrations of traditional healers, is in fear of spells and curses, consumes holy liquids and initiates ceremonies where 'ancient custom was being more than just respected, it was being revived' (Sembéne, 1976, 4).

---

[24] See Samba Gadjigo, 'Ousmane Sembène: The Life of a Revolutionary Artist', an introductory outline of the forthcoming authorized biography of Ousmane Sembène of the same title (www.newsreel.org/articles/OusmaneSembene.htm).

[25] See Sembène's novel *God's Bits of Wood* (1962 [1960]). Inspired by the strike of peasants recruited to work on the construction of the Dakar-Niger railway in 1947–1948, the novel narrates the transformations in consciousness of those who, while still connected to pre-capitalist modes of production and attached to archaic social practices, are in the process of translating their experience of oppression and exploitation into organized resistance. Certainly the novel enacts a moment when agricultural workers pulled from the plough and women separated from their cooking pots discover their capacity for effective agency within a world in the throes of a form of modernization that would consign them to permanent servitude. The novel, however, is not only a reimagining of a new-found militancy: the kaleidoscopic protest march during which the forging of solidarity is interrupted by recurrent clashes between the traditionalists and those amenable to modernization estranges the real by staging the clash between the existent and the emergent.

[26] See David Murphy, 'An African Brecht' (2002).

The satirical evocation of these bizarre concurrences is further and appropriately augmented by allusions to both the fetishism of pre-capitalist societies and modern commodity fetishism, both mysterious attachments transfixing those who while still immersed in past tradition are subject to the traumas of capitalism's intrusions. A victim seeking to dispel the curse of impotence wears 'esoteric writings [...] like fetishes around his waist'—in the film an actual fetish object is displayed[27]—while the marabout's services awaken in him 'the ancestral atavism of fetishism' (Sembéne, 1976, 42, 55). The new African business class, through a distortion of consciousness wrought by their indeterminate social and cultural positions, experience the perceptible artefacts made in Europe—the gold wristwatch, the Mercedes, the tailored suit, the bottled water—as actively 'thinglike', possessing an independent existence disconnected from their original context as products of human labor and their material properties, to be coveted for the imperceptible power they hold.[28]

It is therefore fitting that in such a society, a crime of material dispossession is punished by a metaphysically delivered and potent affliction. The doubleness in the speech of an African registrar in a hospital practicing modern medicine, who modifies his affirmation that science 'is never powerless', by immediately adding 'we are in Africa, where you can't explain or resolve everything in biomedical terms' (Sembéne, 1976, 47), is not a corroboration of the irrational as characteristic of a continent, but a gesture to the continuing power of a received belief system (53). El Hadj, one-time primary school teacher and activist in the independence movement, a member of the Chamber of Commerce and Industry under a self-serving post-independence regime where nationalist rhetoric is still invoked, is presented as a figure of the incomplete fusion of two cultures (4): one a senescent feudalism, the other a pubescent capitalism. His crime has been the theft of communal land from his clan and its conversion into private property—a symbolic act of an individualist money economy replacing pre-capitalist community ownership; his penalty is the 'Xala', the curse of sexual impotence—which is also an allusion to a post-independence regime still reliant on metropolitan capitalism.

---

[27] See Laura Mulvey, '*Xala*, Ousmene Sembène: The Carapace That Failed' (1991).

[28] Marx: 'A commodity appears at first sight an extremely obvious, trivial thing. But its analysis brings out that it is a very strange thing, abounding in metaphysical subtleties and theological niceties'.

34   B. PARRY

Without any sentimentality about premodern consciousness and tradition—patriarchy, polygamy and genital mutilation, the worship of spirits and the belief in gnomes and jinns, seers and saints—the novel unravels the injurious effects of the precipitate arrival of a money economy on precapitalist social relationships. Within a substantial body of commentary,[29] I find the most discerning reading of *Xala* to be that of Fredric Jameson, who detected that

> this tale raises the issue of what must finally be one of the key problems in any analysis of Ousmane's [*sic*] work, namely the ambiguous role played in it by archaic or tribal elements [...] The same double historical perspective—archaic customs radically transformed and denatured by the superposition of capitalist relations—seems to me demonstrable in *Xala*. (Jameson, 1986b, 80)[30]

The paradox of Sembéne's reflections on damaged, no-longer-intact indigenous social formations is that unblinking criticism of anachronistic practices coexists with an appreciation of the qualities in older forms of communal life and regret at their disruption. As Frederic Jameson writes: 'Thus the primordial crime of capitalism is exposed: not so much wage labor as such, or the ravages of the money form, or the remorseless and impersonal rhythms of the market, but rather this primal displacement of the older forms of collective life from a land now seized and privatized. It is the oldest of modern tragedies' (Jameson, 1986b, 84). A refusal to scant the commonality that had sustained earlier ways of living, together with a cool-eyed recognition of its accompanying deprivations, is condensed in an abrupt shift of sentiment in this remark: 'The village had neither shop, nor school nor dispensary; there was nothing at all attractive about it in fact. Its life was based on the principles of community interdependence' (Sembéne, 1976, 69).

This demonstration of affection and respect for pre-capitalist ways of life is anticipated by scenes of a landscape inaccessible to modern transport, 'marked by a grandiose, calm austerity and harmony'; in demonstrations of 'the customary courtesy' of its inhabitants; and in

---

[29] In addition to work cited in text and foonotes, see, for example, Ogundokun (2013), Messier (2011), Sorensen (2010) and Lynn (2003).

[30] For a polemical and pedantic challenge to Jameson's reading, see Edwards (2004).

giving voice to a peasant's recoil from the nearby town, Dakar, over-taken by machines and a 'rhythm of madness' (Sembéne, 1976, 67–9). *Xala*, then, fashions a world in which the residual and the emergent intersect and clash, but where the agents of political revolution are not yet center stage, as they are in Sembéne's *God's Bits of Wood* (1960). The venal African compradors, beneficiaries of independence and servants of metropolitan capitalism are agitating for greater economic power; the urban and rural women subject to their husbands and fathers are chafing at patriarchy; and the maimed and diseased beggars, the redundant men and women who can no longer be harbored in the impoverished villages and are surplus to the towns, rebel against their immediate and visible oppressors. Only in the medical student Rama, principled daughter of the corrupt businessman El Hadj, and who despises polygamy, scorns the pretensions of the French-speaking African elite and promotes the use of Wolof, do we see a radical political consciousness in the making.

The choreographed revenge of the dispossessed against the depriva-tions and injustices they had endured is reminiscent of the gang rape in Luis Buñuel's film *Viridiana* (1961) and is as allegorical.[31] If the surplus of physical affliction among the procession invading El Hadj's villa, overfilled with ostentatious and gaudy commodities, is a symptom of a diseased social order that would engender and tolerate such degra-dation, it also appears calculated to evoke fear and loathing in the reader: a leper, a human trunk on a roller, a 'cripple with a degenerates' head and runny eyes', another whose maggoty face has 'a hole where his nose had been', a woman with 'a cloven heel and stunted toes', a hunch-back, a young man with 'an infected sore on his shin, covered with a zinc plate held in place by a piece of string [giving] off a smell of rotting flesh' (Sembéne, 1976, 108–10). It is noticeable that neither these adverse descriptions nor the beggars' obscene gestures and indecent conduct—causing Rama, who 'was always ready with the words "revolu-tion" and "new social order"', to recoil (1976, 111–2)—are transcribed into cinematic language. Instead, and preceding the assault on property and person, the film visualizes a tableau of crippled beggars in colorful robes, their dignity intact as they make an arduous progress across a bleak landscape, before sharing an austere meal and lamenting the loss of

---

[31] Since writing this I have come across an essay that makes this same point: see Marcia Landy, 'Political Allegory and "Engaged Cinema": Sembène's "Xala"' (1984).

communal funds to a thief who graduates from pickpocket to membership of the Chamber of Commerce.

Moreover, neither sight nor sound of the beggars' banquet in the film betrays a view of the vile and monstrous cohort that emerges from the book's surplus of inimical language. It could be argued that the vitriolic rhetoric is in part mitigated by the recurrent presence and refrain of the dignified beggar from whose community El Hadj had stolen and who in retaliation had laid the curse. Sitting cross-legged on a worn-out sheepskin, as if 'part of the décor' outside the office of the disconcerted businessman who does not recognize him, he is a figure of statuesque poise: hunchbacked with prominent ears and a skinny neck, chanting a never-changing holy complaint 'in a carefully modulated voice' (Sembéne, 1976, 79) and always 'keeping a proud, distant pose' (101), in making his continuous passive protest.

The book also articulates the anger and contempt of the outcastes when in idioms not elegant but eloquent, they castigate the perfidious African elite: 'People like you live on theft. And exploit the poor [...] All your past wealth [...] was acquired by cheating [...] I am a leper! I am a leper to myself alone. To no one else. But you, you are a disease that is infectious to everyone. The virus is a collective leprosy' (Sembéne, 1976, 111). All the same, the hostile representation of the despised and rejected in the novella stands as a sign of deformed bodies incapable of the rational exercise of violence. Whereas the film ends with the ritual abasement of the miscreant by righteous enemies, this in the book is followed by the inevitable defeat of the haphazard rebellion and the restoration of the existing regime's fragile order—'[O]utside the forces of order raised their weapons into the firing position' (114)—intimating that the insurgents are not yet in possession of a class consciousness and the organizational skills needed to challenge entrenched power.

It was my intention to recuperate the novel's world as one where earlier forms of economic and social existence disrupted by capitalist expansion coexisted with antecedent modes of labor, belief systems and customs that defied the pervasive presence of the new. The density in the representation of social conditions in permanent crisis places *Xala* in the tradition of realism from which it also departs by accommodating formal and vernacular linguistic registers, bardic and impersonal address, drama and exegesis, sarcasm and exhortation, naturalism and the prodigious. Such stylistic ingenuity surpasses the imitation or adaptation of entrenched novelistic modes, to emerge as the metamorphosis of a historical moment into aesthetic form that, in turn, allows readers access to the material ground of traumatic existential states and the intimacy of their materialization.

Acknowledgements My thanks to Keya Ganguly and Timothy Brennan for their suggestions and critical comments, and for sharing with me their work in progress.

BIBLIOGRAPHY

Adorno, T. W. (1977), 'Reconciliation under Duress', in *Aesthetics and Politics*. London: New Left Books, pp. 151–76.

Adorno, T. W. (1991–92), *Notes to Literature*, 2 vols. W. W. Nicholsen (transl.), R. Tiedemann (ed.). New York: Columbia University Press.

Adorno, T. W. (1997), *Aesthetic Theory*, G. Adorno and R. Tiedemann (eds), R. HullotKentor (new transl. and ed.). London: The Athlone Press.

Amin, S. (1974), *Accumulation on a World Scale*. New York: Monthly Review Press.

Anderson, P. (1984), 'Modernity and Revolution'. *New Left Review*, 144 (March–April), 96–113.

Appiah, K. A. (1991), 'Is the "Post" in "Postcolonial" the "Post" in "Postmodern"?'. *Critical Inquiry*, 17 (2), (Winter), 336–57.

Bahri, D. (2003), *Native Intelligence: Aesthetics, Politics and Postcolonial Literature*. Minneapolis: University of Minnesota Press.

Barrows, A. (2010), *The Cosmic Time of Empire: Modern Britain and World Literature*. Berkeley: University of California Press.

Berman, J. (2012), *Modernist Commitments: Ethics, Politics and Transnational Modernism*. New York: Columbia University Press.

Berman, M. (2003), *All That Is Solid Melts into Air: The Experience of Modernity*. London: Verso.

Bhabha, H. (1994), *The Location of Culture*. London: Routledge.

Brennan, T. (2001), 'Introduction', in A. Carpentier (ed.), *Music in Cuba*. Minneapolis: University of Minnesota Press.

Brennan, T. (2014a), 'Homiletic Realism', in E. Kent and T. Tomsky (eds), *Negative Cosmopolitanism*. Montreal: McGill/Queens University Press, pp. 24–39.

Brennan, T. (2014b), 'The Case against Irony', in B. Etherington and J. Zimbler (eds), 'The Craft s of World Literature', special issue of the *Journal of Commonwealth Literature*, 49 (Fall), 1–16.

38   B. PARRY

Carpentier, A. (1995), 'On the Marvellous Real', in L. P. Zamora and W. B. Faris (eds), *Magical Realism: Theory, History, Community*. Durham and London: Duke University Press, pp. 75–88.

Cleary, J. (2012), 'Realism after Modernism and the Literary World-System'. *Modern Language Quarterly*, special issue 'Peripheral Realisms', 73 (3), (September), 255–68.

Deckard, S. (2012), 'Peripheral Realism, Millennial Capitalism'. *Modern Language Quarterly*, special issue 'Peripheral Realisms', 73 (3), (September), 351–72.

Doyle, L. (2012), 'Modernist Studies and Inter-Imperiality in the Longue Durée', in M. Wollaeger and M. Eatough (eds), *The Oxford Handbook of Global Modernisms*. Oxford: Oxford University Press, pp. 669–95.

Dussel, E. (1998), 'Beyond Eurocentrism: The World-System and the Limits of Modernity', in F. Jameson and M. Miyoshi (eds), *The Cultures of Globalization*. Durham, NC: Duke University Press, pp. 3–31.

Edwards, B. (2004), 'The Genres of Postcolonialism'. *Social Text*, 22 (1), 1–15.

Elliott, E., Caton, L. F. and Rhyne, J. (eds), *Aesthetics in a Multicultural Age*. Oxford: Oxford University Press.

Esty, J. (2004), *A Shrinking Island: Modernism and National Culture in England*. Princeton: Princeton University Press.

Esty, J. and Lye, C. (2012), 'Peripheral Realisms Now'. *Modern Language Quarterly*, special issue on 'Peripheral Realisms', 73 (3), (September), 269–88.

Everdell, W. (1997), *The First Moderns: Profiles in the Origins of Twentieth Century Thought*. Chicago: Chicago University Press.

Friedman, S. S. (2006), 'Periodizing Modernism: Postcolonial Modernities and the Space/Time Borders of Modernist Studies'. *Modernism/Modernity*, 13 (3), (September), 425–43.

Glissant, É. (1989), *Caribbean Discourse: Selected Essays*, M. Dash (ed.). Charlottesville: University of Virginia Press.

Gramsci, A. (1988), 'The War in the Colonies', in D. Forgacs (ed.), *A Gramsci Reader*. London: Lawrence and Wishart, pp. 112–13.

Harootunian, H. (2000a), *History's Disquiet: Modernity, Cultural Practice, and the Question of Everyday Life*. New York: Columbia University Press.

Harootunian, H. (2000b), *Overcome by Modernity: History, Culture, and Community in Interwar Japan*. Princeton: Princeton University Press.

Harris, W. (1967), 'Tradition and the West Indian Novel', in *Tradition, the Writer and Society*. London and Port of Spain: New Beacon Publications, pp. 28–47.

Harris, W. (1970), *History, Fable and Myth in the Caribbean and Guianas*. Georgetown, Guyana: The National History and Arts Council Ministry of Information and Culture.

Harvey, D. (1989), *The Condition of Postmodernity*. Oxford: Blackwell.

Hayot, E. (2009), *The Hypothetical Mandarin: Sympathy, Modernity, and Chinese Pain*. Oxford: Oxford University Press.

Heath, S. (2004), 'The Politics of Genre', in C. Prendergast (ed.), *Debating World Literature*. London: Verso, pp. 163–74.

Huyssen, A. (2005), 'Geographies of Modernism in a Globalizing World', in A. Thacker and P. Brooker (eds), *Geographies of Modernism: Literature, Culture, Places*. London: Routledge, pp. 6–18.

Jameson, F. (1986a), 'On Magic Realism in Film'. *Critical Inquiry*, 12 (Winter), 301–25.

Jameson, F. (1986b), 'Third-World Literature in the Era of Multinational Capitalism'. *Social Text*, 15, 65–88.

Jameson, F. (1991), *Postmodernism or the Cultural Logic of Late Capitalism*. London: Verso.

Jameson, F. (2002), *A Singular Modernity*. London: Verso.

Jameson, F. (2003), 'The End of Temporality'. *Critical Inquiry*, 29 (4), (Summer), 695–718.

Kent, E. and Tomsky, T. (2017), 'Introduction: Negative Cosmopolitanism', in E. Kent and T. Tomsky (eds), *Negative Cosmopolitanism: Cultures and Politics of World Citizenship after Globalization*. Montreal and Kingston: McGill-Queen University Press, pp. 263–82.

Landy, M. (1984), 'Political Allegory and "Engaged Cinema": Sembène's "Xala"'. *Cinema Journal*, 23 (3), (Spring), 31–46.

Larsen, N. (2001), *Determinations: Essays in Theory, Narrative and Nation in the Americas*. London: Verso.

Lawrence, N. (2015), 'The Question of Peripheral Realism', in S. Deckard, N. Lawrence, N. Lazarus, G. Macdonald, U. P. Mukherjee, B. Parry and S. Shapiro (eds), *Combined and Uneven Development: Towards a New Theory of World-Literature*. Liverpool: Liverpool University Press, pp. 49–80.

Lazarus, N. (2011), *The Postcolonial Unconscious*. Cambridge: Cambridge University Press.

Löwy, M. (2007), 'The Current of Critical Irrealism', in M. Beaumont (ed.), *Adventures in Realism*. Oxford : Blackwell, pp. 193–206.

Lukács, G. (1973 [1949]), *Dostoevsky, in Marxism and Human Liberation: Essays on History, Culture and Revolution by György Lukács*, R. Wellek (transl.). New York: Dell Publishing Company.

Lynn, T. J. (2003), 'Politics, Plunder, and Postcolonial Tricksters: Ousmane Sembène's *Xala* '. *International Journal of Francophone Studies*, 6 (3), (1 December), 183–96.

Mahaffey, V. (2007), *Modernist Literature: Challenging Fictions*. Oxford: Blackwell.

Maiangwa, Y. (1979), 'The Duty of Violence', in Kolawole Ogungbesan (ed.), *New West African Literature*. London: Heinemann, pp. 10–20.

40   B. PARRY

Mao, D. and Walkowitz, R. (2008), 'The New Modernist Studies'. *PMLA*, 123 (3), 737–49. Marcuse, H. (1977), 'Adorno on Brecht', in *Aesthetics and Politics*. London: New Left Books, pp. 178–95.

Martin, G. (1989), *In Journey through the Labyrinth: Latin American Fiction in the Twentieth Century*. London: Verso.

Messier, V. (2011), 'Decolonizing National Consciousness Redux: Ousmane Sembène's Xala as Transhistorical Critique'. *Postcolonial Text*, 6, (4), 1–21.

Mitchell, T. (2000), *Questions of Modernity*. Minneapolis: University of Minnesota Press. Moretti, F. (2006), 'The End of the Beginning'. *New Left Review*, September/October, 41, 71–86.

Moretti, F. (2006), 'The End of the Beginning'. *New Left Review*, September/October, 41, 71–86.

Mulvey, L. (1991), 'Xala, Ousmene Sembène: The Carapace That Failed'. *Third Text*, 16 (Autumn/Winter), 19–37.

Munro, M. (2005), 'Chronicle of the Seven Sorrows (Review)'. *Callaloo*, 28, (4) (Fall), 1103–05.

Murphy, D. (2002), 'An African Brecht'. *New Left Review*, 16, (July–August), 115–29.

Nicholls, P. (1995), *Modernisms: A Literary Guide*. Berkeley and Los Angeles: University of California Press.

Ogundokun, S. A. (2013), 'Cultural and Political Alienation in Sembène Ousmane's Xala'. *Global Journal of Human Social Science Research*, 13 (4-A), 27–31.

Osborne, P. (1995), *The Politics of Time: Modernity and Avant-Garde*. London: Verso.

Rabaté, J.-M. (2007), *1913: The Cradle of Modernism*. Oxford: Blackwell.

Radhakrishnan, R. (2003), *Theory in an Uneven World*. Oxford: Blackwell.

Schwarz, R. (1992), *Misplaced Ideas: Essays on Brazilian Culture*, J. Gledson (ed. with an intro.). London: Verso.

Schwarz, R. (2001), *A Master on the Periphery of Capitalism*, J. Gledson (transl.) Durham: Duke University Press.

Sembène, O. (1962 [1960]), *God's Bits of Wood*, F. Price (transl.). London: Heinemann.

Sembène, O. (1976), *Xala*, C. Wake (transl.). London: Heinemann.

Sembène, O. (2005), 'Interview with Ousmane Sembène'. *Socialist Worker Online*, 1955 (11 June).

Serequeberhan, T. (1997), 'The Critique of Eurocentrism', in E. C. Ez (ed.), *Postcolonial African Philosophy: A Critical Reader*. Oxford: Blackwell, pp. 141–61.

Sorensen, E. P. (2010), 'Naturalism and Temporality in Ousmane Sembène's *Xala*'. *Research in African Literatures*, 41 (2) (Summer), 222–43.

Trotsky, L. (1965), *History of the Russian Revolution*, vol. I. London: Gollanz.

Williams, R. (1989), *The Politics of Modernism*, T. Pinkey (ed. and intro.). London: Verso.

Wood, P. (1992), 'The Politics of the Avant-Garde', in *The Great Utopia: The Russian and Soviet Avant-Garde 1915–1932*. New York: Guggenheim Museum, pp. 1–23.

Wright, G. (2002), 'Building Global Modernisms'. *Grey Room*, 7 (Spring), 124–34.

What is Peripheral about Peripheral Modernisms?

Maria-Irene Ramalho-Santos

'Il n'y a que des mots inexacts pour désigner quelque chose exactement'
Gilles Deleuze and Claire Parnet, *Dialogues*.[1]

Students of Modernism would fully agree with what my epigraph, borrowed from Gilles Deleuze, states: 'there are only inexact words to designate something exactly'. At least since Harry Levin's famous question of 1960—what was Modernism?—and particularly after Maurice Beebe's self-confident reply in 1974—what Modernism was—students of Modernism know that, as concerns their object of study, there are only inexact words to designate something exactly.[2] More than that, they do know that the main problem is not really that there are no exact words,

---

[1] Gilles Deleuze, Claire Parnet, *Dialogues* (Paris: Flammarion, 1977).

[2] Harry Levin, 'What Was Modernism?', *The Massachusetts Review* 1.4 (Summer 1960): 606–630; Maurice Beebe, 'What Modernism Was', *Journal of Modern Literature* 3.5 (July 1974): 1065–1084.

M.-I. Ramalho-Santos (✉)
Faculdade de Letras, Centro de Estudos Sociais, Universidade de Coimbra, Coimbra, Portugal
e-mail: mirramalho@gmail.com

© The Author(s), under exclusive license to Springer Nature Switzerland AG 2024
K. Pizzi and R. Gefter Wondrich (eds.), *Rethinking Peripheral Modernisms*, https://doi.org/10.1007/978-3-031-35546-2_3

but rather that there is no exact *thing*. For students of Modernism, Modernism is never *exactly* Modernism. That is why they tend to use the plural—Modernisms—and frequently resort to modifiers.

The conference at the Institute of Germanic and Romance Studies of March 2012 that is at the origin of this essay was about *peripheral Modernisms*. Exactly at the same time, a similar conference on Modernism was taking place at the University of Oxford, gathering together many renowned scholars from various places, languages, and cultures of Modernism. Andreas Huyssen, who once mapped the geographies of Modernism, was one of them, and for a good reason.[3] The Oxford conference announced itself as a conference on *moving Modernisms*. It claimed to be concerned with 'the most significant directions in which study of *the period* has developed over the past forty years'. I emphasize 'the period' which, together with 'the discipline' mentioned further down, seems to contradict the intended exploration of 'emergent geographies' and 'shifting temporalities'. Is Modernism a period? Can Modernism be considered a discipline? According to *Modernism/Modernity*, the official journal of the Modernist Studies Association, Modernism is both a period ('roughly from 1860 to the present'—I am tempted to ask, where does 'the present' end?) and a discipline ('Modernist studies'). Curiously enough, a very interesting, multilingual- and multicultural-sensitive essay by Susan Stanford Friedman, published in the same journal, ends up romantically describing Modernism as a living organism.[4]

Modernism as a period is, of course, a useful concept, and I would not wish to discard it. When asked to write about American Modernist poetry for the fifth volume of *The Cambridge History of American Literature* (2003), I promptly produced an essay entitled 'Poetry in the Machine

---

[3] Andreas Huyssen, 'Geographies of Modernism', in Peter Brooker and Andrew Thacker (eds.), *Geographies of Modernism. Literatures, Cultures, Spaces* (London & New York: Routledge, 2005). A revised version published as 'Geographies of Modernism in a Globalized World' is in *New German Critique* 34.1 (2007): 189–207.

[4] Susan Friedman, 'Planetarity. Musing Modernist Studies', *Modernism / Modernity* 17.3 (September). To be fair, Friedman's 'living, breathing organism' is 'Modernist studies' as 'planetarity': 493; Friedman's substantial elaboration on the concept, which she insists is to be distinguished from Spivak's use of it in *Death of a Discipline*, just came out as a book: *Planetary Modernisms Provocations on Modernity across Time* (New York: Columbia University Press, 2015), 347, n. 17. Cf. Gayatri Chakravorty Spivak, *Death of a Discipline* (New York: Columbia University Press, 2003), chapter 3 ('Planetarity).

WHAT IS PERIPHERAL ABOUT PERIPHERAL MODERNISMS? 45

Age', explicitly linking Modernism to modernity and modernization. Since Frank Lentricchia had already taken care of his 'Modernist quartet' for this volume (Frost, Stevens, Pound, Eliot),[5] I discussed six more poets: Gertrude Stein, William Carlos Williams, H. D., Marianne Moore, Hart Crane, and Langston Hughes (dates of birth ranging from 1874 to 1902). For me, then, American Modernist poets were clearly of a period. To a certain extent, they still are. But my discovery while writing that essay was that the lyricism of all my six Modernist poets was of more than one period and could be seen to reclaim present, past, and future. Just one example: H. D. 'went back to the Greeks' (as she said) to reinvent the modern woman in her *Helen in Egypt* (1960). Tradition and resistance to tradition are two sides of the same coin. Just like center and periphery.

I find the many qualifiers of Modernism very interesting and never stop wondering about them. Here are some of them: high, classic, canonic, aesthetic, primordial, late, epiphanic, social, hegemonic, bad, reactionary, fascist, peripheral, moving, divergent, relational, alternative, errant, mestizo, cannibal, emergent, gendered, queer, cosmopolitan, international, transnational, transhemispheric, and, last but not least, planetary. Clearly, Jackson Lears' concern with 'this terminological muddle' makes even more sense today than when it was first formulated more than thirty years ago.[6] When, in 2008, António Sousa Ribeiro and I myself put together a collection of essays on the subject, the title we chose for it was also a modified plural: *Translocal Modernisms*.[7] In our Introduction, we too asked questions, even if not expecting them to be graced with exact answers. We asked not only the much repeated old questions—what is? what was?—but also two new ones—why Modernism*s*? and *what will Modernism be*? This latter question of ours signifies that

---

[5] F. Lentricchia's, *Modernist Quartet* (Cambridge: Cambridge University Press, 1994) is the base for 'Modernist Lyric in the Culture of Capital', the essay that Lentricchia and Andrew DuBois contributed to the fifth volume of *The Cambridge History of American Literature*.

[6] T. J. Jackson Lears, *No Place of Grace. Anti-Modernism and the Transformation of American Culture, 1880–1920* (Chicago, Ill: The University of Chicago Press, 1983), XIX.

[7] M. I. Ramalho Santos and A. Sousa Ribeiro (eds.), *Translocal Modernisms. International Perspectives* (Bern: Peter Lang, 2008).

other famous question—Raymond Williams' 'when was Modernism?'[8]—while making sense to us as a survey of the relations of art to production and of modern art's accommodation to bourgeois values, seemed premature to us because of its suggestion of closure. Our wording pointed, rather, to the historicity and fragility of the concept of Modernism as being in constant need of rigorous recontextualization and reformulation—present, past, and future. Although the essays included in our volume had a decisive literary bias (as, incidentally, my contribution here does too), *Translocal Modernisms* covered a wide spatial and temporal range of literary, artistic, cultural, and social fields and perspectives.

Here I hesitate both before the plural (*Modernisms*) and the qualification (*translocal*). I started having serious misgivings when I received an invitation to address the conference calling for papers on peripheral Modernisms. Of course, I was aware of the use of the concept by such distinguished authors as Beatriz Sarlo, Carlos Blanco, Harry Harootunian, and Benita Parry, among others, but I had never really questioned it. Beyond the various kinds of art produced in a geography that is peripheral to the self-appointed center of the speaking subject, what could be peripheral about peripheral Modernisms, I wondered. To speak of the periphery presupposes a center, thereby implying, willy-nilly, a value judgment. Periphery, not being the center, is different, which usually means, in the western culture, somehow inferior.[9]

Andreas Huyssen writes of 'metropolitan culture' being 'translated, appropriated and creatively mimicked in colonial and postcolonial countries'.[10] Could this be a fair description of art outside the speaking center? In Immanuel Wallerstein's understanding of the modern world system, of course, periphery means economically less developed than the centers of international capital and hence at an earlier stage of capitalism. But I submit that artistic creation works differently. Etymologically, periphery also means, literally, at the outer boundary or circumference. Not here, at the center, but out there, at the margins. To claim the circumference, as

---

[8] See R. Williams, 'When Was Modernism?', *New Left Review* I/175 (May–June 1989): 48–52, first delivered as a lecture at the University of Bristol in 1987.

[9] I discuss this problem in M. I. Ramalho Santos, 'Difference and Hierarchy Revisited by Feminism', *Anglo Saxonica* III, 6 (2013): 21–45.

[10] Huyssen, 'Geographies of Modernism': 189.

Emily Dickinson once arrogantly did ('my business is circumference'),[11] is to question the centrality of the center, or rather, to question the reality of the center itself, as Derrida was to do a century after Dickinson: 'the center is not the center'.[12] Which means that the periphery is not the periphery, either. This particular notion of periphery does appeal to me, whether 'peripheral' refers to the *where* of place, the *when* of time, the *what* of content, or the *how* of form. Or even simply suggesting world relevance, impact, and circulation.

Aesthetic Modernism began to be perceived at the turn of the twentieth century as a fairly well contained Western (if not heavily Anglo-American) literary/artistic phenomenon, only soon to explode into the diversity and plurality that has not ceased to grow to this day—or to *the present*.[13] Curiously enough, some of Harry Levin's core, or canonical, Modernists were exiles or expatriates from what Wallerstein would later call the semiperiphery, if not from the periphery itself. Some of these 'high Modernists' had been regularly borrowing from the periphery all along—the so-called primitivism, exoticism, or barbarism.[14] One of the most brilliant borrowers is one of the most quoted definers of Modernism at its earlier stages, Charles Baudelaire, who saw modernity as bridging time and eternity: 'La modernité, c'est le transitoire, le fugitif, le contingent, la moitié de l'art, dont l'autre moitié est l'éternel et l'immuable' (1863). [Modernity is the transient, the fleeting, the contingent; it is one half of art, the other being the eternal and the immovable] This passage is quoted all the time. I go on to cite, before I continue, the next sentence,

[11] E. Dickinson, *Letters*, eds. T. H. Johnson and T. Ward (Cambridge, Mass.: The Belknap Press of Harvard University Press, 1970), 412 (To Higginson, July 1862).

[12] J. Derrida, 'Structure, Sign, and Play in the Discourse of the Human Sciences' was first presented to a conference on structuralism at the Johns Hopkins University in 1966. Later, it was included in *Writing and Difference*, trans. A. Bass (Chicago: The University of Chicago Press, 1978), 278–294 (279).

[13] For a useful survey of the trajectory of 'Modernism', 'Modernist studies', and 'the new Modernist studies', see Carla Kaplan, 'Making It New: Constructions of Modernism', in Paul Lauter (ed.), *A Companion to American Literature and Culture* (Malden, MA, Oxford, Chichester: Wiley-Blackwell, 2010), 40–46.

[14] Several examples can be found in essays collected in Peter Brooker and Andrew Thacker (eds.), *Geographies of Modernism. Literatures, Cultures, Spaces* (London & New York: Routledge, 2005).

which is even more relevant for my purposes here: 'Il y a eu une modernité pour chaque peintre ancien'. [There was a form of modernity for every painter of the past].[15]

Neither Center nor Periphery was the title of one of the panels of the 'Peripheral Modernisms' conference. I, too, would settle for Modernism *tout court*. This is not to say that I would easily discard the many, interlaced narratives of modernity, modernization, Modernism, Postmodernism, and postmodernity. They are all part of the post-Enlightenment narrative of capitalism and colonialism. Capitalism reinforces, rather than replacing, colonialism, and both continue to trace what de Sousa Santos defines as the abyssal line of inclusion and exclusion of what we call modernization.[16] Modernization and its attendant globalization really amount to what I would call 'capitalismization', that is to say, the obsession with accumulation, totalizing structures, and exhaustive, controlling knowledge in its attempt to incorporate the outside world as unaligned or emergent.[17] Or, in other words, peripheral.

Thus, by virtue of the unequal development of capitalism, the outside is kept firmly outside within an omnivorous globalism. Postcolonial scholarship often gilds the impact of colonialism by highlighting the advantages of Imperial development and modernization.[18] One of the facets of aesthetic Modernism is precisely its discontent with modernization, technological development, and infinite progress, the latter actually viewed as decadence. The parable Walter Benjamin composed on Klee's *Angelus Novus* in his 'Theses on the Philosophy of History' (1942) is very eloquent in this regard in that it refuses to let the past be automatically

---

[15] Charles Baudelaire, *Le peintre de la vie moderne*, 1859–1860, first published in 1863, IV, 'La modernité', https://www.uni-due.de/lyriktheorie/texte/1863_baudelaire.html, accessed 29 October 2019.

[16] B. de Sousa Santos, 'Beyond Abyssal Thinking. From Global Lines to Ecologies of Knowledges', *Review* XXX, 1 (2007): 45–89.

[17] Cf. Jon Hegglung, 'Modernism, Africa and the Myth of Continents', in Brooker and Thacke (eds.), *Geographies of Modernism*, 43–53.

[18] For a fine critique of postcolonial studies, see H. Harootunian, *The Empire's New Clothes. Paradigm Lost and Regained* (Chicago: Prickly Paradigm Press, 2004). Cf. as well Benita Parry, *Postcolonial Studies. A Materialist Critique* (London: Routledge, 2004). A different kind of critique, aimed mainly at privileged, exilic intellectuals from the so-called third world, is in Dorothy M. Figueira, *Otherwise Occupied. Pedagogies of Alterity and the Brahminization of Theory* (Albany: State University of New York Press, 2008), esp. chapter 5 ('The Romance of Exile').

redeemed by the future.[19] Indeed, Benjamin saw modernity as fragmentary, as an illusion of progress, and as 'the new in the context of what has always been there'.[20]

To be sure, this is also the discontent of 'reactionary Modernists', e.g. Carl Schmidt and Ernst Jünger.[21] Hitler's *Mein Kampf* can also be, and has been, seen as a good example of a 'reactionary Modernist' text.[22] The truth is that both aesthetic and reactionary Modernism regret the post-Enlightenment sense of an ending, but whereas reactionary Modernism aestheticizes politics by resorting to myths of national purification and regeneration (with the disastrous consequences we all know), aesthetic Modernism provides us with fictions that make human sense, but which never let us forget they are fictions, not myths. As eloquently put by Frank Kermode in *The Sense of an Ending*, fictions 'are not myths, and they are not hypotheses; you neither rearrange the world to suit them, nor test them by experiment, for instance in gas-chambers'.[23] Great poets are fine providers of fictions, Wallace Stevens being for me, as for Kermode, one of the most eloquent: 'The final belief', writes the inventor of the disquieting 'fiction of an absolute' in *Notes Toward a Supreme Fiction* (III, vii), 'is to believe in a fiction, which you know to be a fiction, there being nothing else. The exquisite truth is to know that it is a fiction and that you believe in it willingly'.[24]

If peoples and nations can be considered developed or underdeveloped, and can be oppressors or oppressed and subjected to hierarchization, art on the other hand never is, even if hegemonic criticism would conspire to make it so—for instance, by speaking of center and periphery. What

[19] See Walter Benjamin, *Illuminations*, ed. Hanna Arendt, trans. Harry Zohn (New York: Schocken, 1969), 257.

[20] Apud David Frisby, *Fragments of Modernity* (Cambridge: Polity Press, 1986), 205–207. See also B. de Sousa Santos, 'The Fall of the Angelus Novus. Beyond the Modern Game of Roots and Options', *Current Sociology* 46.2 (April 1998): 81–118 (passim).

[21] *Translocal Modernisms* includes a very interesting analysis of Schmidt and Jünger as 'reactionary Modernists' penned by Isabel Capeloa Gil – *op.cit.*, 185–211.

[22] Cf. Roger Griffin, *Modernism and Fascism. The Sense of Beginning under Mussolini and Hitler* (New York: Macmillan Palgrave, 2007), 260–265.

[23] Frank Kermode, *The Sense of an Ending. Studies in the Theory of Fiction* (New York: Oxford University Press, 1967), 41. Griffin's excellent *Modernism and Fascism* draws generously on Kermode's *Sense of an Ending*.

[24] Wallace Stevens, 'Adagia', in F. Kermode and J. Richardson (eds.) *Collected Poetry & Prose* (New York: Library of America, 1997), 349, 903.

I am suggesting is that the categories of Wallerstein's world system do not apply to art or poetry. This much is already acknowledged by Carlos Blanco, proudly writing 'from the semiperiphery' in 1998. Taking off from Baudelaire's realization that 'the modern' has always been there for art, Blanco recalls the early peripherality of what was to be considered the center. The main characters of the avant-garde's break with the nineteenth century (Marinetti, Picasso, Tzara, Mayakovski, Eisenstein, Piscator, Brecht, the Constructivists, the Dadaists) are all peripheral artists and writers vis-à-vis the metropolitan centers of Imperial capital, whether as regards geography, language, politics, or all three of them.[25] To a certain extent, Gerald Bruns' notion of 'aesthetic anarchy', even if I find it too much circumscribed to the 'period', speaks to this issue as well: 'anything goes, nothing is forbidden, since anything is possible within the historical limits of the particular situations in which (...) art and poetry have been created'.[26]

When Beebe characterizes aesthetic Modernism as 'the international revolution in literature and the arts which began in the late nineteenth century and flourished until the 1950s',[27] his are inexact words to designate inexact things. In this essay, I borrow the inexact word *Modernism* to refer to the permanent revolution in literature and the arts which, being *permanent*, has always been happening at all times and places in many different ways. I focus on poetry in the broadest sense of the word to isolate agreed features of central, western so-called Modernism which I argue can be observed across languages, geographies, and centuries.[28] This is how I understand Rimbaud's meaning when he provocatively

---

[25] Carlos Blanco Aguinada, *Sobre el modernismo desde la semiperiferia* (Granada: de Guante Blanco/Comares, 1998), 67.

[26] Gerald Bruns, *On the Anarchy of Poetry and Philosophy: A Guide for the Unruly* (New York: Fordham University Press, 2006), XXV and *passim*. The elision in the quote refers to 'modern and contemporary'.

[27] M. Beebe, 'What Modernism Was', 1066.

[28] In a very useful book, Astradur Eysteinsson highlights some widely recognized features of canonical Modernist poetry. I take off from there to devise a few of my own, suggesting that they signal great poetry and are to be encountered in every untimely poet—see A. Eysteinsson, *The Concept of Modernism* (Ithaca, NY: Cornell University Press, 1992).

stated that 'Il faut être absolument moderne' [One must be absolutely modern].[29]

My concept of Modernism (a term which I am increasingly tempted to discard) is thus closer to Paul de Man's *modernity* and Giorgio Agamben's *the contemporary*.[30] It comes as no surprise that both these theoreticians of Baudelaire's fusion of presentness and timelessness take off from Nietzsche's complex reflections on history in the second of his *Unzeitgemässe Betrachtungen* (Untimely Meditations; 1874).[31] The meditation in question is entitled 'On the Uses and Disadvantages of History for Life' and its major points are firstly that, though we cannot but be reconciled to history, as Nietzsche himself acknowledges, the value we ascribe to it is 'an occidental prejudice'[32]; secondly, that 'an excess of history is harmful to the living man'[33]; thirdly, that 'it is altogether impossible to live without forgetting'[34]; fourthly, that 'the past and present are one' because of 'imperishable types' and, therefore, that we must act 'counter to our time and thereby acting on our time'.[35] 'Untimely', for Nietzsche, thus means 'beyond all that is ephemeral'.[36] Drawing heavily on Nietzsche's second meditation, Paul de Man comes to the conclusion that, while transcending history, modernity 'acts as the principle that gives literature duration and historical experience' and that since the poet 'is both the historian and the agent of his own language', 'literature has always been essentially modern'.[37]

---

[29] Arthur Rimbaud, 'Adieu' (1873), in Michel Décaudin (ed.), *Une saison en enfer. Oeuvres poétiques* (Paris: Garnier-Flammarion, 1964), 140.

[30] Paul de Man, 'Literary History and Literary Modernity' and 'Lyric and Modernity', in *Blindness and Insight. Essays in the Rhetoric of Contemporary Criticism* (Minneapolis: The University of Minnesota Press, 1983), 142–186; Giorgio, 'What is the Contemporary?', https://folk.uib.no/hlils/TBLRTOTALT-221015/TBLR-Contemp-Paris2015-27.12.15/Agamben%20Contemporary.pdf, accessed 29 October 2019. The site says page not found; but the one I gave in 2012 says the same now as well....

[31] Friedrich Nietzsche, *Untimely Meditations*, trans. R. J. Hollingdale, ed. Daniel Breazeale (Cambridge: Cambridge University Press, 2007), 1997.

[32] *Ibid.*, 66.

[33] *Ibid.*, 67.

[34] *Ibid.*, 62.

[35] *Ibid.*, 66 and 60 respectively.

[36] *Ibid.*, xlv.

[37] P. de Man, 'Literary History and Literary Modernity', 162, 152 and 151 respectively.

Giorgio Agamben, in turn, echoing Roland Barthes quoting Nietzsche, states that 'the contemporary is the untimely'.[38] The contemporary, Agamben adds, implies 'a singular relation with one's own time, which adheres to it and, at the same time, keeps a distance from it [...] Those who coincide too well with the epoch, those who are perfectly tied to it in every respect, are not contemporaries, precisely because they do not manage to see it; they are not able to firmly hold their gaze on it'.[39] The contemporary is the one who interpellates his or her time, transforms it, and puts it in relation to other times.[40] For Agamben, then, untimeliness, or contemporariness, is a question of *timely relevance*. And 'timely relevance' is what I claim for all poetry and art from all times and places. I thus appropriate, in somewhat modified form, Bruns' concept of anarchist aesthetics.

Let me push the theoretician a little further: to be untimely is to be always in time (be it *chronos, aevum,* or *kairos*) and to speak to time at all times. The poet, or, rather, the strong poet, after my much-admired teacher Harold Bloom, is always contemporary precisely because the lack of coincidence of times allows him or her to perceive time's darkness— as in Whitman's 'dark patches' in *Crossing Brooklyn Ferry* (1856)—and thereby disclose the light of time. Strong poetry (and by poetry I mean all strong literary production, that is to say, all the fictions we believe in) is always already untimely, contemporary, modern(ist). Blake's Bard, 'who Present, Past, & Future sees', speaks for the relevance of all *untimely* poets.[41] Untimeliness may well be the most compelling of our fictions.

The Enlightenment promise of modernity as modernization and infinite progress began to be called into question early on by the Romantics. Friedrich Schlegel's ironic concept of *Unverständlichkeit* (incomprehensibility) (1800) inaugurates what would become a major feature of Modernism at the turn of the nineteenth century by explicitly calling into question language's capacity to communicate. Later, Benjamin would further elaborate on this topic in the introduction to his translation of

[38] G. Agamben, 'What is the Contemporary?', 40.

[39] *Ibid.,* 41.

[40] *Ibid.,* 53.

[41] William Blake, 'Introduction', *Songs of Experience* (1794), in Geoffrey Keynes (ed.), *Poetry and Prose* (London: The Nonesuch Library, 1961), 65.

Baudelaire's *Tableaux Parisiens* (1923).[42] Poets, of course, have always been fascinated by the materiality and uncanny opaqueness of language. Wallace Stevens called it 'the poet's gibberish' and 'lingua franca et jocundissima'.[43]

In fifteenth-century pre-Colombian America, Nezahualcoyotl, the Nahuatl poet, *king* and sage (*tlamatini*) of Texcoco, was already expressing anxiety about the possibility of speaking true words; instead, he conjured up flowers, feathers, and stones to say the unsayable.[44] Centuries later, Hart Crane, under the spell of the ancient cultures of Mexico, would hanker after the 'cognate' word in his magnificent *The Broken Tower* (1932).[45] At about the same time, in Brazil, João Guimarães Rosa, in *Sagarana* (1938, 1946), was giving expression to the inexpressible by searching deep into the possibilities of the Portuguese language, hybridizing it and rendering it foreign, and doing violence to its referentiality. As one of his characters, who inexplicably finds himself blind, is desperately trying to get out of the thick forest, by setting one foot carefully in front of the other, foot by foot, the phrase 'pé por pé, pé por si', is rendered foreign and as madly absurd as the character's unexpected situation: 'Pé por pé, pé por si... Pèporpé, péporsi... Pepp or pepp, epp or see... Pêpe orpèpe, heppe Orcy...'.[46] At the same time, in North America, Gertrude Stein, who in *Tender Buttons* (1914) had already made words stand solid and opaque, allowed herself properly to write, in 'What Is English Literature' (1935): 'You do see what I say'.[47] A few years earlier, in 1931, on the other side of the Atlantic, in *Livro do desassossego*, a book of fragments that is really the theory of a poet's practice, Fernando Pessoa, in the person of Bernardo Soares, wrote: 'Gosto de palavras ... As palavras são para mim corpos tocáveis, sereias visíveis, sensualidades incorporadas'. (I love words. Words are for me touchable

---

[42] W. Benjamin, *Illuminations*, 69–82.

[43] W. Stevens, *Notes* II.ix, *Collected Poetry & Prose*.

[44] Miguel León-Portilla, *Fifteen Poets of the Aztec World* (Norman: University of Oklahoma Press), 70–98.

[45] Hart Crane, *Complete Poems and Selected Letters*, ed. Landon Hammer (New York: The Library of America, 2006), 106–107.

[46] João Guimarães Rosa, *Sagarana* (Rio de Janeiro: Nova Fronteira, 1984), 260.

[47] Gertrude Stein, *Writings 1932–1946*, eds. Catherine R. Stimpson and Harriet Chessman (New York: Library of America, 1998), 221.

bodies, visible sirens, embodied sensualities).[48] Ten years earlier, in Peru, César Vallejo composed *Trilce* (1922), arguably the most revolutionary language adventure of the twentieth century, a mestizo poet's mestizo poem, in which Spanish is sacrificed to Runa Simi and Runa Simi sacrificed to Spanish.[49] Seventy years later, one of Vallejo's translators into English, próspero saíz, himself a poet of mixed ancestry from the Navajo County in Arizona, would in turn disfigure the English language and render it foreign in *The Bird of Nothing* (1993), thereby totally subverting the linguistic colonization of the Americas.[50]

Bouncing once again across time and space, I jump back to 1919 Europe to fetch Odradek, the strange creature in Kafka's short story 'Die Sorge des Hausvaters' ('The Cares of a Family Man'),[51] whose name nobody could ever really make out. Neither the name, nor the thing itself. Commentators and interpreters go from an unsophisticated, broken-down, useless item kept in a house for no purpose, to Marxist commodities, to the Freudian return of the repressed, to religious tradition, and more. In a very fine and intelligently argued article in *Translocal Modernisms*, Vivian Liska finds 'The Cares of a Family Man' 'a quintessentially Modernist text'.[52] The narrator's efforts to come to terms both with Odradek and Odradek's unfathomable name prefigure, she shrewdly argues, 'the various attempts to come to terms with modernism'.[53]

---

[48] Fernando Pessoa, *Livro do desassossego, composto por Bernardo Soares, ajudante de guardalivros na cidade de Lisboa*, ed. Richard Zenith (Lisboa: Assírio & Alvim, 2007), 246. My translation, but see also F. Pessoa, *The Book of Disquiet*, ed. and trans. Richard Zenith (London: Penguin, 2002), 224.

[49] César Vallejo, *Obra poética completa*, ed. Américo Ferrari (Lima: Alianza Editorial, 1974). See also a selection of poems translated by próspero saíz, who contributed as well a 'Translator's Preface: The Poet as Translator', *Abraxas* 40/41 (1991): 5–22.

[50] Próspero saíz, *The Bird of Nothing and Other Poems* (Madison, WI: Ghost Pony Press, 1993), 53149.

[51] Franz Kafka, 'Die Sorge des Hausvaters', http://www.textlog.de/32073.html, accessed 14 May 2021.
An English translation is in F. Kafka, *The Complete Stories*, ed. Nahum N. Glatzer (New York: Schocken Books, 1995), 427–429.

[52] V. Liska, 'Making it Mean and Making it Matter: Modernism for the Twenty-First Century', in I. Ramalho Santos and A. Sousa Ribeiro (eds.), *Translocal Modernisms*, 121–138.

[53] *Ibid.*, 122.

My suggestion, however, is that Odradek may well embody no less than language itself, perhaps just like Vallejo's *Trilce*, e.g. the uncanny creature living with us and intriguing us all the time, without letting us know whence it comes or where it goes, a weird thing assuming many shapes without letting itself be fixed, a solid yet living organism that is always changing but never dies, and is never exact either.

Kafka's Odradek has affinities with 'der veste Buchstab' ('the solid, firm, strong letter') which, more than a century before, Hölderlin had tremulously promised the German song at the close of his hymn *Patmos*.[54] Tremulous was the poet's promise, for language is the most precious but also the most dangerous of possessions, as Hölderlin acknowledges in another fragment, 'Im Walde'. That is why, in poetry, the desire for the exact word often goes hand in hand with demystification. Joyce needed the whole of *Finnegans Wake* (1939) to toy with this idea. Dickinson, a century earlier, just a little poem about searching 'philology' in vain while the 'propounded word' waited until revelation came (*J1126/Fr1243*; 1872). Often, poetry takes advantage of the failure of language-as-solid-word with extraordinary results. This is what happens, for example, in the Caribbean/Canadian poet Nourbese Philip's *Zong* (2008), a long poem of shattered words scattered throughout the pages to make the horrifying silences of the Middle Passage speak.[55]

That scholars became uncomfortable with the concept of Modernism very early on can be seen in the emergence of the concept of Postmodernism at the close of the 1960s. Soon, studies of Modernism were speaking of myriad forms of post-, while bringing into their discussion the concept of pre-Modernism as well.[56] Augusto de Campos'

---

[54] Friedrich Hölderlin, *Selected Poems and Fragments*, trans. Michael Hamburger (New York: Penguin, 1998), 242–243: 'der Vater aber liebt/Der über allen waltet/Am meisten, dass gepfleget werde/Der veste Buchstab, und bestehendes gut/Gedeutet. Dem folgt deutscher Gesang'. ('what the Father/Who reigns over all loves most/Is that the solid letter/Be given scrupulous care, and the existing/Be well interpreted. This German song observes').

[55] M. Nourbese Philip, *Zong*! As told to the author by Setaey Adamu Boateng (Middletown, CT: Wesleyan University Press, 2008).

[56] See the special issue of *New Literary History* on *Modernism and Postmodernism* 3.1 (Autumn), especially Ihab Hassan's 'POSTmodernISM. A Practical Bibliography': 5–30.

56 M.-I. RAMALHO-SANTOS

provocatively deconstructive poem 'pós-tudo' (1984)[57] speaks to perfection to the human compulsion to search for the new and to conceptualize what absolutely resists conceptualization, e.g. poetry itself.

What Abel de Barros Baptista and Osvaldo Manuel Silvestre say about Brazilian Modernism—an iconoclastic problematization of the poetic itself—applies to all strong poetry.[58] And no strong poet pushed poetic problematization so far as the Portuguese Fernando Pessoa, whose Lisbon, whether peripheral or semiperipheral, hardly ever joins the 'cities of Modernism'. Problematization, deconstruction, interruption, fragmentation, consciousness of time, Futurism, decadence, defamiliarization, depersonalization, impersonation—these are all identifiable Modernist topoi which in Pessoa transcend one another. Depersonalization—i.e. Pessoan heteronymy—encompasses all of them. The self-interruptive heteronyms deconstruct and render authorship problematic, each one of them contesting the others in turn from different spaces and times. Among several lesser ones, there are: the classical Ricardo Reis, just waiting, in troubled placidity, for time to come and go; the pre-modern Alberto Caeiro, erasing poetry altogether by questioning its conventions; the modern, or Modernist, Pessoa-himself, conjuring up the 'Hour' of timelessness; the Futurist-Decadent Álvaro de Campos, singing his tormented odes of triumph and defeat; the scribbler of *Livro do desassossego*, Bernardo Soares, who praises *imperfected* art and whose headache is also an ache in the universe.[59]

I have suggested elsewhere that Pessoa's *desassossego* (disquietude) is the quintessentially Modernist counterpart of Schlegel's *Unverständlichkeit* (incomprehensibility).[60] The universe, and not just language, has now become untrustworthy. The poet takes refuge in

---

[57] A. de Campos, 'pós-tudo', https://www.google.pt/search?q=augusto+de+campos+quis+mudar+tudo&biw=1242&bih=701&site=webhp&tbm=isch&tbo=u&source=univ&sa=X&ved=0ahUKEwjhxrOfhK_LAhWF6RQKHcbBBDsQsAQIOg&dpr=1, accessed 14 May 2021; see also A. de Campos, *Despoesia* (S. Paulo: Perspectiva, 1994), 35.

[58] Abel Barros Baptista and Osvaldo M. Silvestre (eds.), *Seria uma rima, não seria uma solução. A poesia modernista* (Lisbon: Cotovia, 2005), 38–39.

[59] F. Pessoa, *Livro do desassossego por Bernardo Soares*, 298 (#330; #331).

[60] I. Ramalho Santos, *Atlantic Poets. Fernando Pessoa's Turn in Anglo-American Modernism* (Hanover & London: University Press of New England, 2003), 259. See also I. Ramalho Santos, 'The Tail of the Lizard. Pessoan Disquietude and the Subject of Modernity', in Steffen Dix and Jerónimo Pizarro (eds.), *Portuguese Modernisms. Multiple Perspectives on Literature and the Visual Arts* (London: Legenda, 2011), 264–276.

the *intervalo* ('interval'): the void of nothingness, the inbetweenness-of-being-nonbeing-in-multiplicity, is repeated more than forty times in *Livro do desassossego*. Signifying presence and absence at one and the same time, *intervalo* is the sign of the Pessoan enigma of disquietude. The term carries different meanings in different sketches, and they are all relevant. Whether it be a proper interval, like the intermission of a show, or a space between beings, feelings, or things, an unfathomable twilight zone, as it were, *intervalo* is implicitly and explicitly disquieting: *Entresou* (I-am-between/between-I-am),[61] the poet confesses and the image of human existence in modern society suddenly appears as the I's total vulnerability-in-incomprehensibility. No wonder Harry Harootunian chose *Livro do desassossego* to preside over his *History's Disquiet* (2000).[62]

To conclude, I invoke a moving and hilarious 'Modernism with a human face', a parody embodied in the fictional title of a fictional book by a fictional 'paper architect' created by David Mazzuchelli in his truly untimely graphic novel *Asterios Polyp* (2009).[63] The title is the cleverly concocted name of the puzzling, fascinating protagonist, the prize-winning architect who never saw any of his brilliant designs actually built. The modernist mystery of Kafka's Odradek comes to mind again.

---

[61] F. Pessoa, *Livro do desassossego por Bernardo Soares*, 263 (281).

[62] H. Harootunian, *History's Disquiet. Modernity, Cultural Practice, and the Question of Everyday Life* (New York: Columbia University Press, 2000).

[63] David Mazzuchelli, *Asterios Polyp* (New York: Pantheon Books, 2009). My thanks to João RamalhoSantos for calling my attention to Mazzuchelli's work.

Liminality in the 'Semi-peripheries'

The Literature of Trieste and the Perils of Peripherality

Katia Pizzi

An international phenomenon encompassing travelling cultures and contact zones, Modernism is underpinned by diasporic, exilic and migrant practices. Shifting social, political and economic paradigms challenged traditional aesthetic and discursive forms, debunking national canons, engendering conceptual and psychological displacement, reconfiguring artistic methods and practices. Authors, artists, intellectuals and cultural operators became eminently mobile, caught in the flow of modern migration, the rupture of a technological First World War and the cauldron of financial or industrial crashes, leading to destabilization and more conflict on a global scale. Resisting or embracing this age of traumatic change, the avant-garde dispersed outside state-nation boundaries, interfacing and, even, hybridizing, with other cultures.

As a result, translational, transnational and transcultural criteria have become part and parcel of the critical discourse, following on from

---

K. Pizzi (✉)
Institute of Languages, Cultures and Societies, School of Advanced Study, University of London, London, UK
e-mail: katia.pizzi@sas.ac.uk

© The Author(s), under exclusive license to Springer Nature Switzerland AG 2024
K. Pizzi and R. Gefter Wondrich (eds.), *Rethinking Peripheral Modernisms*, https://doi.org/10.1007/978-3-031-35546-2_4

Bradbury and McFarlane's seminal *Modernism, 1890–1930*.[1] In particular, awareness of plural, spatially and temporally inflected international Modernisms increasingly challenged existing theoretical frameworks, reorienting the debate towards notions of centre and periphery. Fredric Jameson, Benita Parry, Laura Doyle and Laura Winkiel, to cite only a few of the most recent advocates, have all argued for an understanding of Modernism in a peripheral framework. By connecting Modernism directly with the global spread of capitalism, the critical debate became re-focused, re-oriented in geo-modernist directions, encompassing imagined, psychological and new postcolonial geographies.[2]

These debates invited methodological questions, concerning, for example, the new temporalities of Modernism. In *The Sense of an Ending*, Kermode argued that 'because there is something irremediably temporal about literary form [...] Modernist writing [...] uses our normal temporal expectations, and then frustrates or complicates them'.[3] Another methodological challenge lies in the binary centre/periphery, its definition within Modernist studies and the critical methods that best serve specific spatial and temporal contexts.

Setting aside manichean binaries, such as those predicated on colonial imposition of a 'higher' culture over a 'lower' one (or even an 'a-cultural' one), new research needs to remain mindful of the risks inherent in the disconnects between Empire and nation, rendering the Empire peripheral with reference to the centrality of nation, as was, for instance, the case with the Habsburg Empire. The challenge of bi-directionality and cultural translation throws up further challenges.

Notwithstanding these and other paradoxes, it is important to stress that neat cultural and national vectors need to be disabused, if global

---

[1] Malcom Bradbury and James McFarlane (eds.), *Modernism, 1890–1930* (Harmondsworth: Penguin, 1976).

[2] See, for example, B. Parry's essay 'Stylistic Irrealism as Symptom, Mediation and Critique of Peripheral Modernity' included in this volume. See also L. Winkiel, *Modernism, Race and Manifestos* (Cambridge: Cambridge University Press, 2008) and L. A. Doyle, 'Modernist Studies and the Inter-Imperiality in the Longue Durée', in *The Oxford Handbook of Global Modernisms*, eds. Mark Wollaeger and Matt Eatough (New York: Oxford University Press, 2012).

[3] See M. Hollington, 'Svevo, Joyce and Modernist Time', in *Modernism 1890–1930*, eds. M. Bradbury and J. McFarlane (London: Penguin, 1991), p. 432.

Modernism is to emerge in its diasporic and migratory vocation, a 'traveling culture' as suggested by James Clifford.[4] Paradoxically, Modernism is, at once, migratory and rooted, international and local, 'singular' and plural, a case of 'singular modernity' as argued by Jameson.[5] Peripheral players can shift to the centre of a global game. Centres can be eclipsed, bypassed, re-aligned or re-situated, following the inevitable rise of new centres of gravity. If, in the words of Majorie Pryse, 'the challenge to Modernism becomes one of including heterogeneity and global regions in its categories',[6] it must also be one of reconciling within itself a totalizing view, in line with the re-configured times and spaces of imperial capitalism.[7]

These dynamics encompass, of course, wider social and economic trends. Predicated on spatial annexation and controlled circulation of people and goods, the impetus of global Imperialism appropriated the future of others, as Stephen Kern puts it.[8] The Italian colonial experience undertaken in the African Campaign of 1911, the collapse of the Ottoman Empire and acquisition of Libya and the Dodecanese Islands in 1912, engaged Filippo Tommaso Marinetti and the Italian Futurists, providing a cultural, as well as ideological, backdrop, logistics and infrastructure for expatriations that followed in the interwar and postwar years. Furthermore, Marinetti's trust fund allowed for a cosmopolitan lifestyle. Many Italian futurists of the postwar era (Prampolini, Pannaggi, Vasari, Depero, to name only a few) expatriated in search of radical cultural platforms, commissions and salaried labour, lured by the magnet pull of great modernist cities: Paris, New York, Berlin.

The authoritarian turn taken by the Fascist regime after 1924 facilitated a distancing of numerous artists and intellectuals from active politics,

---

[4] James Clifford, *Routes: Travel and Translation in the Late Twentieth Century* (Cambridge, MA: Harvard University Press, 1997), *passim*.

[5] See the 'singular modernity' arising from the global, if uneven, spread of capitalism—see Fredric Jameson, *A Singular Modernity* (London: Verso, 2012), p. 12 *et passim*.

[6] Majorie Pryse, 'Afterword: Regional Modernism and Transnational Regionalism', *Modern Fiction Studies*, 55: 1 (2009), 189–92 (189).

[7] F. Jameson, *Singular Modernity*. See also Andrew Hewitt, *Fascist Modernism: Aesthetics, Politics and the Avant-garde* (Stanford, CA: Stanford University Press, 1993), p. 41.

[8] See also Stephen Kern, *The Culture of Time and Space 1880–1918* (Cambridge, MA: Harvard University Press, 1983), p. 92.

64   K. PIZZI

leading to disengagement and, in some cases, exile, ostracism and expatriations, both enforced and voluntary.[9] Uncertainties over cultural and artistic identity, challenged and threatened by aggressive state politics, the unsituated and chaotic nature of the modern experience, in the wake of Duchamp and Picabia's relocation to the US at the eve of the First World War, led to further expatriations, including permanent exile. Decentralizing and de-localizing, the migratory experience brought about, in turn, a heightened sense of personal dislocation, fragmentation and uprootedness, engendering profound uncertainty.[10] Modernism may well have prompted a precocious 'on-the-road' syndrome, together with its psychic corollaries, anxieties and neuroses.

The tectonics of peripheral Modernism were experienced with particular destabilizing force by a sub-set of avant-garde literati in south-eastern Europe, in Trieste and at the extreme north-eastern borders of Italy. This sub-set responded, or resisted to, specific geo-political constellations in the multicultural lands of southeast Europe, frequently resenting and resisting transcultural *modi operandi*. This chapter revisits a corpus of 1910s and 1920s literary works from Trieste and the surrounding border region. Here, the multilingual legacy of the Austro-Hungarian Empire allowed for the production of a particular syntax of literary creativity wedged between, rather than spread across, heterogeneous cultures and languages. Location may have been configured as 'an itinerary rather than a bounded site – a series of encounters and translations' in a constellation of contact zones, a diverse cultural space and crucible of Modernism. On the other hand, this region's internal translatability became fraught and stunted early on, modulated on the 'extraneous' cultural baggage of its internal 'minorities'. In these 'intercultural frontiers of nations, peoples, locales', 'the making and remaking of identities' was, in fact, easily fragmented and ruptured.[11] The organic

---

[9] See, in particular, key figures of the so-called Futurist second generation, such as Vinicio Paladini and Ivo Pannaggi (see Katia Pizzi, 'Of Men and Machines: Pannaggi, Paladini and the "Manifesto of Mechanical Art"', *The Italianist*, 28: 2 (2008), 217–226).

[10] See Piero Zanini, *Significati del confine: i limiti naturali, storici, mentali* (Milan: ESBMO, 1997), pp. 70–71.

'Dopo la mobilità, ecco un altro degli elementi caratteristici della migrazione, la sua profonda incertezza.'

[11] J. Clifford, *Routes,* pp. 11 and 7 respectively.

translatability of individual cultures at the porous Modernist edge experienced interruptions and breakdowns under the mounting pressure of national, ethnic and identitarian fractures in the geo-political fabric. Shifting from Austrian to Italian rule at the end of the First World War, e.g. from a federal Empire to a nation state shortly to turn totalitarian, this region could not but fail to bring to fruition a multicultural agenda.[12]

This liminal region could be branded a 'double periphery', or 'the periphery of a periphery', given its peripherality both *vis-à-vis* Italy, which acquired Trieste and large parts of the region's multilinguistic and multiethnic hinterland after the War, as well as with respect to the Austro-Hungarian Empire, where this Adriatic harbour town had been geographically and culturally negligible, albeit financially and economically pivotal. At the periphery of the Romance and Germanic areas, looking out to the Balkans, the years straddling the First World War witnessed the emergence of a unique Modernist configuration. James Joyce famously 'ate his liver' during his long stay in Trieste and Pula, on the Dalmatian coast, teaching English to wealthy businessmen with literary ambition, including Italo Svevo, gathering material and beginning to draft his *Ulysses*.

In Joyce's and Svevo's time Trieste was the financial hub of an Empire situated at the fringes of the Mediterranean, a historical cultural and linguistic furnace and cross-roads of exchanges. Issues of internal colonialism, translation and inequality, predicated upon ethnicity, nationality and language, imbricated as they were with identity, were paramount. Global and local identities, the regional, the national and the transnational, the general and the particular, collided and crashed here, and also potentially connected and intersected in decidedly original manners. Trieste was well situated to both generate a particular avant-garde culture of its own, as well as act as vehicle channelling innovations from outside. As Mark Thompson remarked, 'Trieste was the crack through which Modernism seeped into Italy'.[13] It was also, however, an ethnocentric cluster in perpetual mutual strife, a hub of mercantile activities attracting non-autochthonous capital.

---

[12] I am borrowing the notion of 'fractured identity' from John Foot, *Fratture d'Italia* (Milan: Rizzoli, 2009), *passim*.

[13] Mark Thompson, *The White War. Life and Death on the Italian Front 1915–1919* (London: Faber & Faber, 2008), p. 101.

66   K. PIZZI

Trieste's particular history had been ignited by a free-trading decree of March 1717, instantly propelling this non-descript fishermen's village to the nerve of the Austro-Hungarian Empire's trading core. Virtually alone as a maritime outlet in a vast continental expanse, Trieste's port brought a substantial contribution to the fortunes of the Empire, consolidating them both before and after the opening of the Suez Canal. After the First World War, the demise and dismemberment of the Empire, however, this once pivotal harbour became progressively pushed to the margins of global history. The city and large parts of this multi-ethnic region were handed over to Italy in 1920, following the stipulations of the Treaty of Rapallo. The competition of Italian ports, especially the adjacent Venetian harbour, quickly contributed to sinking the Triestine hub into stagnation and, in turn, to relegate the city to a marginal economic role, belying its cultural ambitions.[14] A sense of belatedness, loss and marginality progressively seeped in. Local culture began to look nostalgically inwards rather than across its nearby border, in the dusk of its cosmopolitanism. A growing enthusiasm for Italy perceived as an idealized motherland typified the Italian-speaking middle classes, an affluent and socially prominent class due to Trieste's commercial emphasis. Even under the Empire, the German language had never prevailed in the linguistic fabric of the city, where commercial transactions were carried out in a pragmatic vernacular, that *triestino* dialect creatively taken up and appropriated by James Joyce and his family.[15]

A fascist nationalist agenda implemented in the mid-1920s aimed to quash indigenous groups of competing national, linguistic and ethnic profile, especially Slovenian and Croatian. This agenda contemplated forced nationalization, banning of language, attacks on cultural institutions and closure of schools: a monocultural Italian discourse, which had run high with the Italian middle classes before the War, became hijacked by, and subsumed under, fascist banners. The spread of the Italian language and literary canon became institutional policy.

Aimed at buttressing Trieste's national stakes through pursuing an aggressive monolingual and monocultural agenda, authoritarian measures

---

[14] See K. Pizzi, *A City in Search of an Author: The Literary Identity of Trieste* (London and Sheffield: Sheffield Academic Press, 2001) and K. Pizzi, *Trieste: italianità, triestinità e male di frontiera* (Bologna: Gedit, 2007), *passim*.

[15] This dialect is still the preferred vehicle of communication to this day, as is the case in the broader Veneto region.

inevitably cemented the peripheral vocation of this multilingual and multi-ethnic city. Trieste rapidly morphed into deeply reactionary, steeped in localistic, nationalist and jingoistic discourses, branded as *triestinità* ('Triestinness') and *italianità* ('Italianness'). The city was hailed throughout the 1920s and 1930s as the most loyally fascist of all cities in Italy.[16]

In the cracks of institutional policy and, in some cases, hiding in plain sight, Trieste remained, nonetheless, a fertile contact zone at the intersection of European Modernist trajectories. Geographically tucked away, oblique and removed from the canonical cultural capitals: Vienna and Paris, in particular, but also Florence and increasingly Lubljana, Trieste became perceived by some as a cruel 'stepmother' inhibiting indigenous cultural productivity.[17] The national and ethnic 'fluidity' and relative remoteness from canonical cultural centres of this region did keep the door open to forms of eclectic experimentalism. This experimentalism, however, as we shall see below, remained strictly circumscribed within specific linguistic and cultural circles. Mired in national, ethnic and class polarizations, the social and political arena acted as a stimulus and a springboard to pursue radicalized agendas, mono-lingual at worst, and, at best, pan-European. Antonio Gramsci's insight according to which power is both limiting and productive is particularly apposite here. Caught between the two poles of 'central peripherality' and 'double peripherality', Trieste and its borderlands nurtured eccentric, radical and dynamic literary and artistic cultures. These cultures rarely, however, intersected as communicating vessels. Indeed, Trieste's culture at this time was only sparingly cross-cultural and translational. Not accidentally, the two giants of Modernism, Svevo and Joyce, thrived well outside official cultural circles. The virtue of peripherality of this region typically bypassed cultural translation as a result of polarities, frictions and antagonisms that split Triestine society and politics at large, as the examples detailed below testify to.

The Italian-speaking majority, hegemonic and predominantly middle-class, as well as the Slovenian and Croatian minority groups, increasingly

---

[16] In the late 1920s Trieste counted the largest number of card-carrying members to the PNF (Partito Nazionale Fascista) than any other city in Italy.

[17] The Triestine poet Umberto Saba considered Italy as a stepmother—see U. Saba, *Atroce paese che amo: Lettere famigliari (1945–1953)*, eds. Gianfranca Lavezzi and Rossana Saccani (Milan: Bompiani, 1987), p. 28. See also K. Pizzi, *City in Search of an Author*, p. 137.

68   K. PIZZI

oriented towards individual and specific national and cultural goals, operated largely independently, if not outrightly antagonistically. Local cultures were, on the whole, mutually oblivious, indeed mutually suspicious, following trajectories that clashed and intersected occasionally, but were more frequently developed in segregation, out of synch with one another, resistant to shared epistemologies. Seen through the lens of the fragmented, peripheral and de-centred experience of modernity itself, these very paradoxes and disconnects are conducive. Benita Parry convincingly argues that regions traditionally perceived as the geographical and cultural peripheries of global capitalism are best placed to capture experiences of the most authentic, generative modernity.[18] Within this entrenched and monolithic set-up, largely predicated on political and 'colonial' prevarication of Italian language and culture, Homi Bhabha's notion of a 'politics of difference' seems also fitting.[19] Under the tectonic pressures of Trieste's predicament, the 'politics of difference' of the Italian-speaking majority group, prevailed over the contemporary production of their Slovenian counterparts, also examined here. Towering figures of European Modernism such as Svevo and Joyce slipped in the hiatus between these two poles, playing an all but marginal role within these entrenched binaries.

On the eve of the Great War, the Italian-speaking Scipio Slataper (1888–1915), Carlo Stuparich (1894–1916) and Giani Stuparich (1891–1961) forcefully upheld Trieste's Italian heritage, made up of language, nation and culture. These young intellectuals played an instrumental role in this region, virtually inventing, constructing and producing a literary culture in Italian. All three defected from the Austrian conscript Army in 1914, seeking escape in mainland Italy and attending classes at the University

---

[18] See, in particular, B. Parry, 'Stylistic Irrealism' in this volume.

[19] See Homi Bhabha, 'Staging the Politics of Difference: Homi Bhabha's Critical Literacy'. Interview by Gary Olson and Lynn Worsham, in *Race, Rhetoric and the Postcolonial,* eds. G. Olson and L. Worsham (Albany: SUNY Press, 1999), pp. 3–39. Bhabha's 'politics of difference' is more fitting than Antonio Gramsci's *traducibilità* ('translatability'), a notion predicated on a dialogical, communicative process infused with respect for the culture and language of the interlocutor. I am elaborating here on Gramsci's thoughts on cultural translation, emerging especially from the *Prison Notebook*—I am grateful for the useful overview provided by Birgit Wagner in 'Cultural Translation: A Value or a Tool? Let's Start with Gramsci!', in FORUM: Postkoloniale Arbeiten / Postcolonial Studies, GoetheZeitPortal, pp. 1–14, http://www.goethezeitportal.de/fileadmin/PDF/kk/df/pos tkoloniale_studien/wagner_cultural-translationgramsci.pdf (accessed 21 June 2013).

of Florence, traditional cradle of language and civilization.[20] Slataper and the two Stuparich brothers regarded Florence as an anchor of *italianità*: a powerful stabilizer and legitimizer for the multiple, unstable cultural identity of Trieste. They thrived on Trieste's eccentric peripherality, aware that it afforded them latitude, and a platform of broad intellectual and cultural experimentation, which they oriented towards Italy, engaging in *repéchages* into hackneyed literary canons—Dante and Petrarch in the Middle Ages, but also, seemlessly, Giacomo Leopardi and Gabriele D'Annunzio in the nineteenth century—and also *Sturm und Drang* Romantic rebellions, achieving a composite, syncretic and original 'spiritual encyclopedism'.[21]

Most crucially, Slataper and the Stuparich brothers embraced pan-Europeanism, dipping regularly into cultures that were geographically remote: Slataper, for example, turned to Scandinavian languages and literary cultures and wrote a substantial monograph on Henrik Ibsen; Giani Stuparich researched the Czech nation in depth, bringing out the monograph *La nazione ceca* (1915). Significantly, however, they largely glossed over possible transcultural encounters with their Slovenian neighbours. Daily interactions with Slovenian speakers would no doubt be part and parcel of their daily experience back home. Stuparich posited his research on the cultural and identitarian drive of the Czech nation as a template for the Slovene community closer to home. Members of this community are featured occasionally in his prose works, usually in secondary or servile roles (see especially the novel *Ritorneranno* of 1941).[22] His contemporary Kosovel is all but ignored.

In a well-known 'Triestine Letter' published in the influential Florentine periodical *La Voce* in 1909, Slataper scourged complacent continental Italians who had foggy notions of what the Adriatic region consisted of,

---

[20] In the absence of a local University, middle-class Triestines typically attended Universities in Vienna or Graz nearby.

[21] See Ernestina Pellegrini, 'Aspetti della cultura triestina tra Otto e Novecento', *Il Ponte*, 4 (1980), 354–371 (358).

[22] While Mark Thomson is categorical in highlighting this aspect, going as far as remarking an alleged nationalist bias in Stuparich, which I believe to be unsubstantiated, more recent scholarship rehabilitates Stuparich, mapping his position vis-à-vis the Slovenians onto Angelo Vivante's sound historical account (especially *Irredentismo adriatico* of 1912) as well as his own findings on the development of modern Slav national and cultural consciousness—cf. M. Thomson, *White War* and F. Galofaro, 'Slavi si nasce o si diventa? La costituzione del soggetto in "Ritorneranno" di Giani Stuparich', *E/C*, *VI*, 11: 12 (2012), 97–101.

inviting them to become better informed and aware of its complexity. From *La Voce*, which he edited from 1910, Slataper advocated Trieste's emblematic role, nailing on the head the city's modernity: the seat of a conflict between the 'spirit' of an elusive, undefined culture and the all too tangible 'matter' of its commercial identity. As his name suggests, Slataper was himself an ethnic Italian of mixed roots, whose mother was Slovenian. Mixed language would have informed his cultural and psychological background, as the paradoxes punctuating his prose in *Il mio carso* amply demonstrate.

An *Ur-text* of Triestine literature and Slataper's best known work, *Il mio carso* (1912) is a boldly avant-garde lyrical prose fragmentarily contaminated with *Sturm und Drang*,

Gabriele D'Annunzio's neoclassical rhetoric and vistas of urban and technological modernity, construed in opposition to the alleged self-effacement of the rural Karst. The predominantly Slovenian Karst, where his mother's family hailed from, is evoked as an ethnographic pastoral, a largely psychological, affective and multi-sensory landscape, archaeological to the metropolitan and sophisticated dynamism of Trieste. An unresolved tension between holistic Romanticism and fragmentary urban Modernism underlies Slataper's prose, an ambiguity of symbolic relation with the real. While language, Imperialism and national identity are emergent concerns here, Slataper neglects, for example, to address the psychological import of mixed language, which the reader would expect to find here.

Slataper and the Stuparichs were hardly alone. A group of young women and men moved *en masse* from the Adriatic region to Florence in the years straddling the First World War, including Gemma Harazim (1876–1961), Virgilio Giotti (1885–1957), Biagio Marin (1891–1985), Carlo Michelstaedter (1887–1910), Alberto Spaini (1892–1975).[23] *Futurismo* advocated a place for itself in Trieste and, by default, for the city as a whole in the Modernist arena. In 1908, Marinetti marched on Trieste in demonstration of the city's welcome 'restitution' to Italy. The soon-to-be leader of *Futurismo* spoke at Trieste's Gymnastic Society advocating the cause of an Italian University and was arrested by the public authorities after a brawl. The first Futurist soirées also took place

---

[23] For a full exploration of this milieu, see Walter L. Adamson, *Avant-Garde Florence: From Modernism to Fascism* (Cambridge, MA: Harvard University Press, 1993).

in Trieste between 1908 and 1910, testifying to the key role the avant-garde had assigned to this eccentric new metropolis. An official Futurist group gathered together in Trieste after 1922, under the leadership of Bruno Giordano Sanzin, who worked closely with Marinetti, editing the periodical *Energie futuriste* and penning the pamphlet *Marinetti e il futurismo* (1924).[24] Dynamism, mechanic art, patriotic loyalty to Italy and an intensely urban bias were embraced by Sanzin and his acolyte Vladimiro Miletti, an irreverent and comic fellow Futurist who espoused the linguistic iconoclasm of Marinetti's *words in freedom* and *untied imagination* in celebrating the industrial and national status of Trieste in the 1920s.[25]

The Futurists elected Trieste 'Futurist city' *par excellence*.[26] A city deprived of a past of its own, Trieste was propelled towards a future of uncompromisingly urban and mechanical modernity. The cultural insecurities, the city's endemic resistance to hybridization, however, brought about further contradictions. Ultimately, they pulled the city further into a canonical and jingoistic Italian orbit, laying the ground for a symbolic confusion of Fascism itself with *italianità*, a conflation celebrated with pomp and circumstance on 20 May 1924, when Benito Mussolini was granted honorary citizenship by the Trieste city council.[27] An Italian national agenda continued to prevail in the 1930s and 1940s, barely disguised in the fascist attempts to reconstruct the moribund commercial port and revive *Cittavecchia,* an iconic residential area adjacent to the old dockland quarters.[28]

This full immersion in the very heart of Italian literary culture was, in other words, achieved, to a large extent, at the expense of disengaging with, if not rejecting outright, non-Italian cultural agencies in this region. In a geo-political area that experienced the disintegration and fallout of the Imperial cooker, under the pressure of combusting national forces, a

---

[24] For further detail, see K. Pizzi, *City in Search of an Author*, pp. 124–128.

[25] See, in particular, the poems 'Pioggia veloce' and 'Manicure', in Vladimiro Miletti, *Orme d'impulsi* (Trieste: Società Artistico Letteraria, 1967), pp. 68 and 72. Other collections include *Novelle con le giarrettiere* (1933), *Aria di jazz* (1934), *Fughe nei secondi* (1937) and *Portare le armi* (1940).

[26] See Joseph Cary, *A Ghost in Trieste* (Chicago: Chicago University Press, 1993), pp. 85–86.

[27] See K. Pizzi, *City in Search of an Author*, p. 127.

[28] K. Pizzi, *City in Search of an Author*, pp. 124–127.

wasteland where centres and peripheries continued to be scrambled and reconstituted at the drop of a hat well into the end of the Cold War era,[29] Italian and Slovenian authors and intellectuals were, of course, acutely aware of transcultural dynamics. Their transcultural exchanges, however, more frequently than not articulated remote and abstract agendas, pursued on paper alone. Authors cast their glances further afield, to farther vistas that might just bypass the problem of establishing where is centre and where is periphery, selecting 'acceptable' regional partners. Cultural reception, dissemination and transmission were articulated within strict national boundaries, characterized by chronic patterns of mutual suspicion, leading to enduring mutual impermeability. Paraphrasing Gramsci and Spivak, no 'compassionality' was at work in this periphery, marring, rather than facilitating, cultural translation.[30]

A mirror image of these disconnects can be found, *mutatis mutandis*, in the poetry of Srečko Kosovel (1904–1926). Kosovel embraced a paradigm of regional peripherality at home while, at the same time, kept his gaze fixed on a broader European arena, in manners that echo the ethical Europeanism of Slataper and the Stuparich brothers. Watertight national boundaries, engendered by a history of reciprocal denial, prevented fruitful interactions between neighbouring intellectuals: no evidence exists that Kosovel became aware of Slataper's work. Indeed, why should he have wanted to familiarize himself with it in a frame of a social and cultural discrimination? Kosovel was conversant with the Italian language and literary canon. Yet his awareness of Italian literature could hardly be mediated by those Triestine Italians who had defected to Italy before the war. Kosovel absorbed Italian literature via the influential translations of the Slovene minister and scholar Ivan Trinko (1863–1954), who had translated the classics of Italian literature, his friend and fellow contributor of *Lepa Vida*, Mirijam (Fanica Obid), and his personal relationship with the Neapolitan friend Carlo Curcio.

---

[29] See K. Pizzi, 'Cold War Trieste on Screen: Memory, Identity and Mystique of a City in the Shadow of the Iron Curtain', in *Cold War Cities: History, Culture and Memory*, eds. K. Pizzi and M. Hietala (Oxford: Peter Lang, 2016), pp. 75–95.

[30] See also K. Pizzi, 'A Modernist City Resisting Translation? Trieste Between Slovenia and Italy', in *Speaking Memory. How Translation Shapes City Life*, ed. Sherry Simon (Montreal and Kingston, London, Chicago: McGillQueen's University Press, 2016), pp. 45–57.

THE LITERATURE OF TRIESTE AND THE PERILS ... 73

Like Slataper, Kosovel was a staunch advocate of a pan-European identity. For Kosovel Europe epitomized an ideal geo-political framework predicated on the socialist international, pursuing this ideal relentlessly during his short life. However, Kosovel accessed Modernism via a pathway underpinned by Constructivism and socialism on the Soviet model, in stark contrast to Slataper and Stuparich. Kosovel's intellectual and political militancy had a transnational goal: transcend the region and aim for a progressive, liberal Europe erected on a genuinely international transcultural platform. Growing up in Lubljana in the 1920s, however, Kosovel would have been a witness, albeit at a remove, of episodes of heinous violence perpetrated by the fascist authorities on the Slovenian community in Trieste—one for all, the arson of the Hotel Balkan, or Slovenian House of Culture, ignited by fascist black shirts on 13 July 1920. It has been suggested that Kosovel's most visionary modernist poetry was inflected by the imagery, the sensory experience and powerful symbolic signification carried by this traumatic episode.[31] The opportunity of cultural translation was curtailed when official 'Italianness' began predicating itself entirely on an 'anti-Slavness' in this peripheral region.

Numerous visual artists from this region, including Milko Bambič, Veno Pilon, Ivan Čargo and, especially, Kosovel's close friend Avgust Černigoj looked up to Lubljana as a Modernist centre and capital. Their role was crucial in maintaining a vibrant channel of exchange between Futurism and the central European avant-garde scene, cultivating an international periphery alongside and outside its national ambitions. In 1925 Kosovel considered establishing a new Constructivist magazine with Černigoj. Černigoj wanted to call it *Konstruktor*, while Kosovel's heart was set on a simpler title: *Kons.* This intense poetic and intellectual experience led to the foundation of the journal *Euroslave*, a new European centre for peripheral Slovenia. Together with the sister journal *Mladina* (Youth), edited by Kosovel from 1925, *Euroslave* offered a European and internationalist platform to Kosovel's socialist international politics that, together with fulfilling the national aspirations of the Slovenian nation, further laid fertile seeds of Slovenian experimental Modernist poetry.
In the summer of 1925 Kosovel started composing Constructivist poetry entitled *Konsi* (short for 'constructions'), consisting of *words in freedom* and typographic syntheses, experimental poems sitting at the intersection of

---

[31] Cf. Srečko Kosovel, "Italijanska kultura" (c1925) in *Aspri ritmi* (*Ostri ritmi*), trad. Miran Kosuta (Trieste: ZTT-EST, 2011).

74   K. PIZZI

Constructivism with Modernism consisting in an explosion of syntax, bold typographic innovation, such as block lettering and agitational style, reminiscent of Marinetti's *words in freedom*. *Konsi* became Kosovel's favourite expressive mode. The *konsi* are early examples of radical experimentalism in Slovenian literature. Kosovel, however, did not and could not reference the belligerent Futurists, despite the latter's concomitant flirtations with the international left.[32] As mentioned above, the first Futurist performances were staged in Trieste between 1908 and 1909, prior to Marinetti's publication of his 'Futurist and Founding Manifesto' in *Le Figaro* in February 1909. The very first proper Futurist *soirée* took place at Trieste's theatre Politeama Rossetti on 12 January 1910. Kosovel, who was to become a keen and regular attendee at the Rossetti theatre, would have been too young to have been in the audience. Bruno Sanzin, the already mentioned leader of the Triestine branch of Futurism, edited a Futurist column in the periodical *Italia Nova*, an enterprise later to be repackaged under the title *Energie Futuriste*. This new venture was managed by one of Kosovel's closest friends: Giorgio Carmelich. Kosovel and the Italian avant-garde are skirting close to each other once again. Slovenian and Italian peripheral modernisms will, nonetheless, remain non-dialogical, distant like neighbouring galaxies rotating light years away from one another.[33]

Torn apart by ruptures and contradictions, reflecting the indeterminate and shifting state of its multiple centres and peripheries, the trans-cultural opportunities missed by this region testify to its inability to become a melting pot, a cultural crucible. Trieste was more often than not a 'crucible manqué', as Elio Apih persuasively argued.[34] Torn apart by centrifugal forces, this modernist periphery appears more frequently as a rift, obstacle, barrier rather than a located cultural intersection. Ethnic confrontation was entrenched, even fanatical. A region that was historically unsure of itself, and a city, Trieste, in search of a literary identity it could call its own, became all too vulnerable to the seductive siren

---

[32] In 1922, the first Soviet Commissar of Education, Anatoly Lunacharsky, hailed Marinetti as the only genuine 'revolutionary intellectual' in Europe, prompting Gramsci's interest and a collaboration between communists and Futurists in organizing an exhibition in Turin in the same year—see K. Pizzi, *The Futurist Time Machine: Mechanics, Migration, Modernity and the Italian Avant-garde*, forthcoming.

[33] Due to his premature death in 1926, Kosovel's Constructivist poetry remained unknown until 1967, when it was brought out posthumously under the title *Integrali'26*.

[34] See E. Apih, *Il ritorno di Giani Stuparich* (Florence: Vallecchi, 1988), p. 75: 'Trieste fu frequentemente crogiolo mancato.'

songs of its multiple, mutually exclusive identities, endorsing a 'politics of difference' predicated on the pre-eminence of Italian to the detriment of other groups. This is an all too common feature in border areas, where identity is predicated in the negative, in opposition to the culturally and linguistically alien 'others'.

As painfully evidenced by the skewed dynamics between the Slovenian and the Italian avant-garde, the experimentalism still successfully pursued by Slataper, Kosovel and numerous authors and visual artists in this region at the south-eastern periphery of Europe demonstrate the extent to which its culture needs to be re-assessed in the light of culturally comparative methodologies. The search of a cultural identity, the radical politics, the international and European breadth of the investigation, the fragmented, syncopated, typographically astute style shared by the authors examined here ought to build bridges across divided national and linguistic fronts. They should help, in other words, recomposing the 'fractures' of official history, commemoration and memory between neighbouring linguistic and ethnic groups,[35] achieving that political and humanitarian-oriented cultural translation advocated by Antonio Gramsci.

In constructing a hermeneutics of liminal spaces, Gramsci's cultural translation can be a useful critical tool. In dialogue with the hegemony of the centre, or centres as the case may be, trans-culturality is well placed to advocate for a 'glocal' national that remains aware of the pull of the periphery, or peripheries as the case may be. If it is the case that the experience of modernity is one of marginality, liminality and fragmentation, in its very complex, and divided, identity, in its very disjunction and peripherality from the centres of global capitalism, in its ambiguities and contradictions, this region brings an eloquent contribution to the history of Modernism. Fulfilling this agenda while being largely deaf to the call of its 'alien' neighbour is one of the paradoxes and interruptions of modernism that this peripheral region can no longer afford to sustain, as is increasingly evidenced in its contemporary literature.

In a context of globalization, today's Trieste has turned the national question upon its head as a result of a sustained wave of immigration from Southeast Asia, north Africa and the Middle East. A new generation of writers is emerging here, first and foremost Lily-Amber Laila Wadia. Born in Mumbai, Wadia writes in Italian, her acquired language. Her

---

[35] See also J. Foot, *Fratture d'Italia*.

ironic and tongue-in-cheek autobiographical writings debunk received notions of 'national' and 'cultural' in re-constituted national contexts.[36] Wadia's literary production manages to 'scramble' and re-situate once again received paradigms of centre and periphery, national, regional and multicultural, engaging with them in ironical and playful manners, re-imagining and reconfiguring local cultures into novel and shifting new forms. Rejecting ossified local rhetorics, hybridizing with non-indigenous cultural forms while remaining well aware of Trieste's multiple national and ethnic history, Wadia's writings may well ultimately achieve a form of 'compassional' cultural translation as is advocated by Gramsci, avoiding the perils of a hackneyed peripherality.

[36] Lily-Amber Laila Wadia, *Come diventare italiani in 24 ore. Diario di un'aspirante italiana* (Siena: Barbera, 2010).

"From the Periphery of the Metropolis": On Joyce's Modern/ist Irish Peripherealities

Roberta Gefter Wondrich

When one thinks of the notion of "peripheral modernisms" in the context of Western literatures, James Joyce's work and particularly *Ulysses* stand out as a key, though ambivalent case. Born and grown up in Ireland, the colonial *unicum* as the first colony of the British Empire, though a domestic and 'metropolitan' one, that was also part of North Western Europe, Joyce, like Kafka, was "writing from outside of capitalism's centres" and was later "assimilated by a literati enchanted or disturbed" by his innovative work.[1] As the towering figure of Anglophone modernism, a writer who became a voluntary exile from his insular Ireland to insert himself in the peripheral multiculturalism of Trieste, and later in the cosmopolitanism of Paris, Joyce is perhaps the most significant author to have celebrated the complex interconnectedness of modernity and peripherality. Joyce's Dublin represents, in fact, one of the centres (i.e. capitals) of modernist literature, while still being connoted, at the time of its celebration in *Ulysses* and throughout Joyce's writing career, by

---

[1] See Benita Parry, "Aspects of Peripheral Modernism", *Ariel: A Review of International English Literature* Vol. 40, No. 1 (2009): 27–55, 34.

R. Gefter Wondrich (✉)
University of Trieste, Trieste, Italy
e-mail: gefter@units.it

© The Author(s), under exclusive license to Springer Nature Switzerland AG 2024
K. Pizzi and R. Gefter Wondrich (eds.), *Rethinking Peripheral Modernisms*, https://doi.org/10.1007/978-3-031-35546-2_5

a position of economic and industrial peripherality. Ireland's tormented history of emancipation was to award Dublin a political prominence that problematically projected it onto the contested discourse of colonial modernity, while its cultural position in the controlling British centre-margin ideology was a source of inspiration for all its modernist writers.[2] This allowed Joyce to imbue his whole work with what may be defined as a poetics of the margin—the provenance from the margin/periphery and the thematization of the margin—not simply as a political and cultural condition but as an existential one. Within the formidable, challenging inclusiveness of his work, marginality and peripherality have been claimed as critical tropes along with the more disputed ones of internal colonialism, semi-colonialism, "metrocolonialism" (J. Valente, D. Kiberd)[3]; but, in any case, cosmopolitanism for all that, always intrinsically linked to the idea of modernity.

Joyce's work foregrounds the relevance of the peripheral and the modern in their problematic coexistence on several possible levels: the geopolitical and historical, the existential (in the figure of Bloom who is doomed to marginality and yet qualified by a profession that is representative of modern capitalist consumer society); the intertextual, with the combination of recondite, antiquarian cultural allusiveness and countless references to local topics and minutiae, and the identitarian, starting from

[2] The peripherality of Dublin can thus best be situated in an expanded historical context, as reasserted by the recent study *Literature and the Peripheral City*, Lieven Ameel, Jason Finch and Markku Salmela eds, Basingstoke: Palgrave Macmillan, 2025, 2: "Cities such as Dublin and Prague, as well as cities that function as regional metropolises (e.g. Stockholm, Santiago de Chile, Johannesburg), and capitals of countries that are not the largest or most culturally prominent from a Western perspective, can all be understood as peripheral in a global context. Yet to think of them in this way is always to think in relation to a perceived centre which is elsewhere: it is always only a way of metaphorizing spatial relations. Such cities are not peripheral in any absolute or factual sense".

[3] The term *metrocolonial* was coined by Joseph Valente in a study of Joyce's *Dubliners*, then further developed in his *Dracula's Crypt. Bram Stoker, Irishness and the Question of Blood* (Urbana and Chicago: Chicago UP, 2002), but also analysed by Declan Kiberd in *Inventing Ireland: The Literature of the Modern Nation* (London: Vintage, 1994), as he specifies in *DC*, footnote 9, page 147. This refers to the unique conditions and characters of the colonial and postcolonial history of Ireland, which, "with the act of Union in 1800 (...) ceased to be a distinct if colonized geopolitical entity and assumed the unique and contradictory position of a domestic or 'metropolitan' colony (....). (*Dracula's Crypt*, 3). The metrocolonial condition, of which Valente considers Bram Stoker's "an exemplary case "names an uneasy social and psychic space between authority, agency, and legitimacy on one side and abjection, heteronomy, and hybridity on the other" (*Dracula's Crypt*, 4).

Bloom's and Molly's ethnic and national origins. From a biographical point of view, Joyce's two cities—Dublin and Trieste—were both peripheral, outside the centres of capitalism, although the former was a capital and a provincial city at one and the same time, the largest in the British Empire after London, though about twenty times smaller than London, and the latter was the largest maritime port of the Habsburg Empire. Recent criticism, notably by J. McCourt, has brought to the fore the fundamental influence of Trieste's imperial peripheral identity in many thematic and linguistic respects, for example as the very source of Joyce's textualization of "Tarry East" and part of his treatment of Orientalism and the European exotic. The (auto)biographical background of Joyce's spatial politics, in fact, has been widely investigated over recent decades, generally pointing to "a spatial complexity" that cannot be reduced to either imperialist complicity or postcolonial nationalist resistance.[4]

THE MODERNITY OF THE PERIPHERAL

It is in *Ulysses* that we find one of the most complex and thorough textualizations of a spatially connoted idea of modernity that hinges on the dialectics of centre and margin, urban and suburban civilization, the metropolitan, the cosmopolitan, the peripheral, the metro/semi/postcolonial. Leopold Bloom's cultural and artistic positioning has been variously examined as being concerned with the issues of displacement and community, spatial peripherality, social marginality and equality.

This enumeration of socio-spatial questions, a "happy hunting-ground" for any scholar interested in the cultural phenomena of modernity, should be integrated by the fact that in Bloom's character Joyce makes use of fantasy and utopianism as an impulse, a penchant rather than a cultural expression as such, in keeping with the "minor utopias" of modernism, which were on the whole sceptical rather than assertive.[5] More specifically, *Ulysses* foregrounds an idea of modernity which becomes encoded in relation to the peripheral and to what can be best defined as utopian modes of idealization which are grounded

---

[4] Jon Hegglund, "Ulysses and the Rhetoric of Cartography", *Twentieth Century Literature* Vol. 42, No. 2 (Summer 2003): 164–192, 189.

[5] See Benjamin Kohlman, "Introduction", in Rosalyn Gregory and Benjamin Kohlmann, eds. *Utopian Spaces of Modernism. Literature and Culture 1885–1925* (Basingstoke: Palgrave Macmillan, 2011), 1–18 passim and 2–3.

in subjective desires, and which challenge political, ideological and social discourses.[6] In addition to a pervasive textual presence, this cultural nexus of the modern, the peripheral and the utopian, can be analysed firstly in the "new Bloomusalem" in "Circe", Bloom's fantasmagoric, multicultural and multireligious utopian Ireland, and, secondly (and more interestingly for the purposes of this analysis) in the fancy, blissful, hypermodern fashioning of 'Flowerville', in "Ithaca". As an imaginative projection included in the most overtly materialist and expository of all the episodes, this piece of utopian digression presents a narrative fantasy that engages with different aspects of a peripheral, suburban, capitalistic modernity, on the mutually exclusive, incompatible planes of subjective and private desires and social and political realities.

Since the concept of periphery has come to the fore of critical discussion largely owing to early postcolonial theory (notably since the publication of Ashcroft, Griffiths and Tiffin's *The Empire Writes Back*), the fact that Ireland stands as a much disputed case of colonial and postcolonial status, a case history which calls for a necessary set of historical and critical specifications, is worth mentioning at this stage. Among the many current definitions, the relationship between Britain and Ireland was identified by Michael Hechter as one of internal colonialism,[7] an unequal relationship between a modernized core and an underdeveloped periphery in the same State. Core and periphery can be geographically distinct within the space of the same state, then, although the very understanding of state (and nation) appears problematic in the context of the British Isles, including Ireland, and in the Empire.

A parallel and preliminary reference to the controversial, ambivalent relationship between Ireland and modernity—or, better, Ireland's controversial attitude towards the cultural discourses of modernity between, roughly, 1880 and 1939—is necessary. To focus on a narrower and more specific timeline, one should refer to John Wilson Foster's reminder that

---

[6] The most extensive study to date on utopianism in *Ulysses* remains Wolfgang Wicht's *Utopianism in James Joyce's Ulysses*, Anglistisches Forschungen 278 (Heidelberg, C.Winter, 2000).

[7] Michael Hechter, *Internal Colonialism: The Celtic Fringe in British National Development, 1536–1966* (Berkeley: University of California Press, 1975).

the Celtic Revival and High Modernism basically share the same chrono-logical span: 1880–1925.[8] While on the one hand, the Celtic Revival dictated the cultural agenda of nationalist Ireland with a distinct anti-modern bias, on the other it also showed a great interest in certain tropes such as mythological lore, the mythical past and primitivism which were also cultivated by high modernism. The two poles are not thus radi-cally at odds, as conventional literary history has long considered them, despite the ardent localism and nationalism of the revivalists. Issues of nationality and elective or necessary cosmopolitanism are central to the identity of Irish modernism: as Quigley aptly puts it, "To be modern is to leave Ireland and Irish things behind (…) Simultaneously, nothing is more modern than the Irish condition because in their state of alienation, emigration, and internationalism, Irish writers incarnate the globalism of modernity".[9]

Figures like Yeats, in particular, turn out to be somewhat diffi-cult to accommodate in any dichotomic characterization of Ireland's literary history: torn between the traditionalism of the Celtic Revival and modernist experimentalism, they enrich the complexity of Ireland's peripheral modernism as also constitutive of European core modernism.

"Ithaca" and the Cultural Discourses of Irish Modernity

The seventeenth episode of *Ulysses* is probably the most relevant, and one of the most important of Joyce's whole work with regard to the literary representation and critique of Irish modernity as a *peripheral* modernity. Very little happens in the chapter: Bloom and Stephen, finally reunited, reach Eccles Street, where Bloom takes care of his younger guest, offers him a bed for the night, to no avail; the two urinate together under the canopy of stars, enjoying a moment of bonding, and a long trail of elucubrations and reflections begins and continues after Stephen's leaving, when Bloom meditates on his own predicament, life story, fantasizes and eventually longs for his reunion with Molly.

---

[8] John Wilson Foster, *Colonial Consequences. Essays in Irish Literature and Culture* (Dublin: Lilliput Press, 1991), 44. See also Megan Quigley, "Ireland", in *The Cambridge Companion to European Modernisms*, ed. Pericles Lewis (Cambridge: Cambridge Univer-sity Press), 170–190 (178).

[9] Quigley, 171.

82   R. GEFTER WONDRICH

The very title of "Ithaca" evokes the notion of the return home after long, troubled meanderings, but, significantly, in the context of the Homeric parallel, it also implicitly evokes an idea of the *peripheral* as coincidental with the return to the *real*. In a study on colonization and ethnicity in ancient Greek civilization, Irad Malkin states that "The Odyssey's Ithaca is the limit, or periphery, of Homeric geography" [...]

> "Above Ithaca lies the great Beyond, whence the Phaiakians bring Odysseus back home.
> In the Odyssey it is the transition from Phaiakia to Ithaca that marks the return to the real world".[10]

This reference to a detail of the Homeric framework both introduces and validates the suggestion that the idea of periphery and peripheral is inherent and embedded in that exploration of modernity that is a structural feature of the seventeenth chapter of *Ulysses*, "Ithaca", which has its Homeric correspondence in the theme of a return home and of the returning hero.[11] Moreover, there is another suggestion worth mentioning in Malkin's fascinating study, which focusses on the function of *nostoi* as myths and stories of the returning heroes. This regards the "intriguing fringe category" of the "rather consistent pattern of a 'peripheral' superimposition of myths onto peoples and territories".[12] I would thus argue that Joyce's "Ithaca" seems to re-enact this cultural dynamic *sub specie* of that myth of modernization both superimposed on Ireland and there resisted.[13]

The chapter engages with the dominant discourses of revivalist ideology, imperial science and economy, and is pervasively dominated by the issue of modernity and modernization. It mirrors, or rather mocks, the presumption of absolute authority of materialist scientism through the narrative technique of catechistical analysis, "a mathematical catechism"

---

[10] Irad Malkin, *The Returns of Odysseus: Colonization and Ethnicity Malkin, Irad. The Returns of Odysseus: Colonization and Ethnicity* (Berkeley: University of California Press, 1998), 15.

[11] As Malkin reminds, the word *nostos* holds three different meanings in ancient Greek as the returning hero/es from the Trojan war (*nostoi*), the action of return (*nostos*) and the story or myth about the returning hero.

[12] Malkin, 15.

[13] Andrew Gibson's edited *Joyce's "Ithaca" European Joyce Studies series* (Amsterdam-Atlanta, 1996), offers an in-depth examination of this issue.

in which "all events are resolved into their cosmic physical, psychical etc. equivalents".[14] The question-and-answer pattern which strives to provide hyper detailed responses to highly specific but mostly abstruse questions, eventually produces an accumulation of mostly irrelevant information, which provide some essential background to the preceding chapters but also supplement it with otherwise unnecessary data. Facts are proffered in abundance, but no hierarchical set of principles of value and meaning are invoked to organize them, and the surfeit produces a flattening of meaning and a cumulative parodic effect, which Jon Hegglund has read as a subversion of the "Imperial Archive"[15]. Len Platt epitomizes this process stating that "narrative itself is usurped by the voice and the process of materialist scientism".[15]Yet the narrating voice has much in common with Bloom's: an unswerving faith in the scientific approach and in the positive applications of science and technique to the improvement of civilization.

Civilization as the "precise and unequivocal locus of *Ulysses* 17",[16] is, in fact, a keyword to any analysis of the chapter, and specifically to its relevance to literary configurations of a notion of peripheral modernism. The importance of "Ithaca" in this regard lies mainly in the complexity of the components at work—thematic, ideological and rhetorical—which build up a deflatory and essentially comic critique of modern middle-class urban civilization, while simultaneously rescuing the utopic and affirmative element. They do so—among other things—through a very subtle, multifaceted articulation of the condition of peripherality.

This is best seen when considering how the allegiance between science, scientism and materialist capitalistic ideology, the emptiness and degeneration of modern urban life, which is exactly the kind of scenario that emerges in "Ithaca", was basically the polemical target of the Revival. The revivalist literary politics were based on a set of oppositional tropes (science vs art, urban vs rural, middle class vs peasantry, modernity vs tradition) and middle-class urbanism was its main critical object. As

---

[14] J.Joyce, Letter to Frank Budgen, end February 1921, *Letters of James Joyce*, vol. I, ed. Stuart Gilbert, 159–160.

[15] See note 24.

[16] Len H. Platt, "If Brian Boru Could But Come Back and See Old Dublin Now": Materialism, The National Culture and Ulysses 17". In Andrew Gibson, ed. *Joyce's "Ithaca", European Joyce Studies series* (Amsterdam: Atlanta, 1996): 105–132 (107).

Len Platt epitomizes, "The Ithacan landscape is the revivalist nightmare turned reality",[17] and the chief aspects of science and scientism with which it engages are actually their utility and the ensuing material improvements of civilization.

"Ithaca" is seen by Andrew Gibson as "a massive and sustained assault on science as an English and Anglo-Irish preserve. At the same time, it attempts hugely to supplement the theoretical nature of the Nationalist commitment to science".[18] It attempts to counteract the English and Anglo-Irish Protestant conception of Protestant culture as practical and worldly and of Gaelic culture as ineffectual and abstract, by outdoing—once again—the former's command of scientific and technological knowledge, only to lay bare its pretensions and ultimate ineffectuality. In "Ithaca", "scientific discourse becomes a parody of itself, or collapses under its own weight".[19] Joyce's surfeit of facts, references and terminology—technical, scientific, economic and objectual, on which the chapter is erected, is thus targeted at both the detractors and the champions of an anti-materialist, anti-modernist Ireland.

The focus on the modernity of Ireland, even though it is presented through an impassibly deflatory lens, is, nonetheless, evident: Joyce's attitude to Irish modernity is famously complex, ambivalent and challenging, but this episode reveals his critical awareness of its inherently ridiculous aspects and his satirical exposing of the cultural trope of degeneracy in an anti-revivalist perspective. The modernity which was conceived as a threat to both the Irish nation and Irish art is the very matter which Joyce exploits to expose its limits and its ineluctability, turning it into "an epic demarcation of urban modernity as the Joycean estate".[20] Along these lines, Joyce's literary modernism could also be interpreted, according to Emer Nolan, as a response to the modernizing process of Ireland, in that both Irish modernism and Irish nationalism are connoted by an ambivalence towards modernization, sharing a crucial interest in the issue of

[17] *Ibid.*, 111.

[18] Andrew Gibson, "'An Aberration of the Light of Reason': Science and Cultural Politics in "Ithaca", in Andrew Gibson, ed., *Joyce's "Ithaca", European Joyce Studies series* (Amsterdam: Atlanta, 1996), 133–176 (158).

[19] *Ibid.*, 163.

[20] Platt, 132.

cultural change and regeneration, language and popular culture, the realm of the aesthetic and the role of the artist.[21]

On the whole, then, "Ithaca" can be said to foreground a self-conscious, disorienting version of that basic trait of modernist art that is its ambivalent treatment of modernization, as epitomized by Marshall Berman: "All forms of Modernist art and thought have a dual character: they are at once expressions and protests against the process of Modernization".[22] As usual in Joyce, contrasting and often mutually exclusive versions of the same theme can coexist, by means of formal strategies which undermine what they purport to foreground and represent. "Ithaca" is a case in point, under many respects, as the specific narrative of Flowerville will attest.

SPATIAL COMPLEXITY

Framed in this perspective, the idea of the periphery/al, of the fringe, of the external or marginal, necessarily figures in the taxonomic, normative and controlling discourse of imperial power.[23] Jon Hegglund reading of "Ithaca" as a parodic subversion of the structure of the "Imperial Archive"[24] goes so far as to argue that Joyce, exploring the connection "between represented narrative space and 'real historical space'", imagined an Irish identity through a re-inscription of imperial survey and cartography into the novel.[25] In Hegglund's analysis, Joyce used cartography not as a modernist model of detailed and objective precision, but rather as one of the two terms of an oscillation in form, productive tension between the two equally partial perspectives of the abstract space of the

[21] Emer Nolan, *Joyce and Nationalism* (London: Routledge, 1995).

[22] Marshall Berman, *All That Is Solid Melts into Air* (London: Penguin, 1988), 235.

[23] In this regard, a growing degree of attention has been directed, in the last decades, to mapping and cartography (notably by Eric Bulson and Jon Hegglund) with Joyce's *Ulysses* as an extraordinary case history, a rich repository of challenging and sophisticated textualizations of the cartographic model.

[24] Hegglund refers to Thomas Richard's notion of the Imperial Archive as the imaginary representation of an ideal repository of knowledge through which all sorts of different data about the Empire could be ordered and systematized, and considers it as ultimately a "utopian fiction" whose "existence was impossible to conceive without reference to a real-world geography". Jon Hegglund, *World Views: Metageographies of Modernist Fiction* (Oxford: Oxford University Press, 2012), 61.

[25] *Ibid.*, 84.

map and the specifically placed knowledge of the narrative. This tension is thus one where space is "placed", emerges and exists between geography and literature, a condition that is well suited to the inner colony.[26]

This conceptualization of the oscillating, composite complexity of spatiality in *Ulysses* could be productively applied to the eccentric, escapist fantasy of Flowerville, set as a kind of enclave in the hyper-taxonomic, orderly, catechistical context of the seventeenth episode, which, as will be seen, further complicates this spatial complexity by an intrinsically deconstructive, and yet paradoxically liberating, utopian modernist fancy.[27]

If, on first reading, it appears simply as an escapist, utopian but all-material personal fantasy, on closer scrutiny Flowerville also turns out to be a reminder of the problematic but fruitful coexistence of different, subjective forms of spatial identification and subjective desires. Bloom's *Dasein*, his being in the world as a provincial though ideally cosmopolitan urban colonial subject, unhomed and peripatetic, perpetually displaced, is eventually inscribed in Flowerville as a *narrative*, hence legitimated in its implausibility and its absurdity, within the framework of an all-inclusive irony underscoring the 'catechistical' method of the episode. This occurs precisely within the larger narrative of a chapter evoking the trope of *nostos*, set in the carefully described—i.e. topographic—mapped spaces of his 7 Eccles Street Dublin row house.

The imaginative, fancy and architecturally eclectic Flowerville thus gains a metonymic and synecdochic, and hence highly representative, value in its infringement on the topographic precision of the chapter. It achieves all this by articulating the coexistence and the integration of a utopian projection with the detached objectivity of its catechistical method that invokes a modernist style.

UTOPIANISM, ECLECTICISM, THE IRONY OF STYLE

Though a proper discussion of utopian modes in *Ulysses* would exceed the scope of this article, it is worth mentioning Wolfgang Wicht's mapping of the topic in order to put into perspective the relevance of the Flowerville section to my argument. Wicht identifies four "essential varieties

---

[26] *Ibid.*, 87.

[27] I am using the term enclave in a denotative sense, without reference to the definition of "the utopian enclave" by Fredric Jameson in *Archaeologies of the Future. The Desire for the Future and Other Science Fictions* (London: Verso, 2005).

of utopianism" at work in the novel: "the messianic religious or political design of an idealized place or society" (see "Circe"), an idealized independent national state legitimized by memories of Ireland's Golden Past, biblical messianic messages and messengers, and "the subjective desire of owning an affluence of commodities, and of devising public ameliorations".[28] Yet these varieties are not organically interrelated and often prove self-deconstructive, as Joyce's "fictional discourse establishes a place of heterotopia, negating both utopian promise and social practice".[29] Leaving aside the concept of heterotopia which would not be pertinent to Flowerville, and, focussing instead on Wicht's last variety of "subjective desires", it is worth referring to the link between modernism and utopianism as defined by Kohlman, whereby "The becoming-minor of literary utopias during the modernist period signals a shift of social dreaming into less dogmatic and less confident registers".[30] The notion of *social dreaming* can be deemed as central to Bloom's character and hence to the whole textual structure, as will be illustrated. It brings to mind the well-known imaginative power of conjuring the nation out of existence in Benedict Anderson's notion of "imagined communities", and it is something unmistakably present in "Circe"'s idealistic, utopian and messianic fantasy of Bloomusalem, which, as we have seen, can be considered as somehow proleptic of the subsequent materialistic and private version of "Flowerville" in chapter seventeen:

> BLOOM I stand for the reform of municipal morals and the plain ten commandments. New worlds for old. Union of all, jew, moslem and gentile. Three acres and a cow for all children of nature. Saloon motor hearses. Compulsory manual labour for all. All parks open to the public day and night. Electric dish scrubbers. Tuberculosis, lunacy, war and mendicancy must now cease. General amnesty, weekly carnival, with masked licence, bonuses for all, esperanto the universal brotherhood. No more patriotism of barspongers and dropsical impostors. Free money, free love and a free lay church in a free lay state.[31]

---

[28] Wolfgang Wicht, *Utopianism in James Joyce's Ulysses*, Anglistisches Forschungen 278, (Heidelberg: C.Winter, 2000), 8.

[29] *Ibid.*, 10.

[30] Kohlman, 6.

[31] James Joyce, *Ulysses*, The Gabler Edition. Edited by H.W. Gabler (New York: Random House –Vintage, 1986), 399; 1685–93.

This progressive marginalization of the utopian projects in modernist literature, as a result, stands as a cultural background to the idea that the utopian "impulse" is often located within the dimensions of the margin, of the peripheral, as well as within a host of subjective desires hinged on an apparently all-materialist, factual idea of modernity which takes shape through Bloom's incessant wool-gathering.

The essentially utopian nature of Bloom as a dreamer and an idealist has been emphasized—among others—by Patrick Parrinder, who brings this side of his personality to light against the business-like, practical and finance-concerned one: "But Joyce's archetypal petty-bourgeois is neither a moneygrubber nor a frightened litter clerk. Rather, like Wells's Mr Polly and Dickens' Mr Wemmick, he is a dreamer".[32] Bloom's fantasies are wide-ranging and far-reaching, mostly targeted at ways of making money. It should be reminded, however, that in the context of the competing and conflating treatments of economics, science and cultural ideology at work in "Ithaca", he "fantasizes about being a gentleman pursuing literary work". His unswerving materialism, is "a robust and resilient doctrine",[33] his political utopianism is one in which Western bourgeois civilization can be sweetened by a dose of international socialism, his private utopia (in Flowerville) is based on the fetishization of capital and the landed property,[34] yet there is never any doubt as to Bloom's preserving his humanity and empathy despite his secular pragmatism, his fundamental endorsement of a materialistic, enthusiastically modern, urban middle-class identity.

While, first in "Cyclops" and later in "Circe", especially in the utopian fantasy of Bloomusalem, Bloom's stance towards the inherent violence of nationalism could partly be ascribed to a form of escapism, in "Ithaca" this distancing from the hard core of social reality, from the ineluctability of imperial and capitalist politics remains safely lodged within an analytic, dry, thoroughly referential prose that allows only limited glimpses of poetical outlets, such as the famous "heaventree of stars hung with humid nightblue fruit" seen by Bloom and Stephen.

---

[32] Patrick Parrinder, *James Joyce* (Cambridge: Cambridge University Press, 1984), 144.

[33] *Ibid.*, 144; 149.

[34] Wicht, 224.

FLOWERVILLE

In the incommensurably proliferating bulk of Joycean criticism, this section of chapter seventeen has received comparatively little attention in terms of an in-depth analysis.[35] Yet, this piece of utopian fantasy, embedded as an imaginative projection in the most overtly materialist and expository of all the episodes, actually comprises some of the most decisive aspects of a notion of a peripheral, urban, capitalistic modernity. But it also preserves a transnational dimension of identitarian and social fluidity which represents a form of creativeness, semi-comically pulling different strains together. It is a self-satisfactory, graphic transposition of modernity at its most gratifying combination with the class system and a sense of tradition, both bourgeois and gentrified, luxurious and generous, egotistical and ultimately revealing of a need for the human connectedness of the city. When tackling a textual analysis of Bloom's fantasy of Flowerville, its inception starts under the rubric of Bloom's "ultimate ambition "to which "all concurrent and consecutive ambitions had coalesced",

> Not to inherit by right of primogeniture, gavelkind or borough English, or possess in perpetuity an extensive demesne of a sufficient number of acres, roods and perches, statute land measure (valuation #42), of grazing turbary surrounding a baronial hall with gatelodge and carriage drive nor, on the other hand, a terracehouse or semidetached villa, described as Rus in Urbe or Qui si Sana, but to purchase by private treaty in fee simple a thatched bungalowshaped 2 storey dwellinghouse of southerly aspect, surmounted by vane and lightning conductor, connected with the earth, with porch covered by parasitic plants (ivy or Virginia creeper), halldoor, olive green, with smart carriage finish and neat doorbrasses, stucco front with gilt tracery at eaves and gable, rising, if possible, upon a gentle eminence with agreeable prospect from balcony with stone pillar parapet over unoccupied and unoccupyable interjacent pastures and standing in 5 or 6 acres of its own ground, at such a distance from the nearest public thoroughfare as to render its houselights visible at night above

---

[35] Two recent readings of Flowerville have rather tangentially considered the question of peripherality and modernism in *Ulysses* 17. See William J. Kupinse's environmental perspective in "Private Property, Public Interest: Bloom's Ecological Fantasy in "Ithaca", *James Joyce Quarterly* Vol. 52, No. 3/4 (Spring–Summer 2015): 593–621 and Kiron Ward' analysis of the androcentric and totalising visions contained in the two fantasies in "Paradise and the Periphery: The New Bloomusalem and Bloom Cottage." *James Joyce Quarterly* Vol. 55, No. 1 (2017): 115–133.

90 R. GEFTER WONDRICH

and through a quickset hornbeam hedge of topiary cutting, *situate at a given point not less than 1 statute mile from the periphery of the metropolis*, within a time limit of not more than 5 minutes from tram or train line (e.g., Dundrum, south, or Sutton, north, both localities equally reported by trial to resemble the terrestrial poles in being favourable climates for phthisical subjects), the premises to be held under feefarmgrant, lease 999 years, the message to consist of 1 drawingroom with baywindow (2 lancets), thermometer affixed, 1 sittingroom, 4 bedrooms, 2 servants rooms, tiled kitchen with close range and scullery, lounge hall fitted with linen wallpresses, fumed oak sectional bookcase containing the Encyclopaedia Britannica and New century Dictionary, transverse obsolete medieval and oriental weapons, dinner gong, alabaster lamp, bowl pendant, vulcanite automatic telephone receiver with adjacent directory, handtufted Axminster carpet with cream ground and trellis border, loo table with pillar and claw legs, hearth with massive firebrasses and ormolu mantel chronometer clock, guaranteed timekeeper with cathedral chime, barometer with hygrographic chart, comfortable lounge settees and corner fitments, upholstered in ruby plush with good springing and sunk centre, three banner Japanese screen and cuspidors (club style, rich wine-coloured leather, gloss renewable with a minimum of labour by use of linseed oil and vinegar) and pyramidically prismatic central chandelier lustre, bentwood perch with a fingertame parrot (expurgated language), embossed mural paper at 10/-per dozen with transverse swags of carmine floral design and top crown frieze, staircase, three continuous flights at successive right angles, of varnished cleargrained oak, treads and risers, newel, balusters and handrail, with stepped-up panel dado, dressed with camphorated wax, bathroom, hot and cold supply, reclining and shower: water closet on mezzanine provided with opaque singlepane oblong window, tipup seat, bracket lamp, brass tierod brace, armrests, footstool and artistic oleograph on inner face of door: ditto, plain: servant's apartments with separate sanitary and hygienic necessaries for cook, general and betweenmaid (salary, rising by biennial unearned increments of #2, with comprehensive fidelity insurance annual bonus (#1), and retiring allowance (based on the 65 system) after 30 years service), pantry, buttery, larder, refrigerator, outoffices, coal and wood cellarage with winebin (still and sparkling vintages) for distinguished guests, if entertained to dinner (evening dress), carbon monoxide gas supply throughout. (...)[36]

---

[36] Joyce, *Ulysses*, cit, 585; 1497–1550 (my emphasis).

"FROM THE PERIPHERY OF THE METROPOLIS" ...   91

This latter-day, Anglo-Irish, hypermodern Dublin suburban Strawberry Field, replete with luxurious *dernier-cri* commodities, foregrounds some significant standards: an economic and social class status (the purchase of a lordly mansion); hybridity of context and fashion (a distincly English-styled Irish estate); the combined allusion to the urban and the rural, and to the parodic implication of a pastoral tradition as a trope of the Celtic Revival and cultural nationalism. In particular, the first part of the descriptive fantasy ends with the topography that comically epitomizes the various cultural strains with which the whole chapter is polemically concerned:

> *What might be the name of this eligible or erected residence?*
> *Bloom Cottage, Saint Leopold's. Flowerville.*[37]

Wolfgang Wicht reads this toponomastic emphasis, progressing from the unpretentious "Bloom's cottage" to the "exaggeration of Flowerville", as symbolizing "Bloom's fantasy of upward mobility".[38] Although this is partly reinforced by the fact that Bloom desires to buy into the gentry and "purchase" his own dream mansion, I would rather argue that this is a case where Bloom's mind typically proceeds by accumulation and combination, and that the syntagm does condensate an ideal progression, but also, and significantly, one unitary and imaginary combination of the different Irish geographical and spatial identities: rural, sacred, (sub)urban. The rural tradition is in fact established within the religious topography of an urban bourgeois *periphery*. A consideration of the cultural implications of this materialistic fantasy thus brings forth the issue of *location*: Flowerville is built "rising, if possible, upon a gentle eminence...at such a distance from the nearest public thoroughfare as to render its houselights at night ...situate at a given point no less than 1 statute mile *from the periphery of the metropolis*, within a time limit of not more than 15 minutes from tram or train line".[39]

As the Edenic, utopian dream mansion and ideal dwelling place, Flowerville is safely positioned not in the heart of the Hibernian metropolis

---

[37] *Ibid.*, 587;1579–80.

[38] Wicht, 223.

[39] Joyce, *Ulysses*, 585, 1509–1516. (emphasis mine).

92   R. GEFTER WONDRICH

but on its fringe, the periphery of today's middle-class suburban neighbourhoods. While proclaiming its unique distinctiveness as a parodic version of the patrician Anglo-Irish big house, its "Lord" wisely administering justice and intellectual pursuits, unlike the absentee landlords of the Protestant Ascendancy, Flowerville is in fact a sort of *reductio ad absurdum* of both the pretensions and the aspirations of the urban, materialist, metrocolonial middle class of which Bloom can be considered a member. Yet the peripheral is here firmly established as a privileged, even natural location, as the elective dwelling place of the modern *and* the traditional, the rural *and* the urban, the aristocratic *and* the average man, the entrepreneur *and* the dreamer, the technophile *and* deviser of improbable schemes for earning money. Bloom, in fact, is keen on devising new, appropriate, innovative and highly remunerative systems of connections, and transportation systems that would pay for his dream house by linking Dublin's productive activities such as cattle marketing throughout Ireland, Britain and the Continent:

> A scheme for the repristination of passenger and goods traffics over Irish waterways, when freed from weedbeds. A scheme to connect by tramline the Cattle Market (North Circular road and Prussia street) with the quays (Sheriff street, lower, and East Wall), parallel with the Link line railway laid (in conjunction with the Great Southern and Western railway line) between the cattle park, Liffey junction, and terminus of Midland Great Western railway 43 to 45 North Wall, in proximity to the terminal stations or Dublin branches of Great Central Railway, Midland Railway of England, City of Dublin Steam Packet Company, Lancashire Yorkshire Railway Company, Dublin and Glasgow Steam Packet Company, Glasgow Dublin and Londonderry Steam Packet Company (Laird line), British and Irish Steam Packet Company, Dublin and Morecambe Steamers, London and North Western Railway Company, Dublin Port and Docks Board Landing Sheds and transit sheds of Palgrave, Murphy and Company, steamship owners, agents for steamers from Mediterranean, Spain, Portugal, France, Belgium and Holland and for animal transport and of additional mileage operated by the Dublin United Tramways Company, limited, to be covered by graziers' fees.[40]

Transposed from fantasy to metaphor, this is a crucial aspect of the relevance of this utopian fantasy to the complexity of Joyce's vision of the

[40] *Ibid.*, 590–1; 1724–1743.

Empire as essentially structured and connoted by mobility and circulation (notably of goods and commodities). Despite the limited extension of Dublin as a (peripheral) capital, less than a twentieth of London at that time, there is a strong sense in *Ulysses* of a constant buzz of activity that generates moments of what Richard Alter calls "pure mimesis of urban life",[41] and which proclaims the centrality of Bloom's urban mind's concern with dynamism and mobility. While Bloom's fantasy about new transportation networks also reveals how money lies "at the back of Bloom's utopian plans",[42] this aspect extensively reveals Joyce's concern with the themes of urban and metropolitan mobility and his critique of Ireland's isolation within the wider European scene. It reveals his conception of the periphery as both potentially and fittingly modern, in so far as intrinsically dynamic and open, connected, porous, separate but also part of that "metropolitan shuttle" that Alter considers as central to Joyce's "celebratory sense of urban life".[43]

Overall, the peripheral private enclave of the Anglo-Irish Bloom, the idealist–pragmatist cosmopolitan of Jewish blood, who hosts the helleno-hibernian Dedalus in the privacy of the (real) home, is a fantasy sustained by the capacity to devise a network, a connectedness between the margin, the core, and an imagined open world-picture. It is, thus, not a self-secluded, solipsistic fantasy of isolation and compensation, remote from the "Cityful passing away, other cityful coming"[44] of the Hibernian metropolis, but, among other things, an implicitly comic exposure of the "actual poverty belying the claims and enthusiasms of the Nationalist 'modernizers' around the turn of the century."[45]

The amusing side of this fantasy reads, in fact, in the context of Ithaca's cultural critique of late nineteenth-, early twentieth-century Ireland and the discourse of imperial science and nationalist rhetoric, which is repeatedly evoked, implied, and engaged with through Bloom's amateur, resourceful, but muddling inventiveness. Pairing up with the more direct and violent indictment of nationalist rhetoric in "Cyclops",

---

[41] Richard Alter, "Joyce. Metropolitan Shuttle"in R. Alter, *Imagined Cities. Urban Experience and the Language of the Novel* (Yale: Yale UP, 2005), 124.

[42] Osteen, Ibid., 415.

[43] Alter, 125.

[44] Joyce, *Ulysses*, 153.

[45] Gibson, "An Aberration", 157.

"Ithaca" tackles nationalist modernizing rhetoric. This is exposed in its inconsistency through the enumerative tour de force of Bloom's long list of improbabilities and incongruities and the narrative technique of the catechistical method of questions and answers.

As the embedded fantasy in the gigantic piling up of facts and detailed exposition of the chapter, Flowerville, that is, the apotheosis of Bloom's appetites as a socially elevated consumer—a champion of early twentieth-century consumer culture—is described in the language and modes of an advertisement for real estate. The descriptive mode of the eclectically styled mansion is basically that of the estate agent advertising: Bloom's is a dream house, a material "utopian fantasy in the genre of the 'lifestyles' sold by the modern advertising industry",[46] the one we are all familiar with from magazines' columns and websites.

The *architecture* of Flowerville is, in fact, significant and illuminating. It is an amalgam of styles, largely based on the tenets of nineteenth-century architectural eclecticism. It combines and conflates the bungalow and the cottage, the townhouse and the English country mansion, though evidently located in an Irish peripheral context. It also displays something of the aesthetic excess which Parrinder rubrics under the grotesque, in that "it is a dream house in the double sense that it would be both impossible to build as such and not affordable by Bloom".[47] Grotesque is, perhaps, too complex a cultural notion, but there is no doubt that Bloom's description often becomes comical and constantly verges on the parodic. One of the highlights would be the "bentwood perch with finger tame parrot (expurgated language)", which, by evoking another "lord of the mansion"'s pet (Robinson Crusoe's), implicitly recalls both the notion of mimicry that could be extensively debated in the Anglo-Irish context and the fantasy of accumulation and isolation shared by Robinson and Bloom. The farcical edge of this "Crusoe-like narrative of bourgeois-like proprietorship"[48] is also reinforced by the echoing of the immense New Bloomusalem building with crystal roofs—itself clearly a parody of the Crystal Palace as an imperial symbol of the metropolitan convergence of all the wonders from the remote and peripheral parts of the empire.

[46] Parrinder, Ibid., 156.

[47] Ibid.

[48] Austin Briggs analyses other intertextual connections between Ulysses and Robinson Crusoe in "Bloom's Dream Cottage and Crusoe's Island: Man Caves", *European Joyce Studies* Vol. 24 (2016): 63–75.

To some extent, this architectural eclecticism of Flowerville as a private residence both reflects Bloom's own encyclopaedic, heterogeneous, random tastes and competences—and metonymically announces the eclecticism and composite, multifaceted nature of this construct on the level of cultural critique. Architectural eclecticism signals utopian implausibility and reflects Bloom's political and religious moderation and his own inbetweenness. Significantly, the architectural absurdism of Flowerville reveals a parodic and ironic critique of the nineteenth-century bourgeois conception of the residence as an expression and container of the subject, replete with all sorts of commodities and ornaments, according to the Victorian cult of domesticity. It targets that "traditionally idealized concept of dwelling" "as a false promise, one that modern art forms reject in order to strive for a more authentic definition of human existence in its spatial dimension"[49]. David Spurr thus sees Flowerville as a "deconstruction" and "as a merciless parody of the traditional myth of dwelling, exposing it as something that can only be realized in a banal and commodifed form", aiming at "the frantic pursuit of middle-class leisure activities",[50] which, nonetheless, ultimately results in an affirmative need for the sense of connection that is still afforded by the city.

In this parodic gentrifying fantasy, Bloom—the middle class, urban Catholic Irishman of Jewish origin—fancies himself as the Anglo-Irish lord of the manor, thus implicitly recalling the historically forfeited ideals of loyalty and concern, which are directly referred to,[51] in a role culminating in "his civic function(s) and social status among the county families and landed gentry" as resident magistrate or justice of the peace with a family crest and coat of arms and appropriate classical motto (*Semper paratus*). The fact that Bloom imagines himself as the Lord of Flowerville in his "capacity" as Magistrate, administering justice, is a significant addendum to the hermeneutics of this specific part of the chapter as a piece of cultural critique, nestled in what would otherwise read as a kind of private escapist and utopian fantasy:

---

[49] David Spurr, *Architecture and Modern Literature* (Ann Arbor: The University of Michigan Press, 2012), 53.

[50] Spurr, Ibid., 64.

[51] Joyce, *Ulysses*, 17 588; 1606–11.

the dispensation in a heterogeneous society of arbitrary classes, incessantly rearranged in terms of greater and lesser social inequality, of unbiassed homogeneous indisputabile justice.[52]

Loyal to the highest constituted power in the land, actuated by an innate love of rectitude his aims would be the strict maintainance of public order, the repression of many abuses though not of all simultaneously (...) the upholding of the letter of the law (common, statute and law merchant) against all ...orotund instigators of international persecution, all perpetuators of international animosities, all menial molesters of domestic conviviality, all recalcitrant violators of domestic connubiality.[53]

Gentrified Bloom is basically loyal to the Crown, and his anglophile allegiance is clearly a crucial aspect of the contradictory and complex character of this construct: it implies his compliance to the established class system in a typical case of (incoherent) divergence from his utopian vision of a classless society proclaimed by the New Bloomusalem of "Circe". As Mark Osteen noted, the Flowerville fantasy thus fulfills Bloom's desire for "home rule",[54] in a typically idiosyncratic way. In it, he plays his political part in his imaginary contribution to the common welfare through the repression of abuses, although ineffectually, with no real bearing. It has been argued that his public persona as a magistrate and his activities "turn into imaginative nonsense" as the legal jargon uncovers absurdities of sorts[55] in his mentioned "social dreaming". It should be noted, though, that this legal side of the Flowerville fantasy is no exception to the rule of Joyce's deconstructive techniques, the undermining of discourse through the accumulation of inconsistencies, absurdities and linguistic inconclusiveness, i.e. the ironic display of a host of conceptual and discursive nonsequiturs. It is, as Osteen remarks, "another of Bloom's 'counterfactuals', a 'what if' story designed both to project him into the future"[56] and to celebrate him. Once again, irony is the inclusive discursive strategy that pulls the strings together, even in the Flowerville section. Not only is

---

[52] *Ibid.*, 588; 1617–209.

[53] *Ibid.*, 588; 1633.

[54] Mark Osteen, *The Economy of Ulysses. Making Both Ends Meet*, Syracuse University Press (Syracuse, NY: 1995), 415.

[55] See Wicht, *ibid.*, 227.

[56] Osteen, *Ibid.*, 415.

it "an attribute both of the representation and the critique of individual utopian desires",[57] but notably of Joyce's problematization of the utopian modes of idealization regarding modernity. This also applies to the role played by the aspiration to epistemological totality and the encyclopedism suggested by a copy of the Britannica on the shelf. In a way, while Bloom's Anglo-Irish gentrification and his idealistic—or unconscious—collusion with the hegemonic colonial system casts a dubious light on the political value of the 'modernity' of Flowerville, it also challenges any reductively nationalist, all-Irish agenda, and projects on the brittle screen of private utopian fantasy a form of inclusiveness which embraces the Anglo-Irish "Other" of Gaelic Ireland, and the reverse, rather than reading as mere delusional gentrification.

Still, the fact that Flowerville is also a private, domestic fantasy, is recalled by the closing reference to the violations of domestic harmony; while Parrinder argues that "this is a clear signal that Flowerville, the fantasy retreat, represents a utopian opposite to the actual conditions of his life",[58] the characteristic inconclusiveness of this episode also allows for a milder interpretation. It reads not as an absolute, private utopian elsewhere, perhaps, but as an ideal alternative to the repeated frustrations of the more common—and affecting—"international persecutions" and "animosities", to which Bloom bears witness and which figure prominently in the anti-nationalist critique of "Cyclops", only to mention the most relevant episode. Despite his fantasy refuge, Bloom never really desires seclusion, but connection, as the final nostos, returns home and to Molly, attests.

The Flowerville section of the seventeenth chapter thus narrows the cosmic, wandering focus of "Ithaca" to a utopian, subjective projection which still features significantly in Joyce's concern with those geographical visions that interrogate the limits of the nation-state, a strategy that begins with Stephen's hierarchy of self and world at the beginning of *A Portrait*.[59] As Joyce "stretches the 'local' scale of the novel to the

---

[57] Wicht, *Ibid.*, 228.

[58] Parrinder, *Ibid.*, 157.

[59] "*Stephen Dedalus/Class of elements/ Clongowes Wood College/Sallins/County Kildare/ Ireland/Europe/ The World/ The Universe (…) Stephen Dedalus is my name,/Ireland is my Nation./Clongowes is my dwelling place/and heaven my expectation*". James Joyce, *A Portrait of the Artist As a Young Man*, ed. Jeri Johnston (Oxford: Oxford Classics, OUP, 2008), 12. See J.Hegglund, "Scale Bending", in Rosalyn Gregory, and

point where it can encompass many other scales, ranging from the urban all the way to the cosmological",[60] to the very minimum symbolism of the concluding typographical globe of the dot at the end of the chapter, Flowerville ironically projects yet another version of the individual and the modern nation. This is a private narrative of spatial, utopian imagining, which reasserts, through and despite its paradoxes and irony, that the nation is also constructed (and exposed in its aporias) by individual representations of the many spaces, borders and margins that gravitate around a challenging and challenged centre. Thus, as Hegglund puts it, "Joyce suggests that the nation-state, while a necessity of history, need not limit the bounds of spatial imagination".[61] Flowerville is then much more than a parenthesis in a complex chapter, but an important signifier of Joyce's inventive and provocative reflection on the modernity of Ireland as metrocolonial and peripheral.

On the whole, that dominant feature of *Ulysses* which is the coexistence between ironic distance, intellectual sophistication and critical detachment and the characters' full, imperfect but ultimately affirmative humanity, would appear to be a fruitful interpretive key to the cultural discourses which sustain the (peripheral) modernism of "Ithaca". Ironic parody and the prolonged oscillation between conclusiveness and inconclusiveness, dry scientific and technical explicatory obsessions and escapist fantasies are ultimately accommodated within the challenging construction of a periphery that is both modern and modernist. A periphery that hinges on a problematic, complicated im/possible idea of a modern home and nation which, from the real, urban and middle-class prosaic materiality of Eccles Street, extends to encompass—and perhaps to integrate—the deceptively abstruse Flowerville, only a mile off.

Benjamin Kohlmann, eds. *Utopian Spaces of Modernism. Literature and culture 1885–1925* (Basingstoke: Palgrave Macmillan, 2011), 180.

[60] Hegglund, *ibid.*, 182.

[61] Hegglund, *Ibid.*, 191.

Do Australian Modernisms Strike Back? Still Harping on 'Margins'

Marilena Parlati

"What Was Post-Colonialism?" is a famous question posed by Vijay Mishra and Bob Hodge in 2005. It both followed and triggered a long series of critical and political interventions attempting to sound out the porous boundaries of that concept.[1] In this paper, I question the "When, Where and How" of Australian modernism, offering a glimpse of another open debate concerning 'it', in intensely problematic confines. I will read through the work of two famous writers, Christina Stead and Eleanor Dark, the first a well-known hypermobile citizen of the world, the second a differently well-known sedentary resident of New South Wales, more specifically the Blue Mountains area. While my main focus lies in the writings these two artists dedicated to the city of Sydney, in many ways a cradle for discourses and practices of modernisation and vitalist rejuvenation in the interwar years, I will expand more widely on Eleanor Dark's

---

[1] V. Mishra and B. Hodge, "What Was Postcolonialism?", *New Literary History*, 36, 3 (Summer 2005), pp. 375–402 and previously S. Hall, "When Was the Post-colonial? Thinking at the Limit", in I. Chambers, L. Curti (eds.), *The Post-Colonial Question*, London, Routledge, 1995.

M. Parlati (✉)
University of Padua, Padua, Italy
e-mail: marilena.parlati@unipd.it

© The Author(s), under exclusive license to Springer Nature Switzerland AG 2024
K. Pizzi and R. Gefter Wondrich (eds.), *Rethinking Peripheral Modernisms*, https://doi.org/10.1007/978-3-031-35546-2_6

novels of the late Thirties. As a matter of fact, I deem them of particular interest due to their experiments with modernist formal techniques, middlebrow cultural modernity and the social and political commitments which were animating the literary and artistic scene worldwide in that decade.

Modernism in the singular is undoubtedly the object of numerous and well-motivated attacks due—among other things—to the imperialistic implications inherent in its 'high' Anglo-American canonical version. Fredric Jameson summed up the crucial intertwining of that version of Western modernism with imperialism in an essay which interpellated the mechanisms and privileges shaping much of the experimental artistic and literary output from the late nineteenth century to the late Thirties or early Forties.[2] As he made clear, in fact, already at the end of the war modernism was no longer a pulsating organism. This view has been so widely shared that one still encounters it in school textbooks in many countries of the West (only referring to a few countries and languages I am familiar with). Faced with the narrative of a multifaceted experience mainly rooted in the great capital cities of Western Europe and North America, new modernist studies have insisted on problematising the uses and abuses of the very term 'modernism' and its temporal declensions and on refiguring its geomorphologies.[3] To mention just a few examples, in a book in which T. S. Eliot, Derek Walcott and Kamau Brathwaite are connected in a nonderivative, non-imitative move, Charles W. Pollard has opted for "New World modernisms".[4] Laura Winkiel and Laura Doyle have also argued in favour of "geomodernisms" to revisit the canon in the radical sense of not merely allowing room for voices other than white, Western, male, but of dismantling the traditional centre-periphery route with its alternating journeys in and out of the metropolitan core and invalidating the very narrative which sees non-Western modernism 'striking back' at very insensitive cultural sources.[5]

---

[2] F. Jameson, "Modernism and Imperialism", in *The Modernist Papers*, London, Verso, 2007.

[3] Douglas Mao and Rebecca L. Walkowitz, "The New Modernist Studies", *PMLA*, 123, 3 (2008), pp. 737–48 and Peter J. Kalliney, *Modernism in a Global Context*, London, Bloomsbury, 2016.

[4] C. W. Pollard, *New World Modernisms*, Charlottesville, University of Virginia Press, 2004.

[5] Laura Doyle and Laura Winkel (eds.), *Geomodernisms: Race, Modernism, Modernity*, Bloomington and Indianapolis, Indiana University Press, 2005.

In this line, Susan Stanford Friedman has very convincingly argued in favour of "A full spatialization of modernism [which] changes the map, the canon, and the periodization of modernism dramatically".[6] She suggests a relational mode of reading modernisms, and the even more elusive term 'modernity', to accommodate "the possibility for polycentric modernities and modernisms at different points of time and in different locations".[7] In her thoughtful discussion, Friedman takes partial issue with Dilip Parameshawar Gaonkar's collection of essays on *Alternative Modernities*, which she generally praises. Yet, she laments his eventual surrender to a distorting logic which reads those *other* modernisms as intrinsically doomed to belatedness and vindicational lamentation.[8] In this paper, I side with Friedman's critical position on modernities as "planetary",[9] "with many multidirectional links, affiliations, and often brutal inequities of power (...) each [reflecting] the particular indigenizations of its own location".[10] Thus, alerted to such rhizomatic polycentric constellations, I wish to turn to some versions of (white) Australian modernisms, which both mark and depart from the centre-periphery frame, while still leaving almost undisputed the sore issue of Aboriginal Australian dispossession and obliteration in years which saw the consolidation of the Federation, together with and founded on a white Australia epistemics of violence.

In her thorough survey of the "alternative modernisms" of Australia, Canada and New Zealand, Anouk Lang acknowledges the new awareness that has shaken the secure pillars of canonical 'high modernism'; she also accepts that global modernist productions may bear a certain amount of derivative quality and mutual influences which may seem to imply a hierarchical value biased in favour of the Western metropolitan centres. Yet, Lang vehemently states that "investigating modernism's development in Australia, New Zealand, and Canada is much more than an exercise in

---

[6] Susan Stanford Friedman, "Periodizing Modernism: Postcolonial Modernities and the Space/Time Borders of Modernist Studies", *Modernism/Modernity*, 13, 3 (2006), pp. 425–443, p. 426.

[7] Friedman, cit., p. 426.

[8] See Dilip Parameshawar Gaonkar, "On Alternative Modernities", in Dilip Parameshawar Gaonkar (ed.), *Alternative Modernities*, Durham, Duke University Press, 2001.

[9] See Susan Stanford Friedman, *Planetary Modernisms: Provocations on Modernity Across Time*, New York, Columbia University Press, 2010.

[10] Friedman 2006, cit., p. 435.

102   M. PARLATI

postcolonial inclusivity".[11] Her argument fleshes out my own point here, in that "once we begin thinking of modernism in terms of its transnational conversations, these so-called 'alternative' modernisms *stop looking peripheral* and *start looking* increasingly *transformative*, offering the possibility of revealing new insights about a movement that, even after a century, retains the power to surprise and disturb."[12]

VITAL CELEBRATIONS AND STOLID OBLITERATIONS

After the birth of the Commonwealth Federation in 1901, the state of Australia found in the Great War another quintessential celebratory myth related to the sacrificial participation of its young men in the global war effort, more famously at Gallipoli on 25 April 1915. John Williams maintains that the military intervention in the distant conflict both earned the country international credit and removed the stain of having long been the 'penal colony', inhabited by the scum of the British 'homeland'. The post-war years also saw the continuation of a previous debate over the very existence of a 'national type', a specially indigenised (in the sense Friedman suggests, but with no reference whatsoever to the actual indigenous peoples of the continent) young, athletic, modern human type which was to enact both a return to the land it also had the duty to populate (with white offspring), and an ongoing quintessential relation with Britain. To some white Australians were eventually nothing but "transplanted Britons".[13] Whatever they identified with, in the first decades of the new century Australians could indeed have access and contribute to global cultural revolutions mainly via their literary, cultural and also middlebrow magazines, like any well-informed reader and spectator of the world. In his interesting survey of the visual arts on the continent, Williams suggests that from 1919 onwards any previous trace of openness and curiosity towards experimentation receded in favour of an isolationist culture, of racial self-closure and a nostalgic thrust towards an agrarian

---

[11] Anouk Lang, "Modernist Fiction/Alternative Modernisms: Australia, Canada, New Zealand", in Coral Ann Howells, Paul Sharrad, and Gerry Turcotte (eds.), *The Oxford History of the Novel in English: Volume 12: The Novel in Australia, Canada, New Zealand, and the South Pacific Since 1950*, Oxford, Oxford University Press, 2017, pp. 190–204.

[12] Lang, cit., p. 195, my italics.

[13] J. F. Williams, *Quarantined Culture. Australian Reactions to Modernism 1913–1939*, Cambridge, Cambridge University Press, 1995, p. 2.

arcady and a mythical outback.[14] To him, Australia thus became a "quarantined culture", intent on excluding, both at a political and at a generally social level, whatever it perceived and displayed as pathological. That quarantine, he argues "(...) was propagated by an inchoate grouping of racial supremacists, anti-Semites, anti-bolshevists, protectionists, anti-industrialisers (...) men, mostly, who as individuals often manifested many or all of the foregoing traits".[15] These men intended to protect the alleged purity of the country both via the 1920 Anti-Alien Laws and, in a more restrictedly cultural sense, by attacking "modernism at every opportunity or ridicul[ing]... those they saw as *infected with the modernist virus* and (...) brand[ing] them with (...) the undesirable contagions of bolshevism and Judaism (...)."[16] In this version of the cultural history of post-first-world-war Australia, artistic modernism had to be rejected for the sake of a very predicated national character, paradoxically both oriented towards the British 'Mother Land' and in search of its own specificity. In fact, this entailed the creation of another powerful myth, that of "internal exploration" and exploitation, performed by swarms of squatters, diggers and bushmen, again literally effacing the original inhabitants of the continent.[17]

As David Carter has claimed, Australia's colonial status seemed doomed to perpetual belatedness, to remaining what he terms "always almost modern".[18] On the other hand, many deemed Australia "always already modern", since not endowed with a long enough history or a cultural heritage worth acknowledging. What to some was a drawback was often transformed into a positive vision of freedom from the

---

[14] It is indeed remarkable that in both the 'return to the land' propaganda and in the forms of quarantine Williams recounts, Aboriginal Australians have completely been figuratively dispelled—as indeed they have been—beyond discourse and away from sight. A different view on 'Aboriginal modernism'—with a special focus on the visual arts, again— has been suggested by Ian McLean in "Modernism without Borders", *Filozofski Vestnik*, 35, 2, pp. 121–139. I also wish to acknowledge that I am aware that attaching the term 'modernism' to Aboriginal cultures may repeat a dangerously Eurocentric ensnarement in 'mimicry', and this must therefore remain a very contested and contestable terrain.

[15] Williams, cit. p. 5.

[16] Williams, cit. p. 6.

[17] M. Leer, "Imagined Counterpart: Outlining a Conceptual Literary Geography of Australia", *Australian Literary Studies*, October 1991, p. 3.

[18] See D. Carter, *Always Almost Modern: Australian Print Cultures and Modernity*, Melbourne, Australian Scholarly Press, 2013.

104 M. PARLATI

shackles of paralytic artistic and literary traditions and into allegedly fresher and healthier futures. In this connection, for example, Carter mentions a later essay by H. P. Heseltine, who candidly states that "Due to certain circumstances of history and geography, Australian literature (…) early took as its central subject what is still one of the inescapable concerns of all modern literature."[19] That subject—"the terror at the basis of being"—would therefore instantiate a radical 'Australianness', whose pervasiveness and whose very existence Carter warns against and which I see as continuously fluctuating between modern, antimodern and modernist, at least in the decades between the two world wars. In an attempt at capturing and partaking of the modern, many expatriate artists (not only Australian, of course) set out on transnational itineraries that would take them to Europe and to North America, among other locations, as in the famous case of Christina Stead. Other writers, instead, such as Eleanor Dark, stayed at home and created a locally-engaged version of modernism that Melinda Cooper has very interestingly defined "interwar settler modernism".[20] I wish to address these two differing modes and moves which seem inherent in Australian modernism, and which mirror the road these two women writers attempted to carve out for themselves.

JOURNEYS IN?

Many scholars have seen Australian modernism as surrounded by an aura of nostalgic longing and outofplacedness, suggesting that it never really took (its) place at home, but was only fully realised when it was associated to artists who left Australia behind.[21] Writing at the end of the Fifties, Patrick White situated his own experimental writing with that of Christina Stead in sneering opposition to the "journalistic realism" and the national-provincial slant he saw in much of the artistic and

[19] H. P. Heseltine, "The Literary Heritage", *Meanjin*, 21, 1 (1962), pp. 35–49, quoted in Carter, cit., p. 9.

[20] M. Cooper, "'Adjusted Vision': Interwar Settler Modernism in Eleanor Dark's *Return to Coolami*", *Australian Literary Studies*, 33, 2 (2018), pp. 1–28.

[21] To name just one, D. Modjeska, who stated that "there was very little writing during the thirties to equal the enrgy that surrounded 'the modern' in painting, deisgn or the decorative arts (…)", adding that "the only novelists who can really be said to have made a shift into an idiom and aesthetic of modernism were those who left the country". "'A Hoodoo on That Book': The Publishing Misfortunes of an Eleanor Dark Novel", *Southerly*, 57, 2 (1997), pp. 73–96, p. 74.

literary production in Australia.[22] The contribution of expatriate writers to the cultural life and literary vivacity of imperial centres is the object of continued study, which has also recently started to change the traditional views on the hierarchical connection between peripheral and 'central' sites, in favour of more sophisticated appreciation of the relational, more-than-just-transnational articulations of those encounters. For instance, Rebecca Walkowitz has focussed on the conversations which involved many women artists travelling to the 'centre'. This may provide an essential lens for reconfiguring both transnational modernisms and more recent critical readings of the entanglement of transnationalism, international political and feminist movements, colonial stereotypes, nationalistic thrusts and radical epistemic violence against indigenous peoples and cultures.

The 'journey in' is a frequent trope implying the 'return' to the perceived and political homeland that Britain still signified to many colonial subjects, at the time in which Stead moved to London in 1928.[23] Quite convincingly, Anna Snaith has argued that expatriate writers, more evidently women artists, took the 'journey in' as a means for "subverting the logic of imperial movement", at a time in which imperial propaganda—in and beyond Britain—was very keen on inviting robust, young and potentially fertile men and women to relocate and reproduce in some of the immense expanses the Commonwealth 'offered'.[24] Yet, rather than being a more modern version of the classical Grand Tour, the long journey towards this fraught 'home' could and did produce a number of unpredicted outcomes, such as bitter disappointment, cultural marginalisation and seclusion, racist and sexist encounters and harassment.

As John McLeod suggests in relation to post-decolonisation London, and as Snaith proves, one must acknowledge the extent to which that 'centre' was a fictitious imaginary land, and certainly not a home to many.

---

[22] P. White, "The Prodigal Son", in A. Lawson (ed.), *Patrick White. Selected Writings*, St. Lucia, University of Queensland Press, 1994, pp. 268–271, p. 270.

[23] In Australia, in a number of different senses the issue of 'national' belonging is all but seamless. One might wish to remember the British monarch's visage still stamped on Australian currency, not to mention the unconceded nature of Australian land on the part of Aboriginal first inhabitants.

[24] A. Snaith, *Modernist Voyages. Colonial Women Writers in London, 1890–1945*, Cambridge, Cambridge University Press, 2017, Introduction, p. 1.

106   M. PARLATI

To be sure, it was not a seamless monolithic centre confirming the stability of the British Empire in obviously 'superior' relation to any other world metropolis.[25] In the capital city, contesting networks and resistant sites were available to some (if not always to all) of the expatriates who arrived there, at times to represent their home country, their activist international connections, and themselves as writers ambitiously trying to 'make it' in the publishing global market managed from London and New York.[26] To sum up, the city was not, at least not only, *the* monumental centre of power and culture, but a more controversial and immensely more complex space of cultural confrontation and contamination.

If life could be hard for colonial men facing snobbery and racism in their ordinary life in the city as well as in their attempts at contributing to its cultural life, it could be even more so for women (especially when 'unaccompanied') trying to rent rooms and find jobs and publishers, not to mention the intensely-fraught position non-white women were often forced to occupy. Christina Stead left Australia with the clear agenda of having her novel on Sydney published in Paris, where she lived for a few years with her partner, Bill Blake, before moving to London and later the United States. Stead would later and privately make it bluntly clear that to her London was "the seat of a vicious Empire, oppressor of many nations and author of many crimes" and that the English were "the most bootlickingest, most class-saturated, most conceited and ignorant people" she had ever met.[27] Yet, it was in London that she transformed her original *Death in the Antipodes* into *Seven Poor Men of Sydney*, eventually published in 1934, a radical, politically engaged and formally experimental novel in which she moves away from the bush tradition of the Australian novel still popular at that time and keenly surveys the teeming metropolis and the national celebratory discourses of the time.

> International modernity was gradually adapted and Australianised in Sydney then proudly performed to the rest of the country and returned to the world (...) Rather than the last station on the line, a backwater ten years behind Europe and America as some (...) have asserted, Sydney was

---

[25] See J. McLeod, *Postcolonial London. Rewriting the Metropolis*, London, Routledge, 2004.

[26] Snaith, cit., in particular pp. 4–12.

[27] C. Stead, *Letters*, p. 126 and pp. 73, 313, quoted in Snaith, cit., p. 188.

a busy port of call in the ceaseless international ebb and flow of commerce and ideas that underpinned cosmopolitan modernity.[28]

"Flotsam and Jetsam": Topograhies of Destitution

I am interested in the ways in which Stead and Dark locate themselves and their writing in intimate distance and proximity to such a vibrant new centre of cosmopolitan modernity. I focus on the ways in which they relate, use, readapt the modes of writing the fragmented terrain of such urban life, and the possibilities and responsibilities of art as well as the often difficult class confrontation they could see agitating its gigantic and technologically advanced panoramas. In the view of Sam Matthews, Stead's novel looks back to Balzac's *Illusions perdues*, which displays a young writer-to-be from the province confronting the great metropolis, its squalors and banality.[29] Stead's Sydney is a palimpsest, a "busy port of call", and also a gigantic organism capturing humans in all the greedy activities that make it *just like* any other modern city of capitalism in the years preceding the Great War and at the time of global Depression in the late Twenties. In her novel, Sydney is ready for the impending war, marked by the very visible and audible presence of the searching lights and of its military apparatus. Moreover, one of the seven poor men of the title, Michael Baguenault, also brings into the text the devastating burden of his traumatising experience in Europe.[30] The seven destitute protagonists of the novel are connected by poverty itself, first and foremost, by the city slums and streets, and by its suburban spaces—both new and already derelict. More impressively, Sydney is represented by its immense harbour and also by the radical Tank Stream Press, located at a fictional version of Macquarie Place, one of the real topographic foci both of the novel and of the foundation of white Australia.

Slums and suburban spaces alike seem to attest to the very modernity of the city, its wealth and affluence necessarily founded on the exploitation and marginalisation of the unemployed, deranged, disturbed

---

[28] Jill Julius Matthews, *Dance Hall & Picture Palace: Sydney's Romance with Modernity*, Sydney, Currency Press, 2005, p. 1 quoted in Carter, cit., p. XI.

[29] H. de Balzac, *Illusions perdues*, volume 8 of *La Comédie humaine*, 1843, quoted in Matthews, p. 40.

[30] C. Stead, *Seven Poor Men of Sydney*, with an introduction by M. Harris, Bondi Junction (NSW), Imprint, 1999 (first edition, London, Peter Davies, 1934).

108   M. PARLATI

post-Depression proletarian classes. One of the protagonists, Kol Blount, is described as affected by a paralysis caused by indigence: "He should never have been in a chair all these years, it seems; a pure case of neglect and poverty".[31] Joseph Baguenault, one of the seven, looks at himself to see:

> The sole of one boot was attached by a hair-pin, the worn knees of the trousers showed the colour of his pale skin when he sat down. His hat was an old one of his cousin's. The rest of his attire fell in with these items and produced a sort of harmonious costume, the uniform of misery. The children of Fisherman's Bay shouted after him, "Joey, Jo, Jo, Ullo Jo," when he went past in the evenings. He knew what this song meant; it meant, "*You are rubbish thrown out by men,* and we are allowed to play with you, no one even has a salvage interest in you." The Clown of the Universe had produced a man in his image. The accumulated misery, shame, hunger and ignorance of centuries straddled the path as he advanced against the evening sun (...)[32]

The novel is steeped in socialist and Marxist references and agendas, as one of its first Australian reviews also highlighted: "In *Seven Poor Men of Sydney*, the reader is introduced to a section that is rebellious in spirit, Communistic in policy, and intensely introspective in its outlook. (...) *Seven Poor Men* is stark realism".[33] Yet, the novel also looks back, though obliquely, to the metropolitan culture carried by two of the secondary characters, the English socialist activists Marion and Fulke Folliot, who "talked Cezanne, Gauguin, Laforgue, T. S. Eliot, Freud and Havelock Ellis."[34] Stead seems to be taking an ironical distance from this eloquent list in her connecting it to a happy, middle-class couple, "provided for by" their families before becoming "industrious" and even "protected rather than harassed by the police".[35] Yet, Stead actually introduces some pages of the stream-of-consciousness technique in which the shell-shocked

---

[31] Stead, cit., p. 310.

[32] Stead, cit., p. 96, my italics.

[33] 'Bookman', *The Courier-Mail*, Friday 30 November 1934, p. 16.

[34] Stead, cit., p. 57.

[35] Stead, cit., p. 58.

Michael falls prey to his hallucinated memory.[36] Very interestingly, the review I just mentioned praises the novel for unexpected reasons: "The plot is *negligible*: in fact, the book consists very largely of philosophical dialogues and musings, all with a distinctly pessimistic and rebellious tendency. The merit of the book lies in its characterisation and its brilliant writing. Miss Stead is certainly a master of English and a master of phrasemaking—".[37] To some, then, Stead was 'just' a realist, and yet she managed to innovate Australian fiction in content, mode and form.[38] She succeeded in creating "a startlingly new vision of Sydney quite in opposition to the mainstream duncoloured realism of Australian fiction in the thirties".[39] To other reviewers, namely the very famous novelist Miles Franklin, the novel had dressed the city with "post-Freudianism" and had taken the "vomit from Bloomsbury and Washington Square" and "belch[ed] it upon Sydney".[40]

Franklin had possibly been upset by many passages of this long novel, in particular its last pages, in which Kol Blount recounts the millennial history of "a nameless land (...) abyss, awash, awhist and away (...)[41]:

> Fires were lighted, murder done, ships cast away, cargoes plundered, robbers clothed in silk, rafts seaswept, women lost, sacrosancts profaned, mutinies smothered, hostages taken, chartings made, short-lines plumbed, reefs struck, wreckers enriched, the Chinese rolled from port to port, the Kanakas perished in the cane, mountain bluffs were climbed, the blackfellows destroyed, the plains bore flocks, the deserts of spinifex sprouted gold, the new world began. And after all this notable *pioneer tale of starvation, sorrow, escapades, mutiny, death, labour in common, broad wheatlands, fat sheep, broad cattle-barons, raw male youth and his wedding to the land,*

---

[36] Stead, cit., pp. 230–236.

[37] 'Bookman', cit., p. 16.

[38] M. Wilding, "In writing about Sydney [she] is *creating a new world, a new myth* to replace or complement the outback myth; and she is making a personal and national assertion in putting Sydney on the fictional map", "Christina Stead's *Seven Poor Men of Sydney*", in *The Radical Tradition: Lawson, Furphy, Stead*, Townsville, James Cook University of North Queensland, 1993, pp. 160–186, pp. 160–161, my italics.

[39] Matthews, cit., p. 41.

[40] M. Franklin, "*Seven Poor Men of Sydney* by Christina Stead", in P. Brunton (ed.), *The Diaries of Miles Franklin*, Crows Nest, Allen & Unwin, 2004, pp. 26–28.

[41] Stead, cit., p. 304.

110 M. PARLATI

in the over-populated metropolis the sad-eyed youth sits glumly in a hare-brained band, and speculates on the suicide of youth, the despair of the heirs of yellow heavy-headed acres. What a history is that; what an enigma is that?"[42]

In this section of the novel, many centuries coalesce around the "flotsam and jetsam" of a "land [which] should never have been won" (as a matter of fact, it was obviously *not won*, but illegitimately *appropriated*).[43] Stead imagines the historical presence of Aboriginal Australians before the "pioneer tale" of colonisation in the pages preceding the passage quoted before, but sees them as already sadly "destroyed", in line with many other contemporaries who sided with eugenicists, and therefore saw them as doomed in the confrontation with the "white race".[44] That story and all the stories in the novel are brought to very bitter and disappointing conclusions: Michael commits suicide by jumping off the Gap; his sister Catherine retires to a mental asylum; another protagonist, the Jew Baruch Mendehlson, leaves for Europe like the Folliots, who 'must' take their due place (and family inheritance) back in England. As already suggested, the city waterway functions as an essential chronotope, marked by a seamen's strike which temporarily stops the growing flow of merchandise, books, international drugs, and ocean liners connecting "Singapore, Shanghai, Nagasaki, Wellington, Hawaii, San Francisco, Naples, Brindisi, Dunkirk and London".[45] Yet, none of these routes provides any evidence nor hope of a future, apart from Joseph Baguenault's return home to Ultimo, to be welcomed by a caring wife who listens to the tale he has to spin, again and again: "We were seven friends, at that time, yes, seven poor men...".[46]

[42] Stead, cit., p. 308, my italics.

[43] Stead, cit., p. 308.

[44] Among them, Eleanor Dark herself, as I will briefly refer to later in this essay. On this issue, see S. Garton, "Sound Minds and Healthy Bodies: Re-considering Eugenics in Australia, 1914–1940", *Australian Historical Studies*, 1994, pp. 163–182.

[45] Stead, cit., p. 2.

[46] Stead, cit., p. 319.

Journeys Out?

Like Stead's Joseph Baguenault, the other writer I turn to—Eleanor Dark—also stayed on, leaving Australia only for a brief spell. She lived most of her life at Katoomba, in the Blue Mountains area, at a relative distance from the city of Sydney. In my view, Eleanor Dark is a much more interesting and experimentally courageous writer than Stead, even if she remains sorely little known in Europe. She was the first Australian author to be twice awarded the Australian Literature Society Gold Medal before Patrick White. She can be conceived of as "the first modernist writer in Australia".[47] Her first novel, *Slow Dawning*, was published in 1932, soon to be followed by a series of other novels which consolidated her reputation: *Prelude to Christopher* (1934), *Return to Coolami* (1936), *Sun Across the Sky* (1937), *Waterway* (1938), among others. Her most famous work is a trilogy she dedicates to post-settlement Australian history, whose first volume, *A Timeless Land* (1941) was so immensely popular that it was sent to Australian troops to revive their national pride. In many different ways, I argue, Dark's writings of the Thirties are entangled in local national issues while also problematically experimenting with some of the literary techniques generally associated with 'high modernism', such as stream of consciousness, multifocal narrative, compacted time frames, flashbacks and narrative discontinuity. Instead of a 'revenant modernism', Dark creates her own consistent version of novel writing and cultural intervention: she picks, adapts, manipulates and negotiates with those techniques and themes, thus destabilising and reconfiguring any clearly drawn boundary between high and low, national and transnational issues and agendas. In this context, I decisively side with Melinda Cooper's well-wrought suggestion related to "interwar settler modernism" which is, in her view, "a distinctive convergence of aesthetic modernism with more vernacular modes and settler nationalist desires

---

[47] In her monograph study on Dark, Marivic Wyndham uses the words of Cusak to remind how "in 1977, Dymphna Cusack, prompted by the award of the Order of Australia to Dark in belated recognition for her services to Australian literature, remarked How can it be that a country is so oblivious of one of her greatest writers, admired in Great Britain, Europe and America, that in the last three years of the academic list is represented by one book in one provincial university?" D. Cusack, "The Novels of Eleanour (sic) Dark", *Education*, 25 May 1977, pp. 173–174, quoted in M. Wyndham, *'A World-Proof Life': Eleanor Dark, A Writer in Her Times, 1901–1985*, Sydney, University of Technology Press, 2007, p. 12.

112   M. PARLATI

(...) it works to destabilise these very distinctions, expanding cultural-nationalist aesthetics beyond the bounds of realism (...)".[48] Cooper focuses more specifically on Dark's third novel, *Return to Coolami*, in which Dark takes a step back from the controversial issues she had handled in 1934 in *Prelude to Christopher*. There she delved into modernist techniques while tackling madness, eugenics, and suicide. Her amazing feat had already been publicly recognised by her first ALS prize. Her 1936 text is a very different road novel, oscillating between suburbia and the outback, between technological advances and romantic intrigue and interlacing the lives of its protagonists with two almost fatal car accidents. This text earned Dark her second ALS Prize, thus shining a brilliant national and international light on her. Wyndham suggests that the two following, interlinked novels (*Sun Across the Sky* and *Waterway*) did not receive the same attention, while others also lament that they did not reach similar standards of experimentation and novelty.[49]

In my view, instead, even if less controversial in its choice of themes, *Waterway* is a remarkable novel which also intersects local national(istic) and international preoccupations with style, as well as with global capital and modernisms. According to Wyndham, Dark illuminates some of the means by which Australia was trying to come to grasp its Federation plan and to figure out its position in global geopolitics and cultures. In fact, she focussed on issues such as

> (...) nationalism versus internationalism, populism versus elitism, nation versus empire, the advocacy of a popular distinctive national culture without empowering the masses, liberalism versus socialism, indigenous versus European Australia, Old World versus New World values, bush versus city culture. What kind of society was Australia to be: an outpost of empire still, an American clone, or an independent society?[50]

At the cusp of such questions, the palimpsest city of Sydney and its harbour take central stage in *Waterway*, rightly defined by Modjeska "Eleanor Dark's marvellous Sydney novel."[51]

---

[48] Cooper 2018, cit., p. 2.

[49] Wyndham, cit. p. 8.

[50] Wyndham, cit., p. 6.

[51] D. Modjeska, *Exiles at Home. Australian Women Writers 1925–1945*, Sydney, Allen and Unwin, 1981, p. 5.

The Entangled Bank: Ghostly Terrains and Aquapolitical Solutions

Set in one day and one space (though socially and morphologically highly variegated), *Waterway* pivots on and fluctuates around Sydney waterway, in its concoction of salt and fresh waters, and the transnational routes and rites of passage which cross it. Its numerous protagonists roam along its banks, beaches and streets, in visual pursuit of its local ferries and the ocean ships and battleships which traverse its waters. Their lives are already intertwined or *become* suddenly connected by the single main eventual punctum of its plot, a ferry accident. The novel is divided into five parts, which start at "Sunrise" and conclude at "Sunset", and which take the "Cove", the "City" and the "Ferry" as their respective foci. This careful partition follows the author's intention of imitating a musical polyvocal "fugue".[52] Each part is prefaced by excerpts from historical documents written by the early colonisers who 'first' took 'possession' of the already-dispossessed Port Jackson, their names being David Collins, Arthur Phillip, and Lord Sydney, and dating back to years from 1788 to 1863. Colonial history thus unfolds as a discourse contrapunctal to *and* radically foundational of the modern city and nation and its own fraught national and international interconnections, plus, most relevantly, the cruel practices of violence it had rooted itself on and was practising in growingly 'scientifical' tones. Quite famously, the original owners of those lands had encountered Phillip's exploration party with their very vociferous "'Warra warra', Go away".[53,54] In close connection to *Sun*

---

[52] Dark's version of fugue is also littered—like Stead's harbour waters—by the flotsam and jetsam of global capitalism: "It was, in a sense, a flight. He realised that as he walked along the path beside the Bay, thinking with one part of his mind that it must have been a much prettier beach, a prettier Bay altogether, in the days of that Robert Watson after whom it had been named. Now the high-water mark was littered with rubbish—bits of coke, bits of orange-peel, driftwood, seaweed—all the flotsam and jetsam of a great harbour where ships came and went." Dark, cit., p. 33.

[53] D. Collins, *An Account of the English Colony in New South Wales*, 1798, Chapter 1, quoted in Dark, cit., p. 10.

[54] Among the many who have confronted these 'original' texts, Rachel Stanfield highlights the many crucial predicaments Collins gives voice to. She suggests that "In the Account's first mention of encounter with Aboriginal people, Collins initiated a complex discourse combining a record of Aboriginal displeasure, a suggestion that the people were peaceful, and also an expression of concern about the impact of colonisation on the Indigenous population. Collins first mentioned Aboriginal people while describing an

114 M. PARLATI

across the Sky, in which he had been the protagonist, the novel starts with an aerial view impressed upon the eye and memory of Dr. Oliver Denning and which resonates with the unheeded "shouts of defiance and prohibition" of the first epigraph.[55]

> (...) It was so queerly silent. Humanity was asleep all along those dark, mysterious shores (...) It was as quiet now (...) as it must have been on the dawn of that day a hundred and fifty years ago which had marked the end of its *primeval solitude*. Now, with the aid of dim light, narrowed eyes, and a little imagination, you could annihilate the city (...) You could become a different kind of man, tall and deep-chested, black-skinned and bearded (...) the headlands were not Blue's Point and Pott's Point, Longnose Point and Slaughter-house Point. They were Warringarea and Yarranabbe, Yeroulbine and Tarrah (...) not Pinchgut (...) not a foolish little fortress, staidly renamed Fort Denison, but a lovely soaring column of weather-worn rock, holy place of your people --- Mattewaya....[56]

In this denial of coevalness and of the "simultaneous uncontemporaneities" Patrick Williams focussed on in 2000,[57] Denning *becomes* an unnamed Eora man, by imaginatively taking his position and corporeal stance while surveying Country. In this very crucial passage, Dark *unnames* the sites of the 'original' first dispossession in a move which triangulates the British colonisers/invaders with First Nation inhabitants and the representatives of a new and intensely white (or better, beautifully tanned by their active and sporty lives) Australian indigeneity.[58] In

---

exploration party, headed by Phillip and including Collins, travelling north along the coast from Botany Bay searching for a site for permanent settlement". In "'These Unoffending People': Myth, History and the Idea of Aboriginal Resistance in David Collins' *Account of the English Colony in New South Wales*", in A. Curthoys, F. C. Peters-Little, and J. Docker (eds.), *Passionate Histories: Myth, Memory and Indigenous Australia*, Canberra, Australian National University Press, 2011, pp. 123–140.

[55] Dark, cit., p. 10.

[56] Dark, cit., p. 12. One may also wish to remember that 1938 was the centenary of the Myall Creek Massacre, in which 28 Indigenous people were murdered by white perpetrators who were famously the first to be arrested and sentenced to death.

[57] P. Williams, "Simultaneous Uncontemporaneities: Theorising Modernism and Empire", in H. J. Booth and N. Rigby (eds.), *Modernism and Empire*, Manchester, Manchester University Press, 2000, pp. 13–38.

[58] See note 57 and also E. Dark, "Australia and the Australians", in S. Ure Smith and G. Morton Spencer (eds.), *Australia Week-End. Book 3*, 1944, pp. 9–19.

DO AUSTRALIAN MODERNISMS STRIKE BACK? ...   115

her very recent essay on Australian modernism, Melinda Cooper warns against excessively simplistic associations between modernist primitivism and the Australian version of settler colonial modernism one might be tempted by.[59] Another prolonged passage from the novel may serve to further prove such statements:

> When the invaders landed they felt a soil beneath their feet whose very texture was alien; a hard earth which smelled not of grass and flowers and hay (...) but, strangely, of an age-old solitude. Shrubs, ankle-high, waist-high, sombre in colour (...) armed to the very leaves, defied them (...) An inhospitable land, they said; a barren, hostile country.... Hostile --- no. (...) There it was, here it is still, *untouched*.[60]

According to Wyndham, Dark possibly portrayed herself as Lesley Channon, a writer forever fighting for justice and for fame alike. Lesley studies at the Mitchell public library, in a section of the novel which reiterates and expands the first epigraph quotation from Collins and which alternates between the locale described and etched in the eighteenth-century books she is reading, and the panorama view she can master from the windows of that colonial institution. Originally endowed with topical mysterious powers and subsumed by a disturbing *primeval silence* which again annihilates the original owners of the land, the harbour wakes to its modern throbbing life in which all the characters head on, wait, doze, play, receive a terrible diagnosis, employ or waste their time before the momentous event in part four, the "Ferry", takes place. In an essay on "urban ethics" in *Waterway*, Meg Brayshaw draws on Drusilla Modjeska's arguments on the waterway as a vital part of the city, entangled with the suburban dwellers commuting to and from the vibrant financial and cultural centre of the City.[61] I suggest we allow Modjeska's "entanglement" to resonate with the Darwinian undertones I cannot avoid detecting. The waterway functions like the "entangled bank" of the very last pages of Darwin's 1859 *Origin of Species*, in which Darwin visualised

---

[59] See M. J. Cooper, "News from Australia: Global Modernism Studies and the Case of Australian Modernism", in J. Gildersleeve (ed.), *The Routledge Companion to Australian Literature*, London, Routledge, 2020, pp. 230–247.

[60] Dark, cit., pp. 216–217, my italics.

[61] See M. Brayshaw, "Ecology, Urban Ethics and the Harbour: Eleanor Dark's *Waterway* (1938)", in *Sydney and Its Waterway in Australian Literary Modernism*, London, Palgrave, 2021, pp. 105–134.

116   M. PARLATI

and "contemplate[d] an entangled bank, clothed with many plants of many kinds, with birds singing on the bushes, with various insects flitting about, and with worms crawling through the damp earth".[62] Like that bank, both the novel and the intricate harbour/river site may be read as a site for vital and lethal confrontation and "struggles for existence".

Among the protagonists of the novel are family groups such as the Channons, the Sellmans, the Hegartys, the Harnetts, the Dennings, plus some unattached characters such as the leftist intellectual Roger Blair and the unemployed, therefore enraged workman Jack Saunders. All these families are often the result of non-conformist engagements and the deaths of mothers, husbands, and wives. The only truly positive couple in the novel is made by Oliver, a liberal and warm-hearted GP, and his artist wife, Lois, by all means not the standard type of domestic matron contemporary propaganda suggested women (married, in particular) were supposed to comply with. Readers also follow the romantic/sexual attraction between Lesley Channon and the handsome, rich, 'aristocratic' air ace Sim Hegarty, which will eventually be superseded by a more mature liaison with the radical writer and leftist intellectual Roger Blair. The novel is crowded with middle-class intellectuals and radicals, whom Dark also exposes to the plights and voices of the proletarian and unemployed classes.[63] Two moments in the novel, in fact, are truly collective and both uncannily momentous: the first is a classy wedding ceremony, which tangentially relates the city élite to both the low-class women gaping for the sight of a 'celebrity' and a more dangerous mob protesting against unemployment. In and out of this novel, as in Stead's *Seven Poor Men*, class relations were indeed all but peacefully settled at a time of very high rates of unemployment and growing anxieties concerning global peace.

The most pivotal episode in the text is the Ferry crash, which Dark anticipates in her "Author's Notes", where she justifies her historical incongruent references: "For the purposes of my story, I have revived the regular ferry service (which was discontinued some years ago) from Circular Quay to Watson's Bay and intermediate wharves. Although some of the events described in Part IV are based on real happenings

---

[62] C. Darwin, *Origin of Species*, second edition, London, Murray, 1860, p. 490.

[63] Possibly, this was also due to the influence of Eric Dark, Eleanor's husband, who was a convinced socialist and active member of the left.

in November, 1927, all the characters in the book are imaginary."[64] The Harbour had often been the site of shipwrecks, most recently in November 1927, when a Union Steamship Company liner exotically called the Tahiti had collided with a local ferry, the Greycliffe, on service at 4.14 p.m. Casualties had amounted to forty people, ranging from two to eighty-one years old, all commuting back to Watson's Bay. Many of the protagonists whose perambulations and streams of consciousness the novel introduces are rallied together by their empathetic author: gentle lovers, caring parents and abusive husbands, children and elderly ladies, the guilty and the innocent, the rich and the destitute. For Breyshaw, "The *Tahiti* becomes the *Neptune*, which is the first indication that the event can be read *allegorically*, with the ferry as-society confronting the might of the waterway in its capacity as vital force".[65] In this case, Dark was accused by some members of the Australian literary elites of having condescended to a romantic, popular genre by solving many of the novel's most intricate nodes by a single accident, seen from the focalising perspective of various, even marginal, protagonists, a device which is formally reminiscent of Virginia Woolf's post-war 1925 novel, *Mrs Dalloway*.

Yet, in her essay on the "scene of the Ferry Wreck", Brigid Rooney argues that the crash acts as a "communal sacrifice which performs a mythic back-projection, replacing black bodies with white".[66] While apparently a collective scene, the ferry yet again excludes any element and body which might disturb the seamless line of young and healthy whiteness. Although Dark was sensitive to what she saw as the doom of Aboriginal Australians, she could evidently not imagine ways to envisage a different Australia, to atone for the dispossession, destitution and genocide it had deployed to construe *and* imagine itself in the 150 years since its inception. Very relevantly, and in tune with the eugenicist theories I have already referred to, on board the ferry the younger generation is represented by two orphaned boys, Denis and Jonathan Harnett, who seem to literally 'embody' the new 'natural' indigeneity referred to before. Together with the six-year-old Brenda Sellman, the blind daughter of the very ill-assorted marriage between Arthur and Winifred, they dive into

---

[64] Dark, cit., n.p.

[65] Brayshaw, cit., p. 127.

[66] B. Rooney, "Time's Abyss: Australian Literary Modernism and the Scene of the Ferry Wreck", in R. Dixon and B. Rooney (eds.), *Scenes of Reading: Is Australian Literature a World Literature?*, North Melbourne, Australian Scholarly Publishing, 2013, pp. 101–114.

the waters of the bay and save themselves because they have properly adjusted—or Darwinianly adapted—to the land and its waters, because they are the athletic, undaunted, fearless seeds of a new future. To quote Rooney again, truly the Harbour enacts and emplaces "the dark unconscious of colonisation's ground zero".[67]

To sum up, *Waterway* seeks a confrontation with modernity, modernism and the *true* history of Australia, but eventually sweeps it away by the means of a few nostalgic strokes. The novel concludes very uncomfortably, but not very surprisingly, on a note of contentment and general mutual solidarity which extends as far as white subalterns, and the sixty thousand men "slaughtered"[68] at war, but seems unable to step any further. Actually, the soothing nursery song the newly (and luckily) widowed Winifred Channon-Sellman chooses to calm her daughter to sleep again once again disavows Indigenous culture, by describing first Australians as no more than "darkies".[69] Eleonor Dark's version of national settler modernism works as a perfect example of the intricacies of colonial, national and transnational discourse I have been trying to survey She produced a text which romantically eliminates otherness because it simply cannot 'handle' it. Her foundational saga of the war years, *The Timeless Land*, again manifests Dark's attention to and empathetic concern for the impact on humans and environments of Eurocentric violence, yet she seems unable to experiment along more radically innovative paths. To conclude, by engaging with two women writers refocussing modernism and modernity against the Australian primal scene of European-Indigenous Australian unequal encounter, I have tried to address Friedman's response to Cooper's call for "more multidirectional and decentred account would suggest that Australia produced its own distinct modernisms and modernities contemporaneously and in dialogue with those formed elsewhere."[70] In her view, and in mine, rather than being merely and diminutively "peripheral", other-than-canonical modernisms, settler modernisms might instantiate fruitful discussions on such critical terms and help engage with their multiple and very fraught political and cultural legacies.

---

[67] Rooney, cit., p. 108.

[68] Dark, cit., p. 238.

[69] Dark, cit., p. 440.

[70] Cooper 2020, cit., pp. 236–237.

Metropolis, Technology, Cultural Transfer

Geographies of Peripheral Modernism: The Case of the Russian Avant-Garde (Khlebnikov, Eisenstein, Tretyakov)

Andreas Kramer

This chapter explores issues of peripheral modernism by looking at some of the geographical imaginations of the Russian avant-garde before and after the 1917 revolution. The familiar story of the Russian avant-garde in the first three decades of the twentieth century, from Futurism to Constructivism, is that its radical and utopian aspirations for art and society went largely unrealised, on account of a period of unprecedented upheaval from world war to revolution to civil war accompanied by equally unprecedented social and economic transformation, and on account of increasingly prescriptive and reactionary cultural policies developed and implemented under Stalin's leadership that decisively curtailed and suppressed artistic experimentation. This means that the geographical ideas and images the Russian avant-garde produced during this period need to be considered in both aesthetic and political terms, as working on the level of the imagination, and as engagements with the very discourses about geography and geopolitics by which Russia and the Soviet Union sought to define itself and its place in the world.

A. Kramer (✉)
Goldsmiths, University of London, London, UK
e-mail: a.kramer@gold.ac.uk

© The Author(s), under exclusive license to Springer Nature
Switzerland AG 2024
K. Pizzi and R. Gefter Wondrich (eds.), *Rethinking Peripheral Modernisms*, https://doi.org/10.1007/978-3-031-35546-2_7

121

To begin with, the avant-garde geographies explored in this chapter are bound up with shifting ideas of Russia as space, producing a new variant of the familiar narrative whereby the country's vast and unwieldy territory is fatefully connected with, and at the same time symbolic of, the vagaries of Russia's national history.[1] Moreover, these geographic imaginations reflect profound changes in the connections of centre and periphery within the vast territory dominated by Tsarist Russia and then the Soviet Union. In doing this, they engage with long-standing debates and discourses about Russia's liminal spatial identity between East and West, between Asian Russia and European Russia that assumed new urgency in this period of political upheaval and transformation. Finally, the geographic imaginations of the Russian avant-garde engage with the notion of territorial nationality as a normative condition of modernity, in which centre/periphery relations are subsumed into another kind of order. In doing so, the Russian avant-garde explores questions such as whether geographically and culturally diverse topographies should become a unified "territory" and what role geographical difference plays in the construction of a cultural and political nation.

As well as reflecting debates about the true location and pathway of Russian culture and history, the geographical imaginations of the Russian avant-garde reveal something about the place and role of artistic radicalism within Russia and the Soviet Union. This is compounded by the fact that some of these avant-garde artists were looking to such West European avant-garde movements as Cubism and Futurism, and experimented with abstraction and montage, while deliberately turning these styles and devices into distinctive Russian forms. Other Russian avant-garde artists, however, strenuously resisted what they perceived to be colonising ambitions of the Western avant-garde, as the controversy surrounding F.T. Marinetti's visit to Russia in early 1914 demonstrates. In relation to Futurism, then, the story of its emergence and dissemination is fundamentally a geographical story, involving a spatial turn away from the centre of modernist, avant-garde art, Paris, and towards the southern

---

[1] For a broad survey on the ways in which spatial ideas have been shaping debates about Russian identity, see Emma Widdis, 'Russia as Space', in Simon Franklin and Emma Widdis (eds.), *National Identity in Russian Culture: An Introduction* (Cambridge: Cambridge University Press, 2004), 30–49.

and eastern periphery of Europe.[2] This narrative makes a fundamental link between geographical location and aesthetic radicalism, suggesting that Futurism made itself felt more lastingly on the southern and eastern periphery of Europe where belated industrialisation created both more extreme advocacy of and more extreme resistance to, the avant-garde than elsewhere.[3] My intention then is to explore some of the aesthetic, cultural and political implications of Russian avant-garde geographies and consider whether they might help us revisit a centre/periphery model that is used to account for the twin processes of artistic modernism and politico-economic modernisation. I propose to explore these issues by looking at three examples.

My first example concerns the writer Velimir Khlebnikov (1885–1922), who is, alongside his colleague Aleksei Kruchenykh, usually regarded as a proponent of "zaum" ("transrational" or "beyond-sense") poetry. One of their key concerns was the deconstruction of language and meaning by subjecting them to the device of the "sdvig" ("shift" or "disloca-tion"), a spatial term for a poetic procedure which renders familiar words unfamiliar, and causes the conventions of meaning, time and space to slip, and new content to emerge.[4] In his own brand of "zaum" poems, Khlebnikov deemphasised conventional words in favour of new, ungram-matical ones which he carefully constructed from what he believed to be meaningful grammatical units. Through his exploration of the mate-rial aspects of language, including the shapes and sounds of individual letters, Khlebnikov sought to uncover hidden temporal dimensions he believed were encrypted in the Russian language. One of the distinctive features of Khlebnikov's avant-gardism is the combination of radical mate-riality on the one hand and an equally radical spirituality or utopianism

---

[2] Harsha Ram has explored the aesthetic and political implications of these geograph-ical narratives; see his 'Futurist Geographies: Uneven Modernities and the Struggle for Aesthetic Autonomy: Paris, Italy, Russia, 1909–1914' in Mark Wollaeger (ed.), *The Oxford Handbook of Global Modernisms* (Oxford: Oxford University Press, 2012), 313–340.

[3] For recent versions of this narrative see Martin Puchner, *Poetry of the Revolution: Marx, Manifestos, and the Avant-Garde* (Princeton: Princeton University Press, 2006), 95, and Marjorie Perloff, 'The Audacity of Hope: The Foundational Futurist Manifestos' in Geert Buelens et al. (eds.), *The History of Futurism: The Precursors, Protagonists, and Legacies* (Lanham, MD: Lexington Books, 2012), 12.

[4] Alexei Kruchenykh, 'Declaration of the Word as Such' in Anna Lawton and Herbert Eagle (eds.), *Words in Revolution: Russian Futurist Manifestos* (Washington, D.C.: New Academic Publishing, 2005), 68.

124   A. KRAMER

on the other. He believed this combination to be based on mathematical correspondences between the micro- and the macro-worlds of man and nature, language, history and the universe; accordingly, he speculated on and explored what he took to be universal laws of time.

But this emphasis on a supposed immutable temporality is often quite closely bound up with geography and spatiality. This can be seen in Khlebnikov's Russophile and Slavophile views, specifically in his desire to distil the Russian language and culture to its Slavic essence and strip it of its Western accretions. As part of this linguistic geography, Khlebnikov explored how words migrate across the various Slavic languages and accrue different meanings as they travel across time and space, exploring, in particular, the various ways in which such meanings are enlisted in the service of political and cultural nationalism. The ultimate aim of his "zaum" poetry and its geographical underpinnings was "to freely fuse all Slavic words together".[5] It is important to stress, however, that Khlebnikov's notion of Pan-Slavism is not conservatively fixed on the identity of language and territory, but much more layered and complex, designed to bring old and new into a productive relation. The specific (de-)construction his poems undertake serves to resist fixity and emphasise mobility on every level of language. At the same time, Khlebnikov's view of language is quite distinct from the more technical approach to language found in Italian Futurism, where linguistic experimentation serves to render visible and audible technological forms of speed and mobility. The desire to distinguish a local, Russian Futurism from its Western counterpart also motivates Khlebnikov's choice of the Russian neologism "budetlyanin" (something like "futurian") over the foreign import "futurist".

An early example of the geographical character of Khlebnikov's avant-garde project is an essay of 1913 entitled "Roar about the Railroads".[6] Here, the poet deplores the fragmented and incomplete state of the Russian rail network, especially when compared with the one existing in a similarly vast country like the USA, and calls for it to be expanded as

---

[5] Velimir Khlebnikov, 'Expanding the Boundaries of Russian Literature' (1913) in Charlotte Douglas (ed.), Paul Schmidt (trans.), *Collected Works of Velimir Khlebnikov*, vol. 1: *Letters and Theoretical Writings*, vol. 1 (Cambridge, Mass., and London: Harvard University Press, 1987), 253. See also the manifestos 'The Word as Such' (1913) and 'The Letter as Such' (1913) in ibid., 255–258.

[6] Velimir Khlebnikov, 'Roar about the Railroads', in ibid., 241–242.

quickly as possible. Khlebnikov's specific suggestion is that the railway closely tracked Russia's natural geography, in particular its rivers, so as to create major cross-country routes which would enhance connections between different regions of the vast country. Khlebnikov however is not a hard-nosed moderniser calling for the development of transportation infrastructure in a country desperate to enjoy the fruits of Western-style industrialisation, progress and prosperity. Instead, his vision takes on a geographic and, indeed, geopoetic dimension. In tracking and linking Russia's main rivers, the rail network he envisions redresses the imbalance between centre and periphery. He envisages the creation of routes which would link, for example, the Volga and the Dniepr; the Volga and the Caspian Sea; and the Danube and the Don "to ensure the flowering of the southland" (241). As well as the southern peripheries of Russia, Khlebnikov attends to its northern and eastern peripheries beyond the Urals, calling for a rail link between the mouths of the Volga and the Ob, and mentioning other major Siberian rivers such as the Lena, the Perchera, and the Yenisei. The new rail network tracking the rivers would be directed not from West to East (the quasi-naturalised direction of modernisation along the Western European model whereby progress spreads eastward), but rather from the decentred perspective of a nation abandoning its traditional centre in search of an alternative spatial model. Such a network of cross-country routes, Khlebnikov estimates, would be closer to the North American railroads than to those established in Italy where they mainly track the country's coastline. Yet in Khlebnikov's imagination, the railways are not, as in Western nations, a symbol of how modern technology overcomes the vagaries of natural geography and strengthens territorial nationality, but instead become a sign of how Russia might return to its natural roots as marked by its interior waterways.[7] In this way, the new geography to be embodied by Russia's modern railways is also a very old one, again linking space and time.

In Khlebnikov's conception, however, Russian geographic space is far from uniform. When the poet stresses that the few railway lines that do track Russia's coastline are "only found in partly non-Russian areas",[8]

---

[7] This is an argument Khlebnikov makes in his essay 'A Friend in the West' (1913), in: ibid., 243–245.

[8] Khlebnikov, 'Roar about the Railroads', 241.

126   A. KRAMER

he seems to imply that coastal railways represent a modernity that is somehow "foreign" and unnatural, the implication being that railways running along Russia's rivers contribute to a more natural idea of modern nationhood. Moreover, while the question of how technological modernisation should be mapped onto national geography is clearly important in Khlebnikov's proposals, the key element in his geographical conceptualisation of the railways is that such a network tracking the major rivers would add "sense" to the railway "webs that surround the railroad spiders of Moscow and other cities".[9] Deploring the development of railway networks exclusively around the major cities of European Russia, Khlebnikov envisages a rail network that is able to breach the chasm between urban and rural areas. Moreover, if the urban centres of European Russia, in particular Moscow and St. Petersburg no longer serve as the temporal and conceptual origins of the national rail network, then Khlebnikov's geographic imagination can be said to have metaphorically decentred his nation by emphasising its Southern and Northern, its Caucasian and Asian peripheries. In this way, Khlebnikov repudiates the hierarchical organisation of the nation which places the Europeanised West at the top and the other regions, the underdeveloped South, the Asiatic East and the Siberian North at the bottom. As well as intervening in debates about uneven modernisations, Khlebnikov's meditation on the shape and design of Russia's railways takes on a poetic dimension as the rivers-as-railways—twin tracks formed by old and new forms of transport—form a sort of giant script which will reveal "the unknown letters of an unknown alphabet".[10] Khlebnikov's adoption of the railway, a symbol of the technology of spatial and geographical mobility, enables him to rewrite the relationship between the man-made and the natural world in terms of language, presenting the natural environment as an explanation for the emergence of cultural difference and identity.[11]

[9] Ivi.

[10] Ibid., 242.

[11] Khlebnikov would return to the idea of the river-as-alphabet and celebrate the notion of the universal language of geography in the late poem 'The One, the Only Book' (1920), in Paul Schmidt (trans.), Ronald Vroon (ed.) *Collected Works of Velimir Khlebnikov*, vol. 3: *Selected Poems* (Cambridge, MA and London: Harvard University Press, 1997), 77–78. In another late poem, the transcontinental train re-emerges as a natural tree, linking the soil with the supernatural; 'The Tree', in: ibid., 110–112. This poem is discussed in Anindita Banerjee, 'The Trans-Siberian Railroad and Russia's Asia: Literature, Geopolitics, Philosophy of History', *CLIO* 34: 1–2 (2004–2005): 19–40.

GEOGRAPHIES OF PERIPHERAL MODERNISM: THE CASE ...   127

Another re-imagining of geographic space to reconsider the relationship between centre and periphery is evident in the large body of poems and essays on the subject of Asia. Khlebnikov repeatedly stressed the symbolism of the region of his birth near Astrakhan where the Volga flows into the Caspian Sea, regarding it as a place where East and West, Asian and Slavic peoples meet and intermingle. He would call the Caspian Sea the "Chinese Sea" because it was the ancient homeland of the Kalmyks, a Mongolian Buddhist people who inhabited the grassy steppes on the west bank of the Caspian Sea, Khlebnikov himself having been born into the family of the Russian administrator of the Kalmyk nomads. As do his railway proposals, the poet's Asian imaginations conform to the pattern of de-Europeanisation, or more precisely, dis-occidentalisation. More radically than the railway essays, however, these Asian imaginations tend to dissolve all spatial relationships that produce dominance and subjugation, going so far as to abolish geographic space altogether and create a utopian realm of pure time.[12] If Asia emerges in this way from a geopolitical necessity for European Russia to become the new locus of its cultural and spiritual identity, Khlebnikov's geographical imagination challenges the long-established discourse that separates European Russia from Asiatic Russia, and the assumption that civilised, metropolitan European Russia was culturally separate from its eastern periphery, a primitive, nomadic no-place haunted by memories of Mongol invasions.[13] As a result, the poet envisages the combined land mass of Asia as being at the centre of the world of the future, as that time–space where and when the Slavic cultures would join those of Asia; and Christianity might fuse with the world religions of Islam, Hinduism and Buddhism.[14] Khlebnikov's new geopolitical sensibility, with its focus on Asia rather than Europe, enables him to look both backwards and forward in time, and thus reevaluate the past as much as provide a radical new cartography for the future. In an early dialogue, "The Teacher and the Pupil" (1912), Khlebnikov

[12] See Banerjee, 32.

[13] See Mark Bassin, 'Russia between Europe and Asia: The Ideological Construction of Geographical Space,' *Slavic Review* 50 (1991), 1–17, esp. 4–8.

[14] See e.g. Velimir Khlebnikov, 'Proposals' (1915–1916) and 'Asiaunion' (1918), in Paul Schmidt (trans.), Ronald Vroon (ed.), *Collected Works*, vol. 1, 357–361 and 343; 'Azia Unbound' in *Collected Works of Velimir Khlebnikov*, vol. 2: *Prose, Plays, and Supersagas* (Cambridge, MA, and London: Harvard University Press, 1989), 322–330; 'Azia' and 'Asia' in *Collected Works*, vol. 3, 75–76.

128   A. KRAMER

locates the emergence of an expanded continental subjectivity located in Asia, which he opposes to the limited peninsular reason of Europeans; an idea which corresponds with the geographical image of Europe as Asia's peninsular foreland which he hopes would be dissolved during the latter's evolution into a genuine "continent".[15]

Yet despite such a fantastic geography, the poet remained alert to the geopolitical conflicts of modernity. His tendency towards deterritorialising Europe became more pronounced during the First World War and its aftermath, as Khlebnikov's geographical imaginations took on a utopian and pacifist dimension. The manifesto-essay "The Trumpet of the Martians" (1916) takes issue with the fact that global space is carved up into discrete national territories, and reimagines geopolitical space by seeking to replace a binary model which pits the West against the East, with a notion of fluid interchange of diverse geographies, temporalities and languages.[16] Specifically, Khlebnikov rejects the divisive "states of space"[17] which demarcate and control territory through what he calls "investor/exploiters", and invites his fellow futurists to enter "an independent state" made up of his own "militant vanguard of the inventor/explorers",[18] a global community of poets and scientists united in their challenge of prevailing concepts of time and space (he references Gauss, Lobachevsky and the Montgolfier brothers), and who, in their desire "to form an independent government of time (no longer dependent on space", "have studied the soil of the continent of time, and we found it fruitful".[19] The ideological conflict between the two pairs of actors is again bound up with language, as reflected in the consonantal struggle between letters: "Which is greater: S/T or N/R?",[20] a struggle which further becomes a metaphor for political and economic conflict. In this utopian essay, and a number of other

[15] See Harsha Ram, 'The Poetics of Eurasia: Velimir Khlebnikov between Empire and Revolution' in Madhavan K. Palat (ed.), *Social Identities in Revolutionary Russia* (Basingstoke: Palgrave, 2001), 212–217.

[16] Velimir Khlebnikov, 'The Trumpet of the Martians' in *Collected Works*, vol. 1, 321–324. The manifesto-essay was co-signed by Maria Siniakova, Bozhidar, Grigory Petnikov and Nikolai Aseev.

[17] Ibid., 322.

[18] Ibid., 323.

[19] Ivi.

[20] Ivi.

GEOGRAPHIES OF PERIPHERAL MODERNISM: THE CASE ...   129

similar ones, Khlebnikov's privileging of time over space does not abolish geographic space but re-conceives it in alternative terms. He seems to regard this alternative geographic space as a sort of dynamic cartography which instead of enabling territorial emplacement (as in the roles of "investor" and "exploiter"), engenders a series of nomadic displacements, the latter conceived in both spatial ("explorer") and conceptual terms ("inventors"). Once again, Khlebnikov's (de)constructive strategy allows his imaginative geography to be articulated in temporal terms— new mappings are the results of connections between flexible positions rather than grounded in sites of origin.

A further dimension of Khlebnikov's avant-garde geographies can be seen in his essays on architecture and urban culture.[21] In these essays, the poet turns towards issues closely associated with modernity, such as the city, urban living and transportation, and queries the relationship between urban centres and rural periphery. But what is most remarkable is that he presents Russia as a dynamic space of exploration, mobility and connectivity, as a geography that transcends mere territory. His vision of "Swanland in the Future" (1918) presents a future world where people live in mobile glass cubicles that may be attached to skyscraper-like frameworks, and travel along underwater highways lined with glass walls that connect the fluvial landscape.[22] The titular "swanland" translates "lebedia", the old name for the Tauride region located between the rivers Don and Volga. The root "leb-" additionally establishes a linguistic connection between "swan" and "lion", and it also connotes the constellation of Leo, further deterritorialising the specific geographical region. Overall, Khlebnikov's imaginary geographies of Russia and Russia's place in and relations with the rest of the world, have been called utopian, emphasising their apartness from reality and their residence within the individual imagination. However, given the ways in which these imaginations persistently contest territorial fixity and render geopolitical realities more fluid, it may be more appropriate to call these imaginations heterotopian, designating a kind of geographic space or set of sites that is at once real and set apart

---

[21] See e.g. Velimir Khlebnikov, 'Ourselves and Our Buildings. Creator of Streetsteads. Proclamor' (1920), in *Collected* Works, vol. 1, 347–356; 'The City of the Future' (1920) and 'The Moscow of the Future' (1921), in *Collected Works*, vol. 3, 73–75 and 113–114.

[22] Velimir Khlebnikov, 'Swanland in the Future' in *Collected Works*, vol. 1, 344–346.

130   A. KRAMER

from the real, and that both reflects and inverts the normative regime of the real.[23]

Such heterotopian kind of geography—a geography pinpointing the slippage between the spaces of order and disorder, the spaces constructed by power and at the same time inverting it—features also in my next example. Sergei Eisenstein's (1898–1948) film *The General Line* (1929) is a project which brought him into direct contact with Soviet policy-makers and ideology. Assisted by Grigorii Alexandrov, the director drafted a scenario and began shooting the film in 1926. When Eisenstein was ordered to begin a film on the October Revolution, however, the project came to a halt. It was resumed two years later, and the completed film was finally released in October 1929 under the revised title *The Old and the New*. The film tells the story of how a rural community used to working the land in old-fashioned ways adopts machines and other equipment and sets up a collective to increase productivity. Having been released five months after the announcement of Stalin's first Five-Year-Plan which marked a sharp change in agricultural policy and paved the way for the enforced collectivisation of farming, the film is clearly concerned with a topical instance of the centre/periphery relationship in the Soviet Union, showing how the rural hinterland was subjected to new forms of spatial organisation and control by the socialist centre.

It is not just content, but form and aesthetics as well that makes this a significant film within the Russian avant-garde. Eisenstein explores new possibilities of filmic montage and refines his political aesthetic of "picture-thinking". In order to highlight the narrative structure, Eisenstein sets up a number of visual contrasts and collisions between spaces and their traditional connotations, e.g. the countryside and the city, to show how ideas and technologies of the latter infiltrate the former to transform it beyond recognition. The old methods of working the land (e.g. the strenuous effort required in the manual cultivation of the soil; the possibility of crop disease, livestock infections and other disasters) are juxtaposed and give way to the new methods which deploy tractors and other machines to turn the village and the surrounding fields into a

[23] I adopt Michel Foucault's reading of heterotopian spaces; Foucault, 'Of Other Spaces', *Diacritics*, 16 (Spring 1986), 22–27. See Svetlana Boym's more general proposition that the Russian avantgarde's radicalism "resides precisely in its [...] heterotopian quality;" Boym, *Architecture of the Off Modern* (New York: Princeton Architectural Press, 2008), 24.

modern efficient site of collective production. Yet there are visual signifiers that render such contrasts less clear-cut than they might appear. The film's protagonist, Marfa Lapkina, who is leading the transition from old to new, is aided in this by an agronomist who bears more than a passing resemblance to Lenin. Marfa is rewarded for her efforts with romantic love, but at strategic points, and clearly to disrupt the all-too-clear romantic narrative, Eisenstein uses overtly erotic and sexual imagery in relation to the mechanising process, e.g. when the cream-making machine is seen to be spraying Marfa's face with the end-product.[24] Eisenstein shot parts of the film in Konstantinovo, the birth-place of Sergey Esenin, the modernist poet of rural life who had committed suicide in December 1925, while the director also commissioned Andrei Burov to design a number of strikingly modernist buildings, which have been inserted into the film's rural setting. The artificiality of the "new" architecture in the "old" place indicates the precariousness of Eisenstein's filmic construction of geographic space.

For, in spite of appearances, this is an Eisenstein film without an unambiguous *telos*, as the narrative polarity between old and new, before and after, is constantly being undermined. Instead, the film builds a projective momentum towards the resolution of antagonisms inherent in the peasant population, between the generations and the sexes, and ultimately also between the human and the natural worlds. In creating this momentum, Eisenstein is also vitally concerned with, and draws substantially upon, the disrupting of the classical unities of space and time. The film contains, for example, a stunning montage sequence that correlates the sound and movements of a grasshopper with the noise and mechanism of a combined harvester. Other scenes celebrate the productive, indeed procreative power of the machines used to work the land. Using unusual camera angles, Eisenstein also shows tractors and other farming machines crisscrossing the old agricultural landscape, or moving diagonally through the frame, and he intercuts those shots with shots that show fields of grain

---

[24] In a lecture given in Berlin in 1929, Eisenstein not only defended this scene but described his decision to include erotic imagery as a form of de-localization: "A concrete example of giving pathos to everyday life: the separator in *The General Line*. [...] The principle of construction is derived from the pathos of the situation. Eroticism is far too strong a force not to be utilised. It is 'delocalised'. Not a love situation but a treatment of the unconscious." Sergey Eisenstein, 'Imitation as Mastery' in Ian Christie and Richard Taylor (eds.), Richard Taylor (trans.), *Eisenstein Rediscovered* (London: Routledge, 1993), 70.

132   A. KRAMER

swaying rhythmically in the wind. Such abstract geometric patterning not only establishes a relationship between the natural and the mechanical worlds but contributes vitally to the specific montage method used here. This is a method which Eisenstein himself termed "overtonal montage", a principle he expressly associated with democracy and a compositional technique whereby variations within a given shot and among shots are organised in such a way as to create a multitude of associations and meanings and to stimulate "picture-thinking".[25]

The film's final section entitled "Zemlia daesh" ("Earth, you give") culminates in a stunning montage sequence that shows tractors emerging from the background and riding in circles across a vast field, their tracks gradually inscribing a gigantic spiral in the soil. Not only are the tractors (whose assembly-line production had been the topic of an earlier sequence, which included a Vertovian trick sequence showing a tractor assembling itself) the harbingers of modern farming methods, and symbols of Stalinist industrialisation,[26] their tracks across the field repre-sent an early from of Land Art. Furthermore, the image of the giant spiral that eventually becomes visible in the soil might also encapsulate Eisenstein's philosophy of film, which assumed an analogy between the lines of a spiral, the leaps between the concrete and the abstract, the natural and the technological, and the "organic unity" that a dialecti-cally structured film aspires to in its production and reception.[27] The juncture of tractors and geography in film thus corresponds to a notion Eisenstein suggests in his essay "Beyond the Shot" (1929), where he draws an analogy between cinematic montage and "the implosions of the internal combustion engine", claiming that the individual elements of filmic montage "multiply into a montage dynamic through 'impulses' like those that drive a car or a tractor".[28]

---

[25] For a discussion of *The General Line* in terms of Eisentein's montage aesthetics and further elaboration of individual motifs, see Anne Nesbet, *Savage Junctures: Sergei Eisenstein and the Shape of Thinking* (London: I.B. Tauris, 2007), 94–115.

[26] The tractor's make is identified in one shot as Fordson, which can be read as a subtle reference to the Soviet embrace of the principles of Fordism as an aid rather than a hindrance to socialism.

[27] Eisenstein, 'Organic Unity and Pathos in the Composition of Potemkin' (1939), in X. Danko (trans.) *Notes of a Film Director* (New York: Dover Press, 1970), 53–62.

[28] Eisenstein, 'Beyond the Shot' in Richard Taylor (ed. and trans.), *Selected Writings*, vol. 1: *Writings, 1922–1934* (London: British Film Institute, 1988), 145.

GEOGRAPHIES OF PERIPHERAL MODERNISM: THE CASE ... 133

This forceful dynamic that Eisenstein's tractor montage creates, is given a further element that complicates any straightforward "geography". The montage is internally disrupted by inserts from other spaces and by implication, other times; namely by images showing the assembly-line production of tractors in Stalingrad, and by images showing silos and stockpiled sacks of grain. Eisenstein's film then shows Russian spaces of centre and periphery, the latter is clearly subjected to transformation and change; however, the overall effect is to allow the viewer to discern a subtle resistance to the complete "Sovietization" by inscribing agricultural space with constructivist and geometric patterns and metacinematic images. Eisenstein seems to have envisioned the "earth" as a writing pad, imprinting his own paradoxical message of subversive affirmation into the film. As such the film might confirm what Emma Widdis has identified as a broader tendency in Russian discourses of space: "Images of the territory are defined by a constant slippage between visions of order and chaos, freedom and restriction. The desire to conquer space sits in perpetual tensions with the desire to emphasise its resistance to conquest".[29]

The writer and photographer Sergei Tretyakov (1892–1939), my final example, was similarly concerned with exploring new ways of representing the modernity of Russia's newly socialist spaces. Best known for his theory and practice of "factography", a documentary "literature of fact", and for his notion of the writer as producer, which resonated in Western literary theory with Benjamin, Brecht and Aragon, Tretyakov first entered the Soviet literary scene in 1923, shortly after Khlebnikov's death, by claiming that after the political revolution, "Futurism became the Left Front of Art", and by defining the movement's current trajectory as that of production or industrial art.[30] Like Khlebnikov, he developed a literary geography, though he was less of a poeto-linguistic geography and more closely concerned with the changeful realities of the physical, human and social geographies of the Soviet Union in the late 1920s and early 1930s, the period of rapid industrialisation and enforced collectivisation of agricultural land. Like Eisenstein, Tretyakov had to accommodate his avant-garde inclinations to prevailing political and ideological demands. Like other avant-garde writers committed to socialist aims, he tweaked

[29] Widdis, 43.

[30] 'Whence and Whither (Perspectives on Futurism)', first published in *Lef*, no. 1 (1923), 193–203.

134   A. KRAMER

the literary techniques at his disposal so as to expose contemporary reality as dialectical. He firmly embraced the practice of montage, emphasising "factual" and "natural" material over what he called unnatural or fictional material, and then organising the montaged elements within the spatial and temporal framework of a subject.

Tretyakov responded to the increasing socialisation of space and geography in 1920's Soviet culture by focussing on the ways in which social life, literally, takes place. His writings persistently link features of social or human geography with the physical or natural forms in which they become embedded. Frequently commissioned to travel across the Soviet Union (and beyond) to document examples of the new geography, Tretyakov nevertheless rejected the conventional mode of travel writing. In an essay entitled "Through Unwiped Glasses" (1928), which presents the writer/reporter flying by aeroplane to an assignment in the Caucasus, Tretyakov develops the aesthetic of "factography" specifically in relation to the visual perception and representation of landscape. "Almost no-one sees things or people in art through industrial eyes. This is something we have to start learning".[31] Seated in an aeroplane travelling at speed, Tretyakov takes issue with the global aerial viewpoint, "the inverted binoculars of the flight",[32] as one that turns space and geography into small-scale, distant, and mappable territory, which in turn is conducive to the projection of subjective meanings onto a landscape the writer has never set foot in. As a result, the writer becomes guilty of aestheticising said landscape through the use of clichéd language, e.g. when likening the view of agricultural fields from above to a patchwork quilt. To this kind of "literary", detached geography from above Tretyakov's essay opposes a factual, committed geography from below.[33] In this model, the writer becomes an active rather than a passive observer, his or her vision sharpened by the landscape rather than dulled: "When the eye truly gets sharpened, it will begin to differentiate from above the difference between the crops of the commune and the lone self-employed peasant; it will

---

[31] 'Skvoz' neprotertie očki' ('Through Unwiped Glasses'), *Novyi Lef*, no. 9 (1928), 20–24; reprinted in Tret'iakov, *Literatura fakta*, Moscow, 1929, 235–241 (235).

[32] Tret'iakov, ibid., 240.

[33] See Sylvia Sasse, 'Geographie von unten: Geopoetik und Geopolitik in Sergej Tret'jakovs Reiseskizzen' in Magdalena Marszałek and Sylvia Sasse (eds.), *Geopoetiken: Geographische Entwürfe in den mittel- und osteuropäischen Literaturen* (Berlin: Kadmos, 2009), 261–288.

dictate to the brain the reflex over the consolidated tracts of *sokhoz* fields [...] Then we will become sighted, not only for the biological termite work of man, but for the way that socialism will redraw the face of the earth anew" (241). Tretyakov's factographic aesthetics entails an active relationship to Russian space, to the earth and the landscape. But, as Elizabeth Papazian points out, Tretyakov essay remains ambivalent because of its reliance on some of the same literary methods it denounces (as in the above quotation when he refers to "the termite work of man").[34]

As though aware of an inherent ambivalence, Tretyakov sought to incorporate anti-literary factography within the more complex notion of social and artistic commitment he called "operativism". This incorporation has again a central bearing on his preoccupation with space and geography. The writer-as-factographer is not only opposed to fellow professional writers with their models of literary realism, but he also seeks to disavow his credentials as a professional, trained writer by enlisting or textually documenting non-professionals. Furthermore, he becomes a sort of antitraveller, or anti-tourist who immerses him or herself fully in the life and work of a collective farming community, staying on the ground while documenting developments and changes over time. This approach owes something to the literal meaning of the term "geography", in that it becomes a sort of "writing" or "graphic" study of the earth by means of visual and other signs that is equivalent to agricultural work revolving around the soil. But the most significant refinement Tretyakov undertakes is the switch from observation to participation, from detachment to co-production, from factography to operative writing. The key media predisposed and designed to achieve just this are textual and visual—chiefly, the short literary sketch or essay ("ocherk") and documentary photography, with Tretyakov working simultaneously in these two media. In fact, Tretyakov argued that only through once extraliterary genres such as "memoir, travel notes, [...] reportage, investigations and montage" could the committed writer contribute to the construction of new forms of social life.[35] But beyond the diversity and simultaneity of genres, what was important for Tretyakov was that the "ocherkistoperativnik" ("operative sketchwriter" or "essayist") was to participate directly in the life of the

---

[34] Elizabeth Astrid Papazian, *Manufacturing Truth: The Documentary Moment in Early Soviet Culture* (De Kalb: Northern Illinois University Press, 2009), 41–44.

[35] Sergei Tretyakov, 'What's New' (first published in *Novyi lef*, no. 9, 1928), trans. in Lawton and Eagle, *Words in Revolution*, 271.

136   A. KRAMER

material, operating the literary equivalent of the agricultural "multi-field system".[36]

Though not entirely able to free itself from the role of visitor and associated imbalances in social and expressive power, Tretyakov's "operativism", and the textual and visual representation of changes in Russian space it generates, would supply facts about natural, human and social geographies of any given area. The texts and images resulting from this "operative" approach would produce a sort of synoptic map of how a community lives its life in any given area, a map which projects time onto space and thereby makes visible any changes. In this way, Tretyakov's geographical texts and images, though clearly recognisable as commissioned reportage, serve to emphasise the dynamics of rapid change, and the degree of involvement and cooperation by the people concerned. As Maria Gough has suggested, a similar aesthetic and political approach, and resulting in a similar ambiguity, can be seen in Tretyakov's photo-essays.[37] Some of these photo-essays show clear signs of having been staged as they adopt the traditional traveller/visitor attitude. Many of the images focus on people, dwellings, objects, and machines, with landscape shots providing merely the framework within which the process of change takes place. Equally important in these photographs is the experimentation with viewpoint and light, enabling Tretyakov largely to avoid the kind of monumentalism that characterised contemporary socialist propaganda photographs.

But it is also important to note the extent to which Tretyakov's project of a geography from below collides with a centralising geography from above, with official policies aimed at re-organising the natural and cultural spaces of Russia into a more homogenous, centralised Soviet space. Such collisions are suggested at some points in Tretyakov's writings, for example when he overlays the conventional tropes of the representation

---

[36] These ideas and precepts are developed in Tretyakov, *Vyzov: Kolkhoznye ocherki* (Moscow: IZDvo Federatsiia, 1930), *Feld-Herren: Der Kampf um eine Kollektiv-Wirtschaft* (Berlin: Malik-Verlag, 1931). Material available in English includes Tretyakov, 'The Writer and the Socialist Village' (trans. Devin Fore), *October*, 118 (Fall 2006), 63–70.

[37] Maria Gough, 'Radial Tourism: Sergei Tret'iakov at the Communist Lighthouse', *October*, 118 (Fall 2006), 159–178. A key essay in relation to Tretyakov's photo-aesthetic is his 'Fotozametki', *Novyi lef*, no. 8 (1928), 40, translated as 'Photo-Notes' by John E. Bowlt, in Christopher Philips (ed.), *Photography in the Modern Era: European Documents and Critical Writings, 1913–1940* (New York: Metropolitan Museum of Modern Art, 1989), 252.

of Russia's natural landscape (the steppes, fields, deserts, connoting the vastness of space beyond human habitation) with the economic and political processes that turn such landscapes into stratified geographies. Maria Gough points to the fact that some of Tretyakov's photographs of the industrial and technological sites of the early 1930s, with their snapshot-like quality and their blurring devices, can be read as deliberately going against the official "geography from above" that would present such achievements in a slick, monumentalising style.[38] Elsewhere in his late photographic work, however, such as that which he contributed to the glossy magazine *USSR under Construction*, Tretyakov does seem to have succumbed to state propaganda, where he can be seen to be exploiting the familiar opposition between old and new, before and after to celebrate the achievements of Stalin's regime. In this work we can also find a tendency to exoticise the wild spaces of the Caucasus, presenting them as exercising a barbaric hold over and virtually enslaving the local population, before predictably eulogising the liberation of the indigenous population from the power of elemental nature, a process by which industrialisation and socialist revolution are the forces that liberate the people from the natural forms of archaic feudalism.[39] With these multiple shifts from a "literature of fact" to operative literature, to deliberately "formalist" photography, and his attention to a geography from below, Tretyakov occupies an ambivalent position in Soviet culture around 1930, pitting a late avant-gardist appropriation of plural Russian spaces against the homogenisation of those spaces under the banner of centralist socialism.

The examples of Russian and early Soviet avant-garde geographies I have discussed here engage in different ways with the cultural and political model of centre and periphery. United by the intention to challenge long-held assumptions about and newly emerging definition of centre and periphery, these geographical imaginations, whether overtly fantastic as in Khlebnikov or grounded in specific instances of geographic change as in Eisenstein and Tretyakov, respond to both centrifugal and centripetal forces, picturing a geography in which binary and oppositional models are destabilised so that new models of cultural space, and an awareness of heterotopic sites of modernity, may emerge. As a result, these

---

[38] Gough, 177–178.
[39] See Sasse, 283–284.

138   A. KRAMER

avant-garde approaches to geography bring into sharp relief a disjunction between artistic modernism and political modernity, a disjunction that does not conform to the conventional centre/periphery model. Khlebnikov transforms geographic space into time and language; his geographical imaginations, mindful of the Russian avant-garde's peripheral status in relation to the centre of modernisation in West, produce geographies that seem to challenge the Western norm of linguistically and ethnically homogenous nation-states. Eisenstein's and Tretyakov's geographical imaginations are actively concerned with another kind of centre/periphery relationship, namely the attempt by the Stalinist centre to rapidly modernise and control underdeveloped hinterlands. The film director's and the operative writer's geographies from below seek at least to deflect from official attempts at spatial and social homogenisation from above. Their cinematic, textual and visual geographies may be said to be consistent with Bakhtin's notion of "horizontality", a key term in his spatial aesthetics and one which his 1929 *Problems of Dostoevsky's Poetics* suggests is a precondition for genuine dialogue and democracy.[40] Eisenstein and Tretyakov's constructivist geographies, imagining as they do alternatives to territorial nationality and imperialism, thus complicating what was after all an alternative, post-capitalist and socialist modernity, and the new conditions of production and reception afforded by the system. In other words, the asymmetrical relationship between centre and periphery, in both pre-revolutionary Russia and the post-revolutionary Soviet Union, mirrors and complicates the standard Western model of uneven developments in centre and periphery. Writing about the underdeveloped periphery, a prominent strain of theoretical work from Trotsky to Jameson has persistently suggested that the geographic pattern of the modernist avant-garde movements has been articulated and established itself more lastingly in the periphery that in the Western capitalist, metropolitan core where these movements first emerged. Accordingly, the advocacy of Futurism and Constructivism in Russia and the advanced artistic forms generated there, have indeed been correlated with that country's belated industrialisation. But this is perhaps too abstract a model, and one that fails to account for the interesting reversal that takes place in 1917 when the country's fast-track modernisation was bound up with and legitimated by socialist ideas of modernity. So, while it is difficult

[40] See Sasse, 273.

to find any direct correlation between artistic avant-gardism and political modernity, what might be suggested in the particular case of the Russian avant-garde is this: rather than merely providing artistic resistance effects to the old capitalist and the new socialist "centres", the Russian avant-garde's specific ideas of geographic space speak to its ability to mobilise fluid, flexible, heterotopic geographies that hold in check the idea of spatial conquest and territorial control emanating from the centre, new and old.

Brazilian Modernists and the Avant-Garde: Transcultural Modernism in the Postcolonial Periphery

Patrícia Silva

European artistic production from the early twentieth century was characterised by a crisis of representation, epitomised by the techniques of fragmentation, defamiliarisation and plural perspectivism of the aesthetic object that characterised Cubism and Futurism. These distinctive facets of mainstream European avant-garde movements underscore the underlying contradictions of aesthetic modernism, which arise from the increased complexity of the experience of reality produced by rapid modernisation and the breakdown of the homogenising positivist-illuminist logic when confronted with multiple temporalities and non-Western epistemologies as part of the process of globalisation. My intention in this essay is to examine the re-casting and reframing of avant-garde motifs and procedures deployed by three representative figures of Brazilian modernism, who played a significant part in its emergence, in order to both convey the particularity of the modern Brazilian experience and to claim a place for its cultural production among planetary twentieth-century modernisms. I argue that the Brazilian modernists' aesthetic positioning, artistic practices and creative output constitute early and particularly productive instances

---

P. Silva (✉)
Centre for Social Studies, University of Coimbra, Coimbra, Portugal
e-mail: psm@ces.uc.pt

© The Author(s), under exclusive license to Springer Nature Switzerland AG 2024
K. Pizzi and R. Gefter Wondrich (eds.), *Rethinking Peripheral Modernisms*, https://doi.org/10.1007/978-3-031-35546-2_8

141

142   P. SILVA

of transculturalism in a postcolonial context, displaying exemplary traits of so-called peripheral modernisms occurring in such contexts and informing theoretical standpoints in postcolonial studies.

In 'Aspects of Peripheral Modernisms', Benita Parry argues that '[a]ny inquiry into the generic modes and stylistic mannerisms of modern peripheral literature since the nineteenth century is inseparable from considering the distinctive experiences of *modernity* in spaces *outside* Western Europe and North America, but *within* an imperialist world-system'.[1] Parry attributes the distinctiveness of the experience of modernity in the colonised peripheries to the enforced interruption of local histories caused by imperialist expansion, arguing that 'the extent and degree of the coercions visited on those societies that were seized for their natural and labour resources, or invaded for both material and political reasons [...] inflected the singular accents of the modernisms in these locations'.[2] Moreover, she establishes a causal link between 'the "generic discontinuities" in the art forms of the peripheries' and 'their ground in modernities where traditional and emergent social and cultural values coexisted and clashed, which appear to inhabit manifold material conditions and temporalities'.[3] Such incommensurable asymmetries are responsible, according to her, for the heightened degree of formal complexity and stylistic heterogeneity found in postcolonial cultural production of peripheral modernisms occurring in territories which were subjected to colonisation.

These forms of expression came to prominence in the late nineteenth century as a result of the accelerated expansion of capitalism following the Industrial Revolution. Parry highlights the work of Roberto Schwarz, who in *A Master on the Periphery of Capitalism*, a study of Machado de Assis's 1889 novel *The Posthumous Memoirs of Brás Cubas*, 'examines "the possible correspondence between Machado's style and the particularities of Brazilian society, slave-owning and bourgeois at the same

---

[1] Benita Parry, 'Aspects of Peripheral Modernisms', *ARIEL: A Review of International English Literature*, 40:1, special issue *Thinking Through Postcoloniality* (2009), 27–56, p. 27.

[2] Parry, 'Aspects of Peripheral Modernisms', p. 29.

[3] Parry, 'Aspects of Peripheral Modernisms', p. 32.

time'.[4] According to Parry, 'the connection between the social ground and the stylistics and literary devices of the peripheral novel form' drawn by the Brazilian critic enables 'the insight that its formal qualities – whether realist, fabulist or avant-garde – can be read as transfiguring and estranging incommensurable material, cultural, social and existential conditions attendant on colonial and neo-colonial capitalism'.[5] In the case of Brazil, these incommensurable conditions lasted well into the first decades of the twentieth century, coexisting with the accelerated modernisation of its metropolitan centres. This essay examines the representation and critique of asymmetries arising from uneven modernisation and cultural (neo)colonialism in the literary and artistic production of Mário de Andrade, Oswald de Andrade and Tarsila do Amaral, as case studies of the dynamics of aesthetic modernism in a peripheral postcolonial context.

Else Vieira has argued that 'peripheral manifestations of modernism' in Lusophone and Hispanic America consisted of 'a cultural project aimed at breaking with mental colonialism'.[6] This especially applies to Brazil in the early twentieth century since, as Leslie Barry notes, its gradual transition from colony to republic—although it had gained independence in 1822, it had remained part of a monarchic empire until 1889—meant that nationalism at this time 'was a defensive self-affirmation [...] against European political and cultural hegemony'.[7] Hence, argues Barry, the Modern Art Week which took place in São Paulo in February 1922 and officially launched Brazilian modernism, 'was conceived as a manifesto of cultural autonomy'.[8] The interlinking of modernism and cultural nationalism meant that for the first Brazilian modernists the goal of modernising the cultural field was concomitant with a desire to express a distinctive national consciousness, ascribing an exceptionalist agenda

[4] Parry, 'Aspects of Peripheral Modernisms', p. 36; quotes Roberto Schwarz, *A Master on the Periphery of Capitalism: Machado De Assis*, trans. John Gledson (Durham: Duke UP, 2001), p. 3.

[5] Parry, 'Aspects of Peripheral Modernisms', p. 33.

[6] Else R. P. Vieira, 'Ig/noble Barbarians: Revisiting Latin American Modernisms', in *Postcolonial Perspectives on the Cultures of Latin America and Lusophone Africa*, ed. by Robin Fiddian (Liverpool: Liverpool University Press, 2000), 51–78, p. 52.

[7] Leslie Barry, 'The Tropical Modernist as Literary Cannibal: Cultural Identity in Oswald de Andrade', *Chasqui* 20:2 (November 1991), 10–19, p. 12.

[8] Barry, 'The Tropical Modernist as Literary Cannibal', p. 12.

144   P. SILVA

to the movement. Conversely, they also display what Mariano Siskind describes as 'a desire for the world that points to the modernization of Latin America in cosmopolitan terms', which he identifies as common to Hispanic and Lusophone Latin American modernist discourses.[9] According to this mind-set, which Siskind considers symptomatic of what he terms 'marginal cosmopolitanism', 'literature that is outside Latin American literature' is posited as 'a universal repository of modernist aesthetics where marginal cosmopolitans find the bits and pieces they can put together to articulate a nonparticularistic cultural modernization'.[10] While this cultural positioning led Brazil's first modernists to engage with the advanced aesthetics of the European avant-garde, the aforementioned cultural nationalism compelled them to resist European cultural hegemony, ascribing a dialectical dynamic to Brazilian Modernism.

Generally considered the inaugural literary work of Brazilian modernism, Mário de Andrade's *Paulicéia Desvairada* (1922) [Hallucinated City] is emblematic of the interweaving of local and translocal ideological and aesthetic threads by the first modernists. The epithet hallucinated ascribed to the Brazilian metropolis of São Paulo [Paulicéia] in the title of the collection establishes a parallel between its rapid modernisation in the first decades of the twentieth century and that of emerging European cities at the end of the nineteenth century depicted in Émile Verhaeren's *Les campagnes hallucinés* (1893) and *Les villes tentaculaires* (1895). By alluding directly to these works—which, as shown by Charles Perrone, inspired Mário's debut poetry collection[11]—the Brazilian poet underscores their foundational value in making urbanisation the material of lyric poetry, aligning his work with this tradition of urban poetry. Moreover, Verhaeren's avowed ambivalence towards urbanisation—comprising both 'admiration for the "beauty of the modern" and [...] "enthusiasm" for the industrial and scientific progress mixed with feelings of anxiety, pessimism and regret in the face of the aggressiveness

---

[9] Mariano Siskind, *Cosmopolitan Desires: Global Modernity and World Literature in Latin America* (Evanston, IL: Northwestern University Press, 2014), p. 104.

[10] Siskind, *Cosmopolitan Desires*, p. 104.

[11] Charles Perrone, 'Presentation and representation of self and city in *Paulicéia desvairada*', *Chasqui*, 31: 1 (May 2002), 18–27, pp. 20–21.

BRAZILIAN MODERNISTS AND THE AVANT-GARDE ...   145

and destructiveness of "octopuscities"[12]—provides Mário with an alternative to the facile and over-optimistic representation of the processes of modernisation in Futurism, from which he wishes to distance himself. This notwithstanding, he resorts to futurist imagery and stylistic devices to convey the hallucinating rhythm of São Paulo in 'Paisagem n. 4' ['Landscape 4'], which closes the first part of the collection:

> Os caminhões rodando, as carroças rodando,
> Rápidas as ruas se desenrolando,
> Rumor surdo e rouco, estrépitos, estalidos...
> E o largo coro de ouro das sacas de café!...

> [The trucks rolling, the carts rolling,
> Rapid the streets unrolling,
> Hollow, raucous sound, clatters, crackles ...
> And the grand golden chorus of sacks of coffee! ...][13]

The opening stanza depicts the dynamism of the Brazilian metropolis through a series of accumulating visual and auditory images, evoking the futuristic *topoi* of speed—conveyed lexically by the movement verbs and the adjective 'rapid' used to describe that movement—and noise—conveyed phonetically through the alliteration of 'r' and 's'. Additionally, the asyndetic coordination of clauses and words, which aims to replicate the flux of simultaneous images that pass through the speaker's retina as he strolls through the city streets, resembles the fragmented syntax advocated by Marinetti in 'The Destruction of Syntax – Wireless Imagination – Words in Freedom' (1913). Although Mário emphatically claims not to be 'a Marinetti-styled futurist' in the preface to the collection, these devices illustrate the 'points in contact with Futurism' which he acknowledges, highlighting Marinetti's rediscovery of 'the suggestive, associative, symbolic, universal, and musical power of the liberated word'.[14] However, despite this vivid portrayal of the Brazilian metropolis

[12] Mark D. Steinberg, *Petersburg Fin de Siecle* (New Haven, CT: Yale University Press, 2011), p. 40.

[13] Mário de Andrade, *Hallucinated City/Paulicea [sic] Desvairada: a Bilingual Edition*, trans. Jack E. Tomlins (Kingsport, TN: Vanderbilt University Press, 1968), pp. 74–75.

[14] Andrade, *Hallucinated City*, pp. 7, 11. Mário de Andrade, *Poesias Completas*, ed. Diléa Zanotto Manfio (Belo Horizonte; São Paulo: Itatiaia/Edusp, 1987), pp. 61, 67.

146   P. SILVA

as a frenzied city, corroborating its characterisation as hallucinated in the title of the collection, the poem subverts the futurist expectations to eulogise the city as a symbol of modernity by problematising that very modernity. Hence, the apposition of trucks and carts, symbols of the industrialised city and the agrarian countryside, in the opening line reflects the coexistence of these different realities in São Paulo. According to Marcia Lotito,

> Nos anos 20, São Paulo encarnava a imagem de uma metrópole moderna e a realidade de um país periférico [...], equilibrando-se entre um modelo europeu de urbanidade e o cotidiano inventivo e improvisado das inúmeras etnias e novos grupos sociais que se formavam. São Paulo era a somatória de imagens díspares do arcaico e do moderno, do universal e do particular, da província e da metrópole.[15]

> [In the 1920s, São Paulo embodied the image of the modern metropolis and the reality of a peripheral country [...], balanced between a European urban model and the creative and improvised quotidian of numerous ethnic groups and new social groups being formed. São Paulo was the summation of disparate images of the archaic and the modern, of the universal and the particular, of the countryside and the metropolis.]

The material conditions depicted in the poem and in the above statement correspond to the 'coexistence [...] of realities from radically different moments of history' which Frederic Jameson ascribes to modernism as 'an uneven moment of social development'.[16] Neil Larsen further highlights '*the distinctly Latin American* and perhaps generally "postcolonial" sense of being both modern and traditional, both "ahead of" and yet "behind the times" at once, as if not one but two or multiple histories, were being lived out in one and the same space'.[17] Referring specifically to postcolonial literature, Parry underlines 'the improbable

---

[15] Marcia Padilha Lotito, *Cidade como espetáculo: publicidade e vida urbana da São Paulo dos anos 20* (São Paulo: Annablume, 2001), p. 18, my translation.

[16] Frederic Jameson, *Postmodernism, or, the Cultural Logic of Late Capitalism* (1991), quoted in Parry, 'Aspects of Peripheral Modernisms', p. 32.

[17] Neil Larsen, *Determinations: Essays in Theory, Narrative and Nation in the Americas* (London: Verso, 2001), pp. 139–40, my emphasis.

coexistence of the past and the contemporary in the literatures of societies subjected to imperialist intervention'.[18] By mentioning the 'sacks of coffee', metaphorically equated with gold in the last line of the first stanza, Mário underscores that the city's burgeoning economy relies on products and forms of production inherited from the slave-based plantation economy of its (then) recent colonial past.

While partly celebrating the creation of wealth that distinguishes São Paulo as a metropolis among other Brazilian cities, the following stanza develops the incipient realistic portrayal of the Brazilian metropolis. Notably, it exposes the continued financial control of Brazil by European countries—metonymically and linguistically conveyed in the line 'At the intersection the English cry of the São Paulo Railway...'—depicting the dependency of its economy on the international markets in the line, 'But the windstorms of disillusionment! the drop in coffee prices!...'.[19] This materialistic representation extends to the whole country which by contrast to Brazil's economic hub of São Paulo is depicted as suffering from generalised inaction in the line, 'Far away Brazil with her arms folded...'.[20] Mário's critique of the unevenness of the process of modernisation in Brazil in the early 1920s in this poem illustrates Tele Lopez's claim that *Paulicéia Desvairada* represents 'a first discovery, almost an intuition, [...] intimating, for the remainder of the movement, what Antonio Cândido will term as a "pre-consciousness of our underdevelopment"'.[21]

In the last stanza, the grammatical subject becomes pluralised so as to encompass the ensemble of the city's dwellers, addressed in the lines, 'Let us gird on (Victory!) the necklaces of enemy teeth! / Let us garland ourselves in coffee beans!'.[22] By exhorting them to adorn themselves with their enemies' teeth and coffee beans, the speaker evokes both illuminist Europe's iconographic representation of the indigenous inhabitants of

---

[18] Parry, 'Aspects of Peripheral Modernisms', p. 32.

[19] Andrade, *Hallucinated City*, pp. 74–75: 'Na confluência o grito inglês da São Paulo Railway...'; 'Mas as ventaneiras da desilusão! a baixa do café!...'.

[20] Andrade, *Hallucinated City*, pp. 74–75: 'Muito ao longe o Brasil com seus braços cruzados...'.

[21] Lopez, 'Arlequim e Modernidade', p. 86: 'uma descoberta primeira, quase uma intuição, [...] anunciando, para a continuação do movimento, o que Antonio Cândido chamará de "pré-consciência de nosso subdesenvolvimento"', my translation.

[22] Andrade, *Hallucinated City*, pp. 74–75: 'Ponhamos os (Vitória!) colares de presas inimigas! / Enguirlandemonos de café-cereja!'.

148   P. SILVA

Brazil as cannibals and the major export good of the nineteenth-century Brazilian colonial economy as symbols of the racial discrimination and economic exploitation associated with imperialism, calling to mind Parry's remarks about the 'singular accents' of the modernisms in the colonised peripheries mentioned at the start of this essay. In keeping with the bellicist tone of the stanza, suggested by the word 'victory', he then utters a triumphal chant which expresses at once his 'mockery to the world' and his 'supreme pride in existing São Paulo-wise!!!'.[23] As Júlio Pinto noted, 'to exist São Paulo-wise is the mark of an identity which is built through the sum of dissonant traits and distinct perceptions', which reflects the antithetical structure of the poem moving from praise to criticism of the city.[24] However, as the lines quoted previously suggest, it also involves an attitude of counter-hegemonic challenge to metropolitan Europe which is nonetheless critical of the contradictions arising from Brazil's peripheral and postcolonial condition, notably a form of capitalism which perpetuates aspects of the slave-based economy that characterised the Brazilian colonial experience.

As shown in 'Paisagem n. 4', the hallucinated mode adopted in *Paulicéia Desvairada* is posited as the fitting poetic expression of the contradictions of modern Brazil. Additionally, it is also presented as an aesthetic, which the poet terms 'Desvairismo' [Hallucinism] in the 'Extremely Interesting Preface' that introduces the collection. A Brazilian response to and critique of modernisation, 'Desvairismo' is proposed as a paroxysm of the European aesthetic responses to this phenomenon, competing with various advanced movements, in particular, Futurism, the self-proclaimed harbinger of the ultra-modern. However, at the end of the preface, Mário ironically claims that he is prepared to create another aesthetic within the week, critiquing the proliferation of 'isms' generated by the avant-garde. In effect, he does as much in a letter to Tarsila do Amaral from November 1923, in which he announces the creation of 'matavirgismo' [virgin forest-ism], an aesthetic diametrically opposed to 'Desvairismo' (and to Futurism) that proposes a native primitivism, which

[23] Andrade, *Hallucinated City*, pp. 74–75: 'escárnio para o mundo'; 'orgulho máximo de ser paulistamente!!!'.

[24] Júlio Pinto, 'Ruas de Borges e de seus contemporâneos', *História*, São Paulo, 22: 2 (2003), 121–132, p. 124: '"ser paulistamente" é a marca de uma identidade que se faz pelo somatório de traços dissonantes, percepções distintas', my translation.

would be actualised a few years later in Mário's magnum opera, *Macunaíma: O herói sem nenhum caráter* [Macunaíma: The Hero without Any Character] (1928).[25] According to Vinicius Dantas, '"matavirgismo", like the previous [aesthetics] is a mock-ism which sarcastically signals the relativity of the European *isms* and their Brazilian transplants'.[26] To guard against such ill-fitting imports, he urges Tarsila to abandon Paris, where she was studying painting, as well as 'Gris and Lhote', whom he describes as 'impresarios of decadent aesthetics', and to return to her native virgin forest.[27]

Unlike Mário, who never left Brazil, Tarsila do Amaral and her partner, Oswald de Andrade, were in direct contact with the European avant-gardes. Oswald travelled to Paris in 1912 and upon his return was responsible for the incipient reception of Futurism in Brazil.[28] Tarsila left for Paris in 1920 to study painting at the Academie Julian, returning to Brazil shortly after the Modern Art Week of February 1922 and co-founding the Group of Five with its organisers, Mário de Andrade, Oswald de Andrade, Menotti del Picchia, and Anita Malfatti.[29] She and Oswald returned to Paris, where she spent most of 1923 and part of 1924 studying with Lhote and Gleizes and where she met Cendrars, who introduced her to Brancusi, Cocteau and Léger, whose studio she attended regularly.[30] Despite being influenced by their cubist style, Tarsila developed a predilection for national themes, popular and archaic traditions, and a native figuration infused with a mimetic quality which Vinicius Dantas terms as 'primitivo-construtivismo' [primitive-constructivism].[31]

[25] Mário's letter quoted in Vinicius Dantas, 'Entre "a negra" e a mata virgem', *Novos Estudos* 45 (São Paulo: Cebrap, July 1996), 100–116, p. 103.

[26] Vinicius Dantas, 'Entre "a negra" e a mata virgem', p. 104: '"matavirgismo", como os anteriores, é um ismo-piada que assinala sarcasticamente a relatividade dos radicalismos europeus e de seus transplantes brasílicos'.

[27] Vinicius Dantas, 'Entre "a negra" e a mata virgem', p. 104: 'Abandona o Gris e o Lhote, empresários de criticismos decrépitos e de estesias decadentes! Abandona Paris! Tarsila! Tarsila! Vem para a mata virgem'.

[28] Mário da Silva Brito, *História do modernismo brasileiro*, 26–27; according to Brito, the original manuscript of the poem was lost.

[29] Júlia Silveira Matos, 'As estruturas do cotidiano brasileiro na obra de Tarsila do Amaral', *Historiæ*, 1:2 (Rio Grande, 2010), 85–102 (p. 87).

[30] Matos, 'As estruturas do cotidiano brasileiro na obra de Tarsila do Amaral', p. 90.

[31] Vinicius Dantas, 'Entre "a negra" e a mata virgem', Novos Estudos, 45, 100–116 (pp. 111–112).

150   P. SILVA

According to Dantas, in transposing late Cubism to a Brazilian context, Tarsila

> ao contrário de atender às inquietações desencadeadas pela experiência histórico-social da sociedade industrial, defronta-se aí com o que foi excluido, recalcado ou simplesmente é retardatário em relação à matriz europeia. [...] Tarsila valoriza, bastante ciente dos desajustes entre a circunstância brasileira e o contexto europeu do espírito novo, a presença poética das coisas, figurinhas e paisagem – o que perde em dinamismo simultaneísta, adquire em pitoresco, porque a sua modernidade é menos industrial.[32]

> [instead of heeding the concerns raised by the socio-historical industrial society, she is confronted there with what was excluded, repressed or is simply belated in relation to the European matrix. Quite aware of the incongruences between the Brazilian circumstances and the European context of the new sensibility, Tarsila values the poetic presence of objects, figures and landscape – what she loses in simultaneist dynamism she gains in terms of the picturesque, because her modernity is less industrial.]

Oswald de Andrade's literary works also display a primitivist bias and resort to cubist techniques to express the contradictions of modern Brazil. In 'Atelier', for instance, he conflates autochthonous and foreign elements, as signalled by the title, a borrowing from French. The studio alluded to in the title of the poem is that of Tarsila, portrayed thus in the opening lines:

> Caipirinha vestida de Poiret
> A preguiça paulista reside nos teus olhos
> Que não viram Paris nem Piccadilly
> Nem as exclamações dos homens
> Em Sevilha
> À tua passagem entre brincos[33]

> [Country girl dressed in Poiret
> The laziness of São Paulo abides in your eyes

---

[32] Vinicius Dantas, 'Entre "a negra" e a mata virgem', 109.

[33] Oswald de Andrade, *Poesias reunidas* (Rio de Janeiro: Civilização Brasileira, 1972), 'Obras Completas VII', p. 61.

Which have never seen Paris or Piccadilly
Or the exclamations of the men
In Seville
At your passage in earrings][34]

Despite the cosmopolitan origins of her dress, designed by the Paris-based *haute couturier* Paul Poiret, the portrayal of the artist in the first stanza emphasises her authentic Brazilian origins. This is underscored lexically and semantically by the choice of the word 'caipirinha' [country girl], which originated in the indigenous Tupi language and is used in Brazilian Portuguese to refer to a person from a rural, remote area of some states, including the interior of the state of São Paulo, where Tarsila was originally from. The localist emphasis in Oswald's poem is reinforced by the claim that the girl's eyes display 'the laziness of São Paulo', a trait commonly attributed to the state's country folk.[35] Tarsila's authenticity is also corroborated by the assertion that she has never left Brazil, which reflects her claim that she felt 'more and more Brazilian' in a letter written in 1923, while she was still in Paris.[36]

The term 'caipirinha' also refers to Tarsila's eponymous painting from 1923 (Fig. 1). Highlighting the parallels between the poem and the painting, Jorge Schwartz claims that 'the national/cosmopolitan tension present in 'Atelier' translates itself in the painting by the rural motif moulded on the canvas with the aesthetics imported from Paris', more precisely from Léger, whose distinctive style he sees as informing '[t]he cylindrical forms of the female body – mixed with the angular cut of the houses, the tree trunks, the stripes of the hands and the facade of the house on the left, as well as the green oval volumes of the leaf and the

---

[34] Jorge Schwartz, 'Literature and the Visual Arts: the Brazilian Roaring Twenties', Visiting Resource Professor Papers, Teresa Lozano Long Institute of Latin American Studies (LLILAS), The University of Texas at Austin, p. 8, https://repositories.lib.ute xas.edu/handle/2152/4079 [accessed 13/07/2013].

[35] According to Vânia Carneiro de Carvalho, this trait was specifically associated with the 'caipira' in the state of São Paulo due to the large numbers of its inhabitants who were left without occupation following the end of the expansion inward in the eighteenth century. See *Gênero e artefato: o sistema doméstico na perspectiva da cultura material, São Paulo 1870-1920* (São Paulo: Edusp, 2008), p. 307.

[36] Jorge Schwartz, 'Literature and the Visual Arts: the Brazilian Roaring Twenties', p. 18.

Fig. 1   A Caipirinha (1923)

possible pineapples'.[37] Tarsila's painting documents her growing interest in the pictorial representation of her native land, reflecting the statement in the aforementioned letter, 'I want to be the painter of my land. I'm so grateful to have spent my entire childhood on the plantation. The memories of that time are becoming precious to me'.[38] It is the plantation of her childhood evoked from memory that she depicts in the painting and, by portraying herself as an adult in that setting she actualises her claim in the letter, '*[i]n art, I want to be the country girl from São Bernardo* [...], as in the last picture I'm painting'.[39]

---

[37] Jorge Schwartz, 'Literature and the Visual Arts: the Brazilian Roaring Twenties', p. 19.

[38] Jorge Schwartz, 'Literature and the Visual Arts: the Brazilian Roaring Twenties', pp. 18–19.

[39] Jorge Schwartz, 'Literature and the Visual Arts: the Brazilian Roaring Twenties', p. 19.

Having portrayed the painter as a modern, cosmopolitan but authentically Brazilian woman, the speaker in Oswald's poem proceeds to evoke the national themes in her work:

Locomotivas e bichos nacionais
Geometrizam as atmosferas nítidas,
Congonhas descora sobre o pálio
Das procissões de Minas

A verdura no azul-klaxon
Cortada
Sobre a poeira vermelha

Arranha-céus
Fordes
Viadutos
Um cheiro de café
No silêncio emoldurado[40]

[Locomotives and national animals
Geometrize the limpid sceneries
Congonhas pales beneath the canopy
Of the processions of Minas

The verdure against the klaxon blue
Cut
Across the red dust

Skyscrapers
Fords
Overpasses
The aroma of coffee
In the framed silence][41]

---

[40] Andrade, *Poesias reunidas*, p. 61.

[41] Schwartz, 'Literature and the Visual Arts: the Brazilian Roaring Twenties', pp. 8–9.

154   P. SILVA

In doing so, he lists distinctive aspects of the Brazilian landscape and fauna, and of its traditional popular and religious culture such as the processions in Minas Gerais, which feature in Tarsila's paintings from 1924 to 1925 alongside symbols of the modernisation and industrialisation the country was undergoing.

The references to skyscrapers, fords, and overpasses in Oswald's poem intertextually allude to several paintings by Tarsila about São Paulo, which combine Lhote's cubist stylisation of scenes from everyday life and Léger's simplified mechanical forms with the absence of proportions in naïf primitive art.[42] Additionally, in the lines 'Locomotives and national animals / Geometrize the limpid sceneries', Oswald attempts to re-create semantically the contrast between the monochromatic angular geometric forms of the manmade constructions and the organic colourful forms of the natural landscape evident, for instance, in *Estrada de ferro central do Brasil* [Central Railway of Brazil] (1924) (Fig. 2). In this painting, Tarsila draws on the cubist absence of perspective to juxtapose the disparate elements coexisting in contemporary Brazil, including roads, railroads, train stations, hill-side favelas and baroque churches, synthesizing the archaic and the modern on the flat surface of the canvas. Oswald's elliptic ekphrastic verse achieves a comparable oddness effect to the juxtaposition of differently coloured and shaped planes in Tarsila's painting through the absence of punctuation, the apposition of dissonant fragmentary images, and the use of line breaks such as those around the participle 'Cortada' [cut] to convey the cubist intersection of the green vegetation, the blue sky and the reddish earth depicted in this and other paintings by Tarsila from the same period, like *A Feira* and *Morro da Favela*.

Although the pictorial and poetic techniques developed by Tarsila and Oswald are based on the lessons of Cubism, their aesthetic object consists of the indigenous Brazilian landscape and culture. The native natural element is epitomised by the palm trees that recur in Tarsila's paintings as symbols of Brazil's luxurious tropical vegetation, likewise encapsulated in the expression 'América folhuda' ['leafy America'] used by Oswald in the poem 'Anhangabaú', signalling a hemispheric difference from metropolitan Europe in geomorphic terms. Oswald also underscores this difference in terms of systems of production by referring to the aroma of coffee framed in Tarsila's paintings in the closing lines of

---

[42] These include *São Paulo, São Paulo Gazo, A Gare*, and *Estrada de ferro central do Brasil*, all from 1924.

Fig. 2 Estrada de Ferro central do Brasil (Central Railway of Brazil 1924)

'Atelier'. If on the one hand as a product from the Brazilian soil, coffee can be seen as a metonymic symbol of the land which Tarsila wished to represent, on the other hand, as an economic good it is associated with the country's colonial history and with its access to the global trading market, as seen with regard to Mário's poem quoted earlier. According to Jorge Schwartz, 'the mention of coffee goes beyond mere decoration or the introduction of "local colour" as an affirmation of the national. On the contrary, São Paulo signifies in the years of 1920 the high point

156 P. SILVA

of the coffee baronage'.[43] This view is authorised by Oswald's claim that 'one must understand modernism with its material and inceptive causes, found in São Paulo's industrial park, with its class compromises during the bourgeois golden period of the first high-value coffee crops'.[44] By resuming Mário's imagery from *Paulicéia Desvairada*, Oswald underscores the interrelation between Brazilian modernism and the capitalist world-system.

The emphasis on the native soil pervades the entire poetry collection in which 'Atelier' is included, entitled *Pau-Brasil* [Brazilwood] (1925), which refers to an abundant species of tree native to the coast of South America whose name came to identify the country.

It is also central to the 'Manifesto da Poesia Pau-Brasil' [Brazilwood Poetry Manifesto] (1924), which presents the principles of modern Brazilian poetry, notably '[t]o be regional and pure in our time', emphasising its locality (the term regional here pertaining not to a specific region in Brazil but to that area of the hemisphere), authenticity and actuality.[45] By choosing to name the new type of poetry he proposed Brazilwood, which was the country's major export good of the early colonial economy, Oswald appropriates a symbol of colonial exploitation and inflects it with a libertarian meaning in an ostensive gesture of postcolonial revisionism. Accordingly, he distinguishes between 'imported Poetry' and 'Pau-Brasil Poetry, for exportation', listing the latter among other national export

---

[43] Jorge Schwartz, *Fervor das vanguardas: Arte e literatura na América Latina* (São Paulo: Companhia das Letras, 2013), p. 26: '[a] menção ao café ultrapassa o mero decorativismo ou a introdução da "cor local" como afirmação do nacional. Pelo contrário, São Paulo define nos anos 1920 o apogeu do baronato do café'.

[44] Schwartz, *Fervor das vanguardas*, p. 26: '[é] preciso compreender o modernismo com suas causas materiais e fecundantes, hauridas no parque industrial de São Paulo, com seus compromissos de classe no período áureoburguês do primeiro café valorizado'.

[45] Oswald de Andrade, 'Manifesto of Pau-Brazil Poetry,' trans. Stella M. de Sá Rego, *Latin American Literary Review*, Vol. 14, No. 27, Brazilian Literature (Jan.–Jun., 1986), 184–187, pp. 184, 187. Oswald de Andrade, 'Manifesto da Poesia Pau-Brasil', *Vanguarda européia e modernismo brasileiro: apresentação dos principais poemas, manifestos, prefácios e conferências vanguardistas de 1857 a 1972*, ed. by Gilberto Mendonça Teles. (Petrópolis, RJ: Editora Vozes, 1983), pp. 326, 331: 'Ser regional e puro em sua época'.

goods such as '[c]uisine, ore and dance'.[46] By contrast to the imitative quality of Brazilian poetry in the past (as suggested by the term imported), Oswald proposes the country's modern poetry as an authentic Brazilian cultural product, claiming its access to the literary world-system.

According to Fernando Rosenberg, 'the "Brazilwood manifesto" foregrounds the fact that what stands as artistically new also depends on a sort of validation that is not at all foreign to a global circulation of commodities', which implies 'a world-system of attribution of cultural value'.[47] This critic places Oswald's 'Manifesto da Poesia Pau-Brasil' alongside Oliverio Girondo's 'Manifiesto de *Martín Fierro*' (published in the Argentinian magazine *Martín Fierro* also in 1924) as exemplary of the strategies whereby 'the vanguards, elaborated [...] their own *loci* of enunciation imbricated in the circulation of goods, discourses, and peoples', claiming that these seminal manifestos 'are not only the anchor for a renewed nationalism

[...] but also become vantage points from which to understand an expanded geopolitics'.[48] This expanded geopolitics, argues Rosenberg, counters the narrative of 'modernity as a merely expansionist force' with fixed centres and peripheries.[49] Rendering it more complex, it allows for shifts in the flow of cultural goods, and for the emergence of peripheries as alternative cultural centres, as was the case of the Latin American boom of the 60s and 70s, which was presciently rehearsed in the theoretical and creative output of modernists like Oliverio Girondo and Oswald de Andrade.

At the close of the 'Manifesto da Poesia Pau-Brasil', Oswald characterises Brazilwood poetry as 'Everything assimilated'.[50] The metaphor of

---

[46] Andrade, 'Manifesto of Pau-Brazil Poetry', *Latin American Literary Review*, pp. 185, 187. Andrade, 'Manifesto da Poesia Pau-Brasil', *Vanguarda européia e modernismo brasileiro*, pp. 326, 331: 'poesia de importação. E a Poesia Pau-Brasil, de exportação'; 'A cozinha, o minério e a dança'.

[47] Fernando J. Rosenberg, *The Avant-garde and Geopolitics in Latin America* (Pittsburg, PA: University of Pittsburg Press, 2006), p. 5.

[48] Rosenberg, *The Avant-garde and Geopolitics in Latin America*, p. 6.

[49] Rosenberg, *The Avant-garde and Geopolitics in Latin America*, p. 5.

[50] Andrade, 'Manifesto of Pau-Brazil Poetry', *Latin American Literary Review*, p. 187. Andrade, 'Manifesto da Poesia Pau-Brasil', *Vanguarda européia e modernismo brasileiro*, p. 331: 'Tudo digerido.'

158   P. SILVA

assimilation recurs in the 'Manifesto Antropófago' ['Cannibalist Manifesto'] (1928), where it is embodied by the figure of the cannibal.[51] Amplifying the revisionist stance he had adopted in the previous manifesto, Oswald 'subversively appropriates the colonialist designation of native peoples of the Americas as culture-less [man-eating] savages', which dominated the iconography of colonial Brazil, reversing its pejorative value.[52] Thus, he celebrates the ritualistic cannibalism practised by the Tupí people to absorb the enemy's strength—'The absorption of the sacred enemy. To transform it into totem.' as stated in the manifesto—proposing it as a metaphor for the active assimilation of foreign influences in order to nourish the native culture.[53] The process is exemplified by the statement in English 'Tupy, or not tupy that is the question', which cannibalises Shakespeare's famous line from *Hamlet* and, by replacing the verb 'to be' with the noun 'tupy'—the anglicised form of the name of the most important indigenous people in Brazil and of their language—turns it into a hybrid that combines a major European cultural legacy with an autochthonous one dating back to the Pre-Cabraline period that preceded colonisation.[54] According to Benedito Nunes, Oswald's 'strategy of decolonization is rhetorical'.[55] This is evinced by the dialectical quality of the 'Manifesto Antropófago', which opposes pre-colonial Amerindian culture to European civilisation through a series of dichotomies, namely matriarchy/patriarchy, communal social structure/class system, Paganism/Catholicism, irrationality/rationality, pre-modernity/modernity. In effect, Oswald adopts the iconoclastic tone of the avant-garde manifesto to critique several aspects of European culture, deliberately resuming the aggressive denunciatory tone of Picabia's 'Manifeste Cannibale Dada' (1920). As noted by Irene Ramalho Santos, Oswald's manifesto also subversively appropriates Paul Valéry's gastronomic metaphor, used by the latter poet to

---

[51] The figure of the cannibal in Oswald's manifesto was inspired by Tarsila's painting from the same year entitled *Abaporu*, a Tupi word meaning 'the man who eats people'.

[52] Barry, *Chasqui*, p. 13.

[53] Oswald de Andrade, 'Manifesto Antropófago', *Revista de Antropofagia* 1 (May, 1928), p. 7: 'Absorção do inimigo sacro. Para transformal-o em totem'.

[54] Andrade, 'Manifesto Antropófago', *Revista de Antropofagia* 1, p. 3.

[55] Benedito Nunes, 'Antropofagismo e Surrealismo', *Remate de Males* 6 (June 1986), 15–26, pp. 18, 33.

characterise the ability of European culture to assimilate other cultures.[56] Conversely, the manifesto's celebration of the Amerindians and the primitive New World foregrounds the revalorisation of Brazil's indigenous ancestry and pre-colonial heritage which became central to a faction of Brazilian modernism. It also reflects the nativist, regionalist discourse prevalent throughout Latin America at the turn of the twentieth century, notably in José Martí's *Nuestra América* (1891) [Our America], resumed by Ruben Darío in his invective poem 'A Roosevelt' [To Roosevelt] (1903), and in the *criollista* movement which produced some of its best works in the 1920s.

The syncretic absorption of the Other in the Self underpinning Oswald's cultural cannibalism offers a working solution to the dilemma he and other Brazilian modernists experienced, namely, how to modernise and valorise the national cultural field without succumbing to slavish imitation of foreign models and thereby perpetuate the cultural heritage of the coloniser (or neo-coloniser). That was the strategy adopted by the writers and artists discussed in this essay, who appropriated futurist and cubist motifs and procedures, reframing them in accordance with their 'historical and cultural conditions of enunciation'.[57] Their creative assimilation of European avant-garde aesthetics by combining them with indigenous elements is emblematic of the *nutritive* cannibalism extolled in the 'Manifesto Antropófago', contributing significantly to the renewal of the national cultural field at the time. Hence, the concept of transculturation theorised by Oswald in the 1928 manifesto—based on his and Tarsila's transmedial experiments, and accomplishedly actualised in Mário's experimental novel of the same year *Macunaíma*—can be considered, as Barry argues, a 'counter-hegemonic [...] form of cultural nationalism'.[58] Additionally, the Manifesto enunciates a subversive critique of capitalism comparable to that which Schwarz identified in Machado de Assis's novels, encapsulated in the following passage from 'The Cannibalist Manifesto' which rehearses a definition of 'Anthropophagy', understood by Oswald as '[t]he combat between that which could be called noncreated and the creature – represented by the permanent contradiction

---

[56] Irene Ramalho Santos, *Atlantic Poets: Fernando Pessoa's Turn in Anglo American Modernism* (Hanover, NH: University Press of New England, 2003), pp. 90–91.

[57] Homi K. Bhabha, *The Location of Culture*, New York: Psychology Press, 1994, p. 355.

[58] Barry, *Chasqui*, 12.

160   P. SILVA

between men and his Tabu. Daily love and the capitalist way of life. Anthropophagy'.[59] As such, the cultural cannibalism proposed and practised by the first Brazilian modernists not only allowed them to resist European neo-colonial cultural hegemony in the early twentieth century but was also deployed in a similar manner by subsequent Brazilian avantgardes and counter-cultures, namely the Concrete Poetry movement in the mid-1950s and the Tropicália movement in the late 60s and 70s.

Oswald's use of primitivism to articulate a discourse of resistance to European cultural hegemony in the 'Manifesto Antropófago' ['Cannibalist Manifesto'] displays a transgressive quality which, according to Silviano Santiago, is characteristic of Latin American discourse as a whole. In his 1971 essay 'O entre-lugar do discurso latinoamericano' ['Latin American Discourse: The Space in Between'], the Brazilian critic draws on the rhetorical trope of cannibalism introduced in Oswald's 'Manifesto Antropófago' to convey the ambivalent stance of Latin American postcolonial discourse. Santiago ascribes its specificity to the region's cultural hybridity, claiming that its 'biggest contribution to Western culture derives from its systematic destruction of the concepts of unity and purity' and from its transgressive 'transfiguration' of European cultural commodities.[60] The cultural hybridity underpinning oswaldian cultural cannibalism also anticipates the concept of 'transculturation', proposed by Uruguayan critic Ángel Rama in the early 1980s to describe the ways in which Latin American writers preserve the particularities of 'original' popular cultures while employing the aesthetic resources of North American and European avantgardes.[61] These questions were resumed by influential post-structuralist Latin American critics, such as Beatriz Sarlo, with regard to the notion of 'modernidad periférica' [peripheral modernity]. That same cultural hybridity underpins Sarlo's reading of modernism in Buenos Aires as an instance of peripheral modernity. In the introduction to *Una modernidad periférica*, she posits

[59] 'A luta entre o que se chamaria Incriado e a Criatura—ilustrada pela contradição permanente do homem e o seu Tabu. O amor cotidiano e o *modus vivendi* capitalista. Antropofagia' (my translation).

[60] Silviano Santiago, *The Space in Between: Essays on Latin American Culture*, trans. and ed. Ana Lúcia Gazzola (Durham, NC; London: Duke University Press, 2001), p. 16.

[61] Ángel Rama, *Transculturación narrativa en América Latina* (Mexico City: Siglo XXI, 1982).

una hipótesis que intentaré demostrar se refiere a la cultura argentina como cultura de mezcla, donde coexisten elementos defensivos y residuales junto a los programas renovadores; rasgos culturales de la formación criolla al mismo tiempo que un processo descomunal de importación de bienes, discursos y prácticas simbólicas. El impulso de la suma caracteriza tanto a Martín Fierro como al proyecto pedagógico de "Claridad" o la modernización elegante de *Sur*. La mezcla es uno de los rasgos menos transitorios de la cultura argentina: su forma ya "clássica" de respuesta y reacondicionamiento. Lo que un historiador de la arquitectura llama "la versatilidad y la permeabilidad" de la cultura portena, me parece un principio global para definir estrategias ideológicas y estéticas.[62]

In the discourse that pervaded social and humanistic sciences in Latin America in the late 1980s and 90s, periphery was understood not as much as a 'descriptive geographical reference' or a 'functional notion in the context of dependency', but as the 'experimental metaphor of a perspective from which one experiences and problematizes a specifically heterogeneous modernity'.[63] This reconceptualisation of peripheral modernity based on cultural heterogeneity and hybridity, present in embryonic form in the incipient practices of the Brazilian modernists and conceptualised in Oswald's 'Cannibalist Manifesto', is particularly productive when examining transcultural modernisms arising in (semi)peripheral and postcolonial contexts within the literary world-system.

---

[62] Beatriz Sarlo, *Una modernidad periférica: Buenos Aires 1920 y 1930* (Buenos Aires: Ediciones Nueva Visión, 1988, pp. 28–29.

[63] Hermann Herlinghaus, Monika Walter (eds), *Posmodernidad en la periferia: enfoques latinoamericanos de la nueva teoría cultural*, Berlin: Langer, 1994, introduction, p. 23: 'referência geográfico descritiva'; 'noção funcional no marco da dependência'; 'metáfora experimental de una perspectiva desde la cual se experimenta y se problematiza una modernidad específicamente heterogénea'.

Degrees of Peripherality: The Rhetoric of Architecture in Late Twentieth-Century Iran

Nigel Westbrook and Ali Mozaffari

INTRODUCTION

In this chapter, we revisit existing scholarly material on architectural culture before and after the Islamic Revolution (1979) with a specific purpose—to gauge whether there developed a genuinely local response

---

We first wrote and presented an early version of this work to the Peripheral Modernisms International Conference held at the Institute of Germanic & Romance Studies, University of London in March 2012. Since that time, our position has developed, and we have used the research material and the insights gained, some of which are articulated here, in other works (see Mozaffari and Westbrook 2014, 2020, 2022). The question of peripherality, however, remains important in that it forces us to think in terms of global exchanges rather than, purely in terms of resistance and the parochialism and distortions that this may entail.

N. Westbrook
School of Design, The University of Western Australia, Perth, WA, Australia
e-mail: nigel.westbrook@uwa.edu.au

A. Mozaffari (✉)
Alfred Deakin Institute for Citizenship and Globalization, Deakin University, Northcote, Vic, Australia
e-mail: ali.mozaffari@research.deakin.edu.au

© The Author(s), under exclusive license to Springer Nature Switzerland AG 2024
K. Pizzi and R. Gefter Wondrich (eds.), *Rethinking Peripheral Modernisms*, https://doi.org/10.1007/978-3-031-35546-2_9

to global conditions of modernity. Our exploration works with the theme of "Peripheral modernisms", a term which derives from literary studies, but here we ask how peripherality might be construed and embodied in architecture, placing regionally specific architectural cultures in relation to the Western centres. In the process we shall draw on texts on peripherality, works by Harry Harootounian and Caplan, as well as Critical Regionalism in architecture. The question of regional specificity in architecture pertains to issues and modes of development; that is to say, could processes of design and construction mediate social conditions in developing countries? Further, if, to follow Caplan (2011), it is possible to see in certain forms of peripheral cultures "a return to oral narrative habits" as a form of resistance to the cultural colonization of the West, is it possible to interpret material and intellectual production of architecture in similar terms?

In the early 1980s, a similar rhetoric of resistance, couched under the term "Critical Regionalism", was deployed by leftist critics of Western globalization, firstly by Alexander Tzonis and Liane Lefevre, with their essay entitled "The Grid and the Pathway" (1981), and soon after, Kenneth Frampton's seminal essay, "Towards a Critical Regionalism: Six Points for an Architecture of Resistance" (1983). Both essays argued against both the reduction of architecture to "Pop culture", and cultural trends that are indifferent to specificities of place. In deploying the term "Critical Regionalism", they advocated a conscious local resistance to the global homogenization of architectural culture. Their position was inspired by a Marcusian opposition to the anti-democratic tendencies of global systems. This was a consciously peripheral stance, not rejecting the beneficial aspects of technology and modernization, but also inevitably engaging in a kind of cultural nationalism,[1] which is certainly true of those peripheral architectures that enthusiastically adopted the label, not least the network of architects and theorists associated with the Aga Khan Foundation.[2]

---

[1] Fredric Jameson, *The Seeds of Time*, New York, NY: Columbia University Press, 1994, 202.

[2] See, for example, Robert Powell, ed., *Regionalism in Architecture*, Exploring Architecture in Islamic Cultures 2, Proceedings of the Regional Seminar in the series Exploring Architecture in Islamic Cultures sponsored by The Aga Khan Award for Architecture, Bangladesh University of Engineering and Technology and Institute of Architects, Bangladesh. Held in Dhaka, Bangladesh, December 17–22, 1985, Singapore: Aga Khan

To explore the question of peripherality as resistance within architecture, we will revisit two moments through which Iranian architects and theorists engaged with the question of cultural authenticity in the face of globalizing Western influence. Firstly, we will address the discourses of cultural identity raised in the inaugural International Congress of Architects held in Isfahan, Iran in 1970, *The Interaction of Tradition and Technology,* which was attended by leading local and international architectural scholars and practitioners. Secondly, we will discuss the first nationally significant architectural competition after the 1979 Islamic Revolution, for the complex of the National Academies, which was held in 1991 after an architectural hiatus in architectural activities resulting from the post-revolutionary turmoil and the eight-year war between Iran and Iraq.

DEVELOPMENT AND DISRUPTION

The International Congress of Architects at Isfahan followed a period of rapid socio-economic and cultural changes brought about by State agents and under the aegis of its "White Revolution". Many of the issues dealt with there was material, such as the question of the adoption of advanced prefabrication methods. Others pertained to the impacts that political and economic colonization exerted upon technologically undeveloped or semi-developed societies. The congress sought to understand how developing societies might engage with their traditions and avail themselves of the liberating aspects of technological and social development. In contrast, the Academies competition occurred after the 1979 Islamic Revolution and the subsequent educational reforms of the Maoist inspired "Cultural Revolution".[3] But the revolution was not simply an attempt to return to an ideal Islamic past. A significant cohort of the early instigators of change was inspired by various forms of Marxism and their precepts, and this is reflected in one of the first journals published in the

---

Award for Architecture, 1985. Kenneth Frampton was one of the invited critics for this event.

[3] Anecdotal evidence suggests a connection between the Iranian and communist versions of Cultural Revolution. For example see An early example of this comparison is found in Khosrow Sobhe, 'Education in Revolution: Is Iran Duplicating the Chinese Cultural Revolution?', *Comparative Education,* 18: 3, (1982), 271–280.

post-revolution period, and in the changes to the national architectural curriculum. The Islamist ideology from the outset pursued an agenda of cultural reform, privileging indigeneity and local Islamic tradition over what was seen as the corruptive influence of Western culture, an idea that again had leftist roots.[4] As Javid has revealed, an important tool of this agenda was the reform of architectural pedagogy, both separating it from dependence upon Western models, and reestablishing an engagement with the continuities of traditional culture through methods such as the immersive study of the traditional environments of Iranian rural villages.[5] In order to reveal the development of this discourse within architecture, we will analyse early issues of the post-revolution state-supported architecture journal, *Abadi*, which, in a similar manner to the pre-Revolution journal *Honar-vaMe'mari* ('Art and Architecture'),[6] engaged with these overarching cultural objectives of the new regime. We will focus on the treatment of its coverage of the National Academies competition, the first major post-Revolution architectural event, and will examine the question of whether this event constituted a cultural "rebirth", reflecting the regime's objectives of purging the culture of corruptive Western influences, or whether it constituted a form of continuity in thinking and practice that spanned across the revolutionary divide. Referring to architectural expressions, we probe modes of peripherality and explore whether a distinction could be observed between these modes based on the tenor and use of their products.

[4] Ali Javid, "From French Atelier to Italian Studio: The Impact of Italian Pedagogy and Archaeology on Architectural Pedagogy Revolution in Iran." In *Proceedings of the Society of Architectural Historians Australia and New Zealand: 37, What If? What Next? Speculations on History's Futures*, edited by Kate Hislop and Hannah Lewi, Perth: SAHANZ, 2021, 372–385: https://www.sahanz.net/wp-content/uploads/2D_372-385_JAVID.pdf.

[5] Ali Javid and Nigel Westbrook, '"Pedagogy for Others": Howard University, an Architectural Pedagogy for Third World, and its Legacy in the 1979 Iranian Revolution', chapter accepted for *The Routledge Critical Companion to Race and Architecture*, edited by Itohan Osayimwese and Felipe Hernández, Abingdon; New York: Taylor and Francis, [forthcoming 2022].

[6] The first post-Revolution Iranian architectural journal was *Jame'eh ve Memari*. See Shawhin Roudbari, 'Instituting Architecture: A History of Transnationalism in Iran's Architectural Profession, 1945–1995', In *The Historiography of Persian Architecture*, edited by Mohammad Gharipour, London; New York: Routledge, 2016, 287–332 (309–316).

The Interaction of Tradition and Technology 1970

Architectural discourses in 1970s Iran provide a useful ground for exploring questions of peripherality. Here, we draw upon the records of a Congress held in 1970, under the auspices of the Iranian government.

The 1970 Congress, entitled "The Interaction of Tradition and Technology",[7] was held in the historic Safavid capital of Isfahan.[8] It took place in the context of a period of economic prosperity, which witnessed rapid social change fuelled by the rapid increase in state oil revenue, the details of which are beyond the scope of this writing and are discussed by others. By the 1970s, transformations were apparent in the state's cultural policies and in the context of this chapter, its support and promotion of the fine arts and architecture, a personal passion of Queen Farah (Diba) Pahlavi who, before her marriage, had been an architecture student at the École Spéciale d'Architecture in Paris. To the religious and leftist opposition, the state-initiated suite of development and modernization plans, known as the White Revolution, represented a pandering to Western interests and a deviation from the Islamic traditions of the people.[9]

In this atmosphere in the 1970s, a series of architecture congresses were sponsored by the government, with both local participants and invited participants from Western and Eastern Bloc countries, as well as from Japan, India and Turkey. We have discussed the details of these congresses elsewhere, however, it is worth reiterating that their major concern was to find ways to reconcile the traditions and histories of developing societies such as Iran with modern progress. With hindsight, we can see that a driver for these congresses and the practical and educational responses that ensued (as discussed later), was finding "expressions" that straddled the traditional and the modern. The emphasis on tradition was made explicit in many Iranian delegates' presentations, but also in the

---

[7] Laleh Bakhtiar and Leila Farhad, eds., *The Interaction of Tradition and Technology: Report of the Proceedings of the First International Congress of Architects, Isfahan, 1970,* Tehran: Ministry of Housing and Development, 1970.

[8] Naqsh-e Jahan square and surrounding buildings were given UNESCO World Heritage status in 1979. See "Meidan Emam": https://whc.unesco.org/en/list/115.

[9] In 1963, in reaction to land reform and women's suffrage, two of the principles of the White Revolution, Khomeini, the future leader of the 1979 Islamic Revolution, called for an uprising that led to bloody suppression by the state, and thus marked what his Islamist followers would identify as the beginning of the Islamic Revolution.

choices of location and excursions of the congresses, in historic cities and monumental complexes. For example, Isfahan, which was in the 1970s the subject of intensive heritage studies, thus "served as a demonstration of the ideal, expressed by the conference title, of reconciling modern techniques with regionally authentic cultural forms."[10]

What becomes apparent in the records of the first conference (1970, Isfahan) is the divergence of views regarding architectural solutions and, in particular, how architectural expression could engage with tradition. Dr. Aptullah Kuran, the Turkish architectural historian and the first President of the Istanbul Boğazıcı University, spoke on the topic of "Tradition", as did Ludovico Quaroni, the renowned Italian architectural historian, architect and pedagogue. Kuran emphasized the need for the architect to interpret and build upon "his own cultural environment", producing modern architecture that was "imbued with indigenous characteristics, qualities and accents" but in accordance with universally accepted standards.[11] Kuran could have been talking about his Turkish contemporary, Sedad Hakki Eldem, cited as an exemplar of a regional form of modernism.[12] This resonates with Caplan's account of peripheral literary practices that attempted to bend the grammatical rules of expression in order to accommodate the spirit of local traditions.[13]

In the Iranian context, as the Minister for Development and Housing Kouros Amouzegar remarked, the Congress theme was an attempt to address problems born of liberal (and modernizing) economic and educational policies, and their repercussions for the field of architecture.[14]

[10] Ali Mozaffari and Nigel Westbrook, *Development, Architecture, and the Formation of Heritage in Late Twentieth-Century Iran*, Manchester: Manchester University Press, 2020, 60.

[11] Farhad and Bakhtiar, 1970, 48.

[12] On Sedad Hakkı Eldem, see for example Serena Acciai, *Sedad Hakki Eldem: An Aristocratic Architect and More*, Florence: Firenze University Press, 2018; Adam Himes, 'The Embedded Politics of Type: Sedad Hakkı Eldem and the Turkish House', *The Journal of Architecture*, 24:6 (2019), 756–777, https://doi.org/10.1080/13602365.2019.168 4972.

[13] Marc Caplan, *How Strange the Change: Language, Temporality, and Narrative Form in Peripheral Modernisms*, Stanford University Press, 2011, 25–51.

[14] Farhad and Bakhtiar, 1970, 16.

These remarks could, in retrospect, be characterized as reflecting an identity crisis in Iran. The Congress Chairman, Mohsen Foroughi,[15] noted the absence of a continuity at that time between traditional and contemporary architecture and raised the question of the extent to which the country's patrimony could continue to inform and motivate work in the present.[16] This problem was addressed by a number of the delegates, but would persist into, and through, the period of the Islamic Revolution.[17] In contrast, there was a strong traditionalist camp, spearheaded by Nader Ardalan, an American-Iranian architect and disciple of Seyyed Hossein Nasr,[18] who advocated a "return" to authentic Islamic traditions, a position that was echoed in the following decades by proponents of the Islamic Revolution. What kind of architectural expressions would these positions yield and to what extent could they be consonant with ideas of peripherality? Thus, there was addressed a central question pertaining to the extent to which modern Iranian architecture should emerge from its local cultural roots, and conversely how it might benefit from opening up to global cultural trends. Perhaps just as interesting is to speculate as to the degree to which these camps resonated with later Western positions that may be construed as sympathetic to peripheral conditions, and here we refer to critical regionalism which, as noted above, was theorized a decade later.

Was the emulation of traditional forms any more than a kind of window-dressing of essentially contemporary programmes—what we would now understand as historicist Postmodernism? Similarly, on what basis could contemporary architecture be considered "authentic"? Like the early modernists, was it possible for Iranian architects to derive

[15] Mohsen Foroughi was a prominent architect and Honorary Chair of the Architects' Institute, former Dean of the Faculty of Fine Arts, and an influential politician. He thus formed an effective intermediary between the monarchy and the profession.

[16] Farhad and Bakhtiar, 1970, 20.

[17] On drawing from the "lessons of the past" in the post-Revolution period, see Mozaffari and Westbrook, 'Forming a Future from the Past' In Mozaffari and Westbrook, 2020, 114–120.

[18] Seyyed Hossein Nasr is a noted scholar on Sufism and Islamic Studies. His background was in Science, gaining a Ph.D. in the History of Science at Harvard University. Upon returning to Iran in 1958, he taught in philosophy and Islamic Sciences at the University of Tehran, where he became Vice-Chancellor, and later became President of Aryamehr University (now Sharif University of Technology). He is a significant theoretician of the Traditionalist School of philosophy.

valid principles from their own traditional architecture? The Congress was addressing an issue of global concern, how cultures might benefit from development while retaining a sense of cultural identity, through the example of Iran, a country that sat on the periphery of Western modernism.

The debates sought at once to address ontological questions, such as what might constitute a tradition and what it might require in order to remain vital. On the one hand, for the German delegate Ungers, the tradition was characterized as engaged in a dialectic with historical change and thus both dynamic and evolving but also mutable.[19,20] On the other hand, for Ardalan and others, tradition was seen as a repository of timeless truths. Indeed Ardalan would codify the forms and symbolisms of this tradition in the co-written monograph, *The Sense of Unity*.[21] The American-trained Iranian Ardalan held his national architectural traditions to be founded upon deep cultural and spiritual roots, which needed to be learned from and interpreted in new works. Secondly, the debates engaged with questions of expression, how each of the above positions might be expressed spatially and architecturally. Thus, there was a divergence on how architects should deal with tradition. Perhaps the most subtle distinction was drawn by Aptullah Kuran, who distinguished between "tradition", the body of practices, both conscious and unconscious, which characterized a living culture, and "traditional", which he defined as the "classical" phase of a culture's development.[22] One could

[19] There is, however, a strand in the so-called rationalist movement of the 1970's that indeed sought the timeless and immutable—the analogous city of Aldo Rossi 1973, as seen in the first Milan architectural Triennale of that year. Rossi emphasised architectural autonomy and others, such as Giorgio Grassi defined rationalism in a Platonist vein, as a trace or impression of what is absent. Ungers had already pursued this line through theoretical projects that were based upon abstracted typologies that permitted analogy between new projects and historical precedents, a line of investigation that would culminate in the IBA programme in Berlin, of 197987.

[20] On the IBA, see, for example, Chris Charlesworth, Gernot and Johanne Nalbach, *Berlin Modern Architecture*, Berlin: Senatsverwaltung für Bau- und Wohnungswesen, 1989.

[21] See Nader Ardalan and Laleh Bakhtiar, *The Sense of Unity: The Sufi Tradition in Persian Architecture*, Chicago; London: The Universityy of Chicago press, 1974. In this book, the authors adopted the methods of urban formal analysis of Colin Rowe and others, in seeking to define the quintessential typologies and geometries of traditional Iranian cities and buildings.

[22] Farhad and Bakhtiar, 1970, 85.

maintain a tradition, but the traditional was of the past, a perfected phase that could not be authentically revived.

A similar, but blunter, assessment was given by Iran's Deputy Minister of Housing and Development and the Congress' Secretary-General Nasser Badie, who called for a contextually specific architecture, claiming that mass production and modernism had "dehumanised" architecture and caused its alienation from its natural and cultural context. Positing architecture as a means to maintain continuity with the past, he urged that

> … the city of yesterday must be preserved and maintained in the city of tomorrow, not as a souvenir of a past never again to return, but as the living proof of the artistic sensibilities of the men and of the culture which conceived and created it.[23]

Badie was thus, unlike Kuran, interpreting the heritage of the past not as something frozen in history, as the "traditional", but as a living tradition. His position can also be seen as a reaction against both modern and Western cultural influences. Iranian heritage was seen as something vital.

The question raised by these statements by Iranian architects is what the object was behind these appeals to traditions and the traditional. Could it be understood, to use Goodman's 1978 expression, as World Making—that is to say, imposing certain perceptual and conceptual orders and codes, a symbolic order to guide action in the world?—a kind of ethical framework that seems to speak to our identity, in the face of cosmopolitanism, globalism and genericity?

In concrete terms, what kind of worldly relations are suggested in a project like, for example, Ardalan's Iranian Centre for Management Studies in Tehran?[24] What are the social hierarchies, protocols and rules governing it? As we have discussed elsewhere, the design of the project organizes the dormitories in clusters on either side of what is an interpretation of the traditional Iranian Chahar Bagh, or fourfold garden defined by cross-axes:

---

[23] Farhad and Bakhtiar, 1970, 15.

[24] Mozaffari and Westbrook, 2020, 42, Fig. 1.3.

While Ardalan's project overtly references historical Iranian heritage sites, madrasas and princely gardens, the traditional forms conceal a modern educational programme, while also conveying an overt elitism.[25]

If we were to see Ardalan's output as peripheral modernism, then we would need to take note of not just the surface of the cultural production, which implies a certain invocation of past spatial rules, but also to recognize that in its depth, the work encourages or affirms a particular set of social relations, all of which, as it happens, are set against modernity, if the latter is seen as a move towards the secularization of society, and instead directed towards a return to the utopia of tradition. Here we see a contradiction. The cosmological unity of religious dogma imagines a world founded on what Goodman called "a universal or necessary beginning", thus by implication a utopia. "Worldmaking", in the context of modernity, however, necessitates something akin to drawing upon, juxtaposing, and reimagining the fragments of the past, *re-cognizing*, within the transient context of the present, as indeed the American delegate Louis Kahn seemed to be arguing.[26]

It is clear that, at this and the following two Iran Congresses, a number of non-Western delegates were asserting the need for their regional cultures to approach development and modernization in a manner that was consistent with both their material conditions and their cultural traditions, in what in some cases was "an identity politics of 'resistance'".[27] Kuran effectively argued that the tradition was dynamically evolving and the region existed in a condition of peripheral modernity, noting: Modernity is not about relinquishing cultural specificities in order to arrive at a common global thought, it means rather, that the architect combines his creative spirit and thought and feelings, which are coloured by his cultural

[25] Mozaffari and Westbrook, 2020, 41–45 (43).

[26] Nelson Goodman, *Ways of Worldmaking*, Hassocks: The Harvester Press, 1978, 6–7. Among the foreign Congress delegates, the American architect and educator Louis Kahn called on architects to derive inspiration for their work in the patrimony that surrounds them, mediated by the individual intuition of the designer. Despite the inherently universalizing nature of his design approach, his words served, however, to authenticate the position of those Iranians who were alarmed by the rapid changes of modernity and sought a return to the security of familiar traditions. In the following decades, this quest for authenticity would inform both a social upheaval—the Islamic Revolution—and the official discourse of architecture it espoused.

[27] Mozaffari and Westbrook, 2020, 37.

and social milieu with new materials and modern technology and present a good combination of them in the form of a building.[28]

Kuran's characterization of the refabrication of heritage as a dynamically evolving tradition was thus analogous to the argument we have raised elsewhere, that architects were creating heritage in the present, through the process of design[29]—significantly, like Ungers, he was arguing that tradition was a dynamic and historically immersive process. He went on to suggest that there may be a global culture emerging from the mixture and acknowledgement of different cultural sensibilities and forms of heritage. Quaroni, too, raised the possibility of a global style that is differentiated by its local manifestations in accordance with local traditions and a country's "inherent spirit,":

> Perhaps we are on the eve of a new era in which there will be a veritable world architecture with a few minor differences according to the country and its inherent spirit. Something will remain of each country, that which is vital...[30]

He speculated that perhaps tradition, in its internal sense, no longer existed. Rejecting attempts to imitate traditional motifs, he asserted that the historical relationship between urban culture and architecture was disappearing:

> ...Perhaps even the idea of tradition no longer exists in its inner reality. There is only a false tradition of superficial forms, cut up, compartmentalized, superimposed at will. It is a worldwide crisis.[31]

Also reflecting this argument for the inevitably destabilizing effects of modernization, Sardar Afkhami, a prominent Iranian practitioner and academic (and a 1963 graduate of the Paris École des BeauxArts), located the problems of contemporary architecture in the crisis of tradition and the social discontent arising from modernity, one that was, he argued,

---

[28] Farhad and Bakhtiar, 1970, 2.

[29] Mozaffari and Westbrook, 2020, 119: "citations of the past were attempts to conjure or invent from scratch memories of a tradition through the 'design of heritage'".

[30] Farhad and Bakhtiar, 1970, 57.

[31] Farhad and Bakhtiar, 1970, 57.

social and spiritual.[32] While traditional means and methods were no longer sufficient for today's problems, architecture could not be seen as a field upon itself. His comments were pointed at Traditionalists, like Ardalan and Badie, who advocated return to Islamic traditions of the past.

From this summary, two things are clear. Firstly, the world was seen in polarised terms, however, there were divergent interpretations of peripherality and the mode of existence and action it was seen to demand. Secondly, some of the dominant and later influential positions, may not be easily understood, or may even contradict, what we may understand now as peripheral modernism.

END OF AN ERA? THE ISLAMIC REVOLUTION AND THE RHETORIC OF CULTURAL TRANSFORMATION

[A]lthough I do not feel the same way towards it [Islam] as you, I would like to emphasize, more than you do yourself, your remark that Islam harbours, more than any other social powers of ideological alternatives in the third world (or, with your permission, the Near and Middle-East), both an anticolonialist capacity and an anti-western character ...[33] Frantz Fanon in a letter to the "red Shi'ite", Ali Shariati.

In 1979, the Islamic revolution took place in Iran with the wholehearted support of leftist groups. Under the new regime, the secularizing and Westernizing influences in Iranian society were to be purged from all

---

[32] Farhad and Bakhtiar, 1970, 60–61. Perhaps not surprisingly, Saradar Afkhami's words resonate with what Ali Mirsepassi relates as the Heideggerian spiritual crisis of the west, an idea that many Iranian intellectuals of the 1960's found appealing. See: Ali Mirsepassi, *Political Islam, Iran, and the Enlightenment: Philosophies of Hope and Despair*, Cambridge, New York: Cambridge University Press, 2011, 89.

This group of intellectuals "postulated resistance to deculturation and Westernization; they advanced a critique of Europe and the United States from a radical, populist, Islamic and Third Worldist perspective." Val Moghadam, 'Socialism or Anti-Imperialism? The Left and Revolution in Iran', *New Left Review* 166 (1987), 5–28.

Central to the Islamist self-perception was a false dichotomy between East and West. In its radical form, this would become a futile attempt at distinguishing between the local and the global. This was a line of thought articulated by nativist intellectuals. See: Jalal Al-Ahmad, *On the Service and Treachery of Intellectuals [in Persian]*, Tehran, Kharazmi Publishers, 1979.

[33] Frantz Fanon, letter to Shariati, 1961, in Frantz Fanon, *Alienation and Freedom*, London: Bloomsbury Academic, 2019, 668.

aspects of the society (we can reference my first book in the intro I give a thorough explanation of this). Any deviations from Islamic orthodoxies, including in all forms of artistic expression suspected of such deviation, were banned. Within the field of architecture, most of the leading pre-revolution architects, such as Seyhoun, Amanat, Ardalan and Kamran Diba, left the country. The challenge facing architects in the new cultural climate was how to develop forms of expression that were authentic to Iran's cultural traditions and Islamic identity.[34] But that was, and is, a big challenge, as modes of production were neither traditional nor Islamic (however the characterization is made), and per force, the response would have remained at a shallow depth of expression. In the immediate aftermath of the Revolution, emphasis was placed upon the social role of architecture; here, the fledgling leftist journal *Jame-eh va Memari* emphasized the need for Iran to shed itself of Western influence and collaboration.[35] Instead, the revolutionary Third World became a model.

This Cultural Revolution entailed the resignification of cultural fields like architecture, achieved in part by the Islamization of higher education, which necessitated a wholesale revision of pedagogy and a severe control of forms and sources of information, the closure of universities and the sacking of "ideologically suspect" academics.[36] In addition to suppressing

[34] Revolutionaries in general and Islamists in particular, argue that the monarchy forced people to abandon their authentic culture, traditions and customs, which were their source of innovation, turning them to pure consumers. See N. Roshannahad, *Enqelab-e-farhangidar Jomhuri ye Islami ye Iran [Cultural Revolution in the Islamic Republic]*, Tehran: Centre for Islamic Revolution Documents, 2004, 36–37.

[35] Shawhin Roudbari, Instituting Architecture: A History of Transnationalism in Iran's Architectural Profession, 1945–1995, in Gharipour 2016, 308–314.

[36] Roshannahad 2004, 30. For an example of this kind of rhetoric about intellectuals see: Masoud Khorram, *Identity [Persian: Hoviyyat]*, Tehran, Hayyan Cultural Publishing Institute, 1997. Fanon foreshadowed this position remarking that.

> The colonialist bourgeoisie, in its narcissistic dialogue, expounded by the members of its universities, had in fact deeply implanted in the minds of the colonized intellectual that the essential qualities remain eternal in spite of all the blunders men may make: the essential qualities of the West, of course. The native intellectual accepted the cogency of these ideas, and deep down in his brain you could always find a vigilant sentinel ready to defend the Greco-Latin pedestal.

potential student unrest, this served to cleanse universities of Westernizing forms of modernization and detraditionalization.[37] In a critique that was strangely reminiscent of Nasr's traditionalism, Islamist revolutionaries argued that the universities and their curricula were culturally displaced both from their social and historical context and from an authentic Islamic identity.[38] This emphasis on an authentic Iranian cultural identity became more pressing after Ayatollah Khomeini's Cultural Revolution of 1980–1983 (the period of university closures), a classic example of world-making,[39] in which diverse anticolonialist and traditionalist ideologies, some ironically from Western models, such as French traditionalism,[40] were drawn upon in synthesizing an ostensible cultural unity, a "world", through which emphasis was placed upon the "situatedness of knowledge and experience in relation to the dominant reading of world globalization".[41] This was reflected in the new national constitution which stated that:

> [the nation had] returned to the authentic Islamic worldview and intellectual positions... and was determined to establish its exemplary model society [...] based on Islamic criteria.[42]

The Supreme Leader, Ayatollah Khomeini, in decreeing the Cultural Revolution on 12 June 1980, set out ten key objectives.[43] Two of these, affecting Iranian architecture, were:

[37] Roshannahad, 2004, 88, 106–107.

[38] Roshannahad, 2004, 114–118.

[39] Goodman, 1978, 14.

[40] Mozaffari and Westbrook, 2020, 39.

[41] Waever and Tickner cited by David L. Blaney and Tamara A. Trownsell, 'Recrafting International Relations by Worlding Multiply', *International Relations* 18: 70, 2021, 45–62 at 47.

[42] Constitution of the Islamic Republic of Iran 1979, cited by Mozaffari and Westbrook, 2020, 116.

[43] In March 1980, in his first New Year message after the Islamic Revolution, Khomeini called for a revolution in the higher education system of the country. This revolution would aim at "turning universities to a healthy environment for flourishing of sublime Islamic sciences." Subsequently, all universities were close down in 5 June 1980 and on June 12th, Khomeini decreed Cultural Revolution. The event would be post rationalised as a remedy for the lacking contextual specificity and applicability (usefulness) of knowledge in higher education under the previous regime. See: Roshannahad, Cultural Revolution in Islamic Republic, 102–106.

1. Expanding the influence of Islamic culture in different facets of the society and the reinforcement of cultural revolution and the elevation of popular culture, and
2. Cleansing scientific and cultural environments of materialist thought and rejection of expressions and effects of 'westoxification', an anti-Western term popularised before the revolution,[44] from the cultural sphere of society.

These developments were highly consequential in all fields, including architecture. at universities, a new group of ideologically committed academics and graduates came to power and in the profession, architects were prevented from forming a professional association until 1992 (Roudbari 2016, 318). In this situation, compounded by the economic effects of the drawn-out war with Iran, both architectural pedagogy in the schools, and the professional work of practices became introverted and anachronistic. Rather than adopting a critique of mainstream modernity from the periphery, this was an inward-looking and nostalgic fundamentalism.

(Post-)Revolutionary Architecture, the Persistence of a Discourse of Regional Authenticity in the Islamic Republic

In architectural production and education, global centre–periphery relations were revisited, but without much critical reflection and with little innovation. As we have discussed elsewhere (Mozaffari and Westbrook 2020) one of the first post-Revolution architectural events was the holding of national housing competitions in 1985. Divided into projects for various cities with different population and ethnic compositions, this was an opportunity for demonstrating the principles of Islamic housing/habitat and urban form. (Mozaffari and Westbrook 2020, 120–125). The

---

[44] 'Westoxification' or 'Occidentosis' was an idea initially discussed by the Heideggerian philosopher Ahmad Fardid but later popularized by Al-e Ahmad in his famous book of the same name. It designates a kind of 'disease' that destroys the culture from within but is inflicted upon Iran (and other countries) by the West and its culture of domination. For a succinct treatment of the concept in the intellectual discourse of 1960s–1970s Iran see: Brad Hanson, 'The "Westoxication" of Iran: Depictions and Reactions of Behrangi, al-e Ahmad, and Shariati', *International Journal of Middle East Studies*, 15: 1, Feb. 1983, 1–23.

results were collated into a publication supplemented by essays on the nature of an authentic Islamic architecture. Emphasis was placed upon the need for Iranian housing to represent "Islamic and cultural values", a statement that resonated with some of the pronouncements at the 1970 Congress. Authors advocated for the past to inform the present, in the construction of contemporary forms that both reflected Islamic principles, such as gender segregations, and reflecting their interpretation of Iranian cultural identity. In response, many of the entries incorporated elements common to traditional environments, such as central courtyards, in some cases with a *qibla* orientation, private secluded courtyards, and roof terraces. However, also evident was the influence of European nostalgic postmodernism.[45] In fact, we see in these projects two forking directions: on the one hand, an ideologically laden mimicry of traditional typologies, and on the other, stylistic tendencies that were indistinguishable from post-1980 Western practice. In neither direction was there a critical regional stance vis-à-vis the cultural centres.

However, the widespread promotion of an Iranian identity in architecture did not occur until the inception of the journal *Abadi* ('Development', but also "village" or "settlement") in 1991. It was created by the Ministry for Housing and Urbanism, under President Hashemi Rafsanjani. In its first issue (Summer 1991), the journal's editor, Seyyed Reza Hashemi outlined the need for reforms in architectural education, and for practical solutions to pressing problems. The Journal was to be professional in tone and character, rather than theoretical or political.[46] To promote the profession, Hashemi proposed the institution of awards to promote higher standards of design. His editorials reflected the agenda of the Cultural Revolution, to enforce a singular, state-sanctioned ideological position upon all educational institutions, and reaffirmed the place of instrumental rationality that had been advocated by Islamic modernists who argued for the compatibility between Islam and modern scientific endeavours.

---

[45] For example, the scheme by Ali Akbar Saremi and Tajeer Architects for Isfahan housing bears a strong resemblance to the housing designed by Rob Krier for the Berlin IBA IInternationale Bauaustellung. See Mozaffari and Westbrook, 2020, 126–127 and Fig. 4.3.

[46] Seyed Reza Hashemi, 'Foreword', *Abadi*, 1: 1, 1991, 2–3.

...since we played no part in the international transformations of industrialisation in architecture, we failed to preserve and transfer the traditions of that rich and magnificent and humane patrimony (of past architecture) to a contemporary civilisation.[47]

Hashemi's words do indeed suggest an abdication of the possibility of dialogue, and seemingly a complete rupture in, and with, tradition, one that is perhaps beyond repair. But such abdication of dialogue also amounts to the impossibility of a peripheral condition that is based on critique, agency and exchange, and a conscious choice of cosmologies and forms of expression. Instead, taken at face value, this appears to suggest two possibilities: either a complete rupture with the past or a total return to it.

THE COMPETITION FOR THE IRANIAN ACADEMIES

Alongside the *Abadi* awards programme, the government promoted a series of architectural competitions, returning to the role of design as a representation of cultural identity that had been promoted in the 1986 housing competition. This was the beginning of the so-called "Constructivity Period", an era of economic quasi-liberalism ushered in by the government in the aftermath of the eight-year Iran-Iraq war. The first of these, which we have discussed elsewhere,[48] was a revival of a pre-Revolution proposal for the National Academies (Farhangestan) for the hilly site of Abbas Abad in Tehran, half-way between the historic centre to the south and Tajrish to the north (Mozaffari and Westbrook 2020, 198–206). The three Academies (Science, Medicine and Persian Literature) were located north of the site of the planned National Library, another of the Pahlavi-era projects that had been the subject of a 1976 competition, but not revived until a 1995 competition.[49]

---

[47] This remains a well-known rhetoric about contemporary Iranian history, one that blames nineteenth century Qajar dynasty and its softness toward European colonialism in particular, for the country's ills. In such a narrative, Iran would have had its own indigenous modernity.

[48] Mozaffari and Westbrook, 2020, 198–206.

[49] (Unknown author), 'Competition for the Design of the Iranian Academies Complex', *Abadi*, 3: 12, 1994, 2–3. This was despite the official announcement that, based on their professional standing and experience, up to 18 would receive a small fee to cover basic costs. See: 'Competition for the Design of the Iranian Academies Complex', *Abadi*, 50.

The prize-winning projects are a snapshot of the dominant tendencies in official Iranian architecture at the time. Despite the decade of official isolation from the West, in the context of the official stance of *Gharbzadegi*, there were still networks of influence dating back to pre-Revolution education abroad. Thus, for example, Ali Akbar Saremi had trained at the University of Pennsylvania, initially under Louis Kahn. Seyyed Hadi Mirmiran was a graduate of The Faculty of Fine Arts at the University of Tehran under Houshang Seyhoun, but had substantial experience collaborating with foreign architects, for example on the project for the steel town at the Arya Mehr Steel Complex where he collaborated with the Soviet Giprogor office.[50] Hossein Sheikh Zeineddin also studied under Seyhoun, who brought to his teaching and practice an extraordinary synthesis of Iranian tradition and contemporary Western architecture, with elements of Brutalism.[51] Darab Diba was trained at the University of Geneva and the Royal Academy of Fine Arts in Liège, and was closely connected to the Aga Khan Award for Architecture.[52] Furthermore, a number of other senior architectural educators had studied at Italian universities.[53] There were, then, personal networks that transcended official barriers, and thus permitted a limited degree of interpretation, even spoliation, and transformation within a local context. The collections of university libraries were beginning to be replenished, and private copies of books were photocopied and circulated. In consequence of this architectural *samizdat*, for example, architects drew from the works of James Stirling, and ideas developed by Rob Krier in his typological studies, *Stadtsraum* (Urban Space) and *Elements of Architecture*. It seems that in some cases the leftist discourses of resistance common to, for example, the Italian universities were influential upon what could be described as a search for the expression of a regional identity, perhaps a consciously peripheral position. It could be said that the historicist and postmodernist underpinnings of the "new" scholarship, for example, the writings of the Kriers, Colin Rowe and Aldo Rossi, and indeed characteristic of the leftist-driven cultural project of "The Presence of the Past", the

---

[50] Hamidreza Soufiani, 'Planning Modernity, the Company Town in Modern Iran', PhD thesis uwa, 2020.

[51] Mozaffari and Westbrook, 2022.

[52] https://www.akdn.org/it/architecture/master-jury/10596 (accessed 31 May 2022).

[53] Javid, 2021.

title of the 1980 Venice Architectural Biennale,[54] were seen to be suitable to the cultural and political demands of the country at the time.[55] Given the contestational ideology of the regime and its cultural spokesmen, the question arises as to how a critical position might be established in architectural practice and theory, in what ways might difference as a condition be negotiated and what might be the means and conduits for any such negotiation.

The competition for the Iranian Academies marked a watershed for architectural discourses in post-revolution Iran. The Abadi editor Hashemi openly admitted that in this period Iran had lacked an open debate on architectural tendencies. While this may have been occurring outside official channels, within the press and the universities, discussions were strictly controlled, as was political activity. Hashemi noted that activity had been restricted to what he labelled translations of non-Iranian architects and critics in an unfamiliar language.[56] This reference to "language" also ties such discourse back to a dependence on then-contemporary Western architectural theory, in which a linguistic model was paramount. Within the universities, the curriculum was similarly strictly controlled and standardized, with projects set in line with official dogma. So, the competition promised to open new ground. For Hashemi, the Academies Competition was the first time that Iranian architects were entrusted to design such a complex and significant project.[57]

The competition entries for the Academies were published across two issues of the *Abadi* journal (Volumes 12 and 13), together with substantial analysis by the judges and by *Abadi* itself. This effectively amounted to the first substantive architectural discourse since the Housing Competitions, and certainly the first on civic architecture since the Revolution. In this respect, the exchanges over the projects are revealing for what they

[54] Paolo Portoghesi, ed., *The Presence of the Past*, First International Exhibition of Architecture. La Biennale di Venezia 1980. Architectural Section. Catalogue, 1980.

[55] In this period, some Western pre-war books supportive of a traditionalist viewpoint, such as Amos Rapaport's book *House, Form and Culture* began to be translated into Persian, while the Agha Khan Award for Islamic architecture were taken more seriously by practitioners and academics alike. In conjunction with this, Ardalan and Bakhtiar's 1973 book, *A Sense of Unity*, continued to be read and was used in architectural pedagogy by professors such as Mahdi Hodjat. Anecdotal evidence suggests that this book informed Iranian architects' approaches to design and the formation of architectural styles and taste.

[56] Seyed Reza Hashemi, 'Editorial', *Abadi*, 3: 12, 1994, 2–3.

[57] Seyed Reza Hashemi, 'Editorial', *Abadi*, 3: 12, 1994, 2–3.

reveal about the concern for what might constitute Iranicity, and for the perceived need for the architecture to be of its place and cultural specificity—that is to say, a concern for its authenticity. While the post-war modern architecture of Japan, a model for many Third World developing nations, had been able to develop its own sophisticated synchresis of local and international influences, to such an extent that it was reciprocally influencing the First World, Iranian architectural development had been heavily affected by the flight of its leading architects, notably Seyhoun, Ardalan and Diba, as well as many leading professors, as well as the policy of self-sufficiency, or autarky, necessitated by Western economic sanctions. Within these constraints, architectural discourse and expression were arguably repeating models superseded in the global West, while its emphasis on national identity and Islamicity reflected deep-seated anxieties.

Publication of the submissions in *Abadi* did, in fact, stimulate debates on architecture, tradition, and national identity among architects and academics. These arguments for a regionally and culturally specific architecture, advocated by critics like Darab Diba, also had echoes of similar positions that had been expressed at the 1970 Congress by speakers such as Ardalan and Badi'. Was this a kind of "suspended animation" or did such discourse reflect a kind of continuity that persisted despite, or possibly because of, official discourses? This persistence was apparent in the comments made by jury members, which emphasized, on the one hand, "cultural aspects", as had the judges of the 1986 housing Competitions, but also aspects that were also common to international modernist discourse, such as simplicity in design.

The first prize was awarded to Naqsh-e Jahan Pars group (the office of Seyyed Hadi Mirmiran) on the basis of what the judges thought were "...simplicity in expression, clarity in design and spatial organisation" but also for its monumental urban qualities. The scheme was indeed monumental. A platform laid out like an ancient mastaba tomb rises up out of the hillside, lying in an east-west orientation, its flanks fronted by zigzagging staircases and ramps rising to the north, redolent of the "Stairs of All Nations" at Persepolis, and provides entry into the interior of the platform, which actually contains an arrangement of halls and offices facing a sunken courtyard. At the western end, a shallow dome rises above a low square plinth, and to the east, a gigantic double portal frames the early morning light, creating a silhouetted profile on the horizon that resembles that of the tomb of Cambyses I at Pasargadae. The project is thus both a singular image and a collage of fragmented forms, nostalgically recollecting a vanished past.[58]

Of the other premiated projects, the second prize went to Tajir (Ali Akbar Saremi) for what they judged to be its "...new expression and the creation of consistent and flowing spaces". The third place was awarded to the project of Ivan Hasht-Behesht (Darab Diba) for its "...rational distribution of spaces and simplicity of relationships".[59] This project, in retrospect, is the closest to the architectural language of pre-Revolution Iran. The plan, clearly influenced by Louis Kahn's Dakha Assembly building, uses primary geometric forms- circles, squares and triangles, and a centralized composition. But at a more detailed level, we see abstracted Persian ribbed domes, recalling Safavid and Qajar examples, the same composition of circles, squares and diagonals being reused in several great windows. The judges awarded fourth place to the Bavand office (Iraj Kalantari) for its "...balanced combination of vernacular and modern architectural elements", while fifth place went to the Memar-Naqsh group for "...their attention to cultural and functional [design] aspects".[60]

Regionalist Rhetoric

How can these projects be analysed in relation to the theme of "Peripheral Modernisms"? In analysing these projects, we can realize the modalities of peripherality at work in the architectural context of the time.

The first tendency, articulated by the Mirmiran project, suggested a typological essentialism that ascribed a trans-historical, timeless and essential quality to Iranian architectural typologies and spatial configurations such as the dome.[61] The symbolism of such elements was thought to be immutable, presumably enabling them to be used for the same desired effect. But traditions adapt to change in order to revitalize, otherwise the immutable tradition is as good as dead. The possibility of a living

---

[58] Saman Sayar, 'Assimilating the Authentic with the Contemporary: The Work of Hadi Mirmiran 1945–2006', *Architectural Design*, 82: 3, 2012, 80–87.

[59] Mozaffari and Westbrook 2020, Figs. 6.17 and 6.18.

[60] (Unknown author), 'Competition for the Design of the Iranian Academies Complex', *Abadi* 3: 12, 1994, 49–50, 49.

[61] (Unknown author), 'Architectural Competition for the Design of the Iranian Academies Complex: Introducing Winning Schemes', *Abadi*, 4: 13, 1994, 4–17.

tradition arguably implies an ongoing discursive exchange and interaction between the centres and the periphery, through which both are, over time, transformed. In this regard, Frampton's interpretation of Critical Regionalism, its shortcomings notwithstanding, contains validity.[62] The bedrock of his theory, which is the active and conscious adaptation, within the periphery, of foreign forms and techniques, as indeed many of the architects he identifies, such as Alvaro Siza or Dimitri Pikionis, have attempted, permits their grounding within a new, hybrid context. In this sense, this form of regionalism is not wedded to any mythology of immutable tradition. On the other hand, the deployment of a semiotics of motifs and elements can be decontextualizing. The reliance on a discourse of authenticity, as, in hindsight, appears to have driven the Mirmiran project, freezes meanings and motifs—past and present are conflated outside historical time and space. This blurring of the boundaries between traditional and modern iconography effectively constitutes decontextualization, much like Western Post-Modernism. We have suggested above that the project draws upon ancient typologies and affective forms of Persian archaeological fragments.

But the monumental design, in its combination of the typological elements of courtyard, dome, gateway, and platform, is both reminiscent of certain Western Rationalist projects of the 1970s, and of the monumental forms of late Modernism, such as Oscar Niemeyer's National Congress of Brazil. The ultimate driver is a formal and geometrical order that, rather than internalizing past masterpieces, as Quaroni had advocated in 1970, reproduces and juxtaposes their motifs in a historicist pastiche. This is arguably an ungrounded postmodernist formal semiotics rather than a critique of Western discourses from the margins.

In the second-placed project by Tajir architects (Ali Akhbar Saremi and Taghi Radmard), a "campus" is defined by straight and curving boundary walls incorporating a curving pathway. Within the campus, a series of discrete forms—a square volume surmounted by a circular drum, two shallowly vaulted, rectangular flanking forms, and finally, the main

---

[62] Notable critiques of Frampton's version of 'Critical Regionalism are: Alan Colquhoun, 'Kritik am Regionalismus', *Werk, Bauen und Wohnen*, 3, 1993, 45–52, Keith Eggener, 'Placing Resistance: A Critique of Critical Regionalism', *Journal of Architectural Education*, 55: 4, 2002, 228–237; and Fredric Jameson, *The Seeds of Time*, New York: Columbia University Press, 1994, cf. 183–205.

block, centred upon an Iwan (traditional veranda)like opening, are organized along a central axis that leads to a large rectangular courtyard, or *meidan*. The generally skilful composition combines what are familiar local forms with, arguably, Western case studies—the great drum of Stockholm City Library by Gunnar Asplund, for example, and more closely, Arata Izosaki's Los Angeles' Museum of Contemporary Art, a building opened to the public in 1986, which combines a similarly bricolaged composition and similar forms—vaulted rectangular halls, and facades gridded with rectangular windows. In turn, the latter could be seen as a reprise of Isozaki's use of the grip and vaulted forms at the Gunma Prefecture Museum of 1974, and his similar use of bricolage at the Tsukuba Civic Centre of 1983. Here, it should be noted that at the time Japan, along with India, were cultures that were held up, since pre-revolution times, as models for emulation, for their success in marrying cultural customs and modernity.

Here, it is as if one peripheral culture draws upon the products of another. in fact, in a personal conversation with Ali Mozaffari in the early 1990s, Saremi expressed bewilderment in attempting to make sense of what was unfolding in the global centres of architectural innovation and in the multiplicities of architectural language, which "we do [did] not understand." Admitting his pursuit of contemporaneity in this period, he mentioned that much of the postmodern designs that he and his contemporaries experimented with, looked "dated on paper even as they were drawn".

Darab Diba's third-placed project represents another tendency; the project grounds itself in the assertion of architectural principles that are supposedly inherent to traditional Iranian vernacular building. In his presentation, he borrowed his cousin Kamran Diba's archetypal diagrams used for Shushtar to assert a basis in, firstly, the traditional Iranian courtyard house centred on the walled courtyard, and secondly, the Persian *Chahar Bagh* fourfold garden layout, with its twin axes. Thus, the explanation of the project asserts a cultural continuity between the ancient and mediaeval past, and the present. Diba claimed to have studied traditional Iranian architecture to find its "...timeless artistic richness," and, in particular, traditional Iranian geometric "science"—this was expressed in a diagram that separates the material world, of the elements, light and darkness, and the spiritual, intellectual world. This Platonic discussion was supplemented by recourse to modern architectural exemplars—including some of the architects who attended the Iran Congresses of the 1970s.

But as noted above, the overwhelming reference project seems to have been Louis Kahn's Dakha Assembly project. But, in hindsight, the project suffers from the same placelessness of Kahn's project. Despite Diba's apparently genuine concern for authentic cultural identity, his design approach suffers from an inherent contradiction. While the architect assumed the possibility of a pure and authentic architectural language, this was sought through multiple, and inevitably hybrid sources. The contradiction is apparently overcome by locating authentic meaning in abstract formal and geometrical relations, the same archetypal and mathematical orders that underlay Kahn's later projects, the universality of which renders the very question of local identity invalid.

Kalantari and the Bavand office displayed a fourth tendency that sought an authentic expression through an eclectic citation of historic vernacular forms.[63] The historicist design was, in its organizational hierarchy, reminiscent of traditional cities. At the heart of the project was a tower, containing the book stacks, but hardly practical. The tower sat in a courtyard and was accessed across a sunken court by four bridges, accentuating the analogy with a mediaeval keep. In turn, the courtyard was contained by four walls of walkways, with circular towers marking the corners, and behind which were located the academies' offices. This organization is vaguely reminiscent of traditional citadels such as those in Shiraz, Birjand but notably Manujan castle, with its slender tower inside the enclosing walls. Kalantari's typological reference to the medieval Islamic city and his playful use of its architectural motifs, while essentially postmodernist, accords with one of the possibilities discussed in the 1970 Congress by Kuran, that architects should combine their culturally specific creative spirit with modern building technologies, although here, culture was essentialized into morphological and formal citations of past monuments.

The fifth tendency was apparent in the project by the Memar-Naqsh group, the project that would subsequently be chosen for construction. The principal designer was Kambiz Haji Qassemi, who, aside from his practice, is an expert on traditional Iranian architecture at Shahid Beheshti University. Qassemi's design was based upon a loose grid of three square-planned courtyard structures, comprising the three academies, grouped around a central, rectangular courtyard centred upon a water basin, and conforming to a strict bi-axial symmetry. The rather cumbersome

---

[63] Competition for the Design of the Iranian Academies Complex, 14.

appearance of the facades was not improved by decorative vaults placed centrally to mark the axes. This organization was supposedly designed with reference to the geometrical relations, axiality and central courtyards found in the traditional desert architecture of Iran. On paper, the design approached the expression of authentic identity by the faithful reproduction of traditional geometrical relations and patterns such as axiality and central courtyards and as such, it was a direct reflection of the official projections of national and Islamic identity. In reality, however, as evidenced in the constructed Academies complex, the outcome resembles a period of Western Postmodernist historicism, the short-lived phenomenon that took hold after the 1980 *Presence of the Past* exhibition at the Venice Architectural Biennale. This tendency had its roots in the turn to research into historic architecture and urban design in Italian universities, a reaction against the unbridled commercial speculation of the Late-Modern period in Italy. It then took root in London at the Architectural Association, before spreading globally. Ironically, this movement had its origins in Marxist social realism, rather than an embrace of religiously inspired tradition. In explaining his project, Qassemi claimed that his office sought to attain order, clarity and simplicity in the design, however, these normative principles also recall early modernist creeds rather than the organic basis of traditional Iranian architecture.

Despite their different approaches, the above projects had some commonalities. For example, almost all—with the exception of Kalantari's, were based on abstract geometrical relations. Furthermore, they seemed to have located sources for inspiration in the distant Iranian past conflated in the present time, just as Kahn had invited all to do in 1970 at the Isfahan Congress:

> Tradition can be said to be the result of an inspiration which has lasting value as long as the original inspiration can be felt. The inspirations are born out of a will to be, which develops from man coming in contact with the marvel of the means manifest in the mountains, in the water, in the atmosphere. It is somehow a meeting on a threshold between a way of silence and light.[64]

---

[64] Louis Kahn in Farhad and Bakhtiar, 1970, xiii.

The approach of these architects was consonant with the rising trend of Postmodernist historicism in Western architecture, in which historical time was flattened into synchronicity, and with the juxtaposition of elements of the centre and the periphery, and of different elements of the archaic and the contemporary, that Harootunian has identified as characteristic of peripheral modernity, "in which all societies shared a common reference provided by global capital and its requirements".[65] It is also apparent that certain consistencies exist between pre- and post-revolutionary discourses in architecture as the same set of questions in relation to architectural identity have persisted, emerging as "revenants" in the present. As Harootunian puts it:

> ... these ghosts of a surviving past—the premodern culture of reference—return from a place out of time or a different temporality to haunt and disturb the historical present, to trouble the stable boundaries between past and present, subject and object, interior and exterior.[66]

But while these premiated projects can, as we have demonstrated, be linked back to what Stern in 1980 labelled a "traditional postmodernism",[67] can they, as the Aga Kahn Awards attempted to do for the non-Western projects it premiated in its 1985 awards round, be linked to Critical Regionalism?[68] In this regard, the recent revisiting by Giamarelos of Critical Regionalism in the context of Postmodernism is highly topical:

> [C]ritical regionalism [was] the first sustained attempt to resist and provincialise these 'central' constructs of postmodern architecture in the 1980s

---

[65] Harry Harootunian, *History's Disquiet: Modernity, Cultural Practice, and the Question of Everyday Life*, New York: Columbia University Press, 2000, 163.

[66] Harry Harootunian, 'Some Thoughts on Comparability and the Space–Time Problem', *Boundary 2*, 32: 2, 2005, 23–52 (47).

[67] Robert Stern, cited by Stylianos Giamarelos, *Resisting Postmodern Architecture: Critical Regionalism before Globalization*, London: UCL Press, 2021, 18.

[68] Powell, 1985, 58–59. Although the symposium focused on regionalism in architecture, and three Western regionalist proponents, including Kenneth Frampton, were invited speakers, there was no consensus, and some of the non-Western delegates such as the Indian delegate Romi Khosla, rejected Critical Regionalism, Khosla emphasizing the need for "Asian consciousness" rather than Western rationalism.

by foregrounding the architecture of 'peripheral' sites and practices within Western architectural historiography.[69]

In his reading, Critical Regionalism was self-consciously peripheral. Indeed Frampton, in a 1984 essay argued that

> Critical Regionalism has to be understood as a marginal practice, one which, while it is critical of modernization, nonetheless still refuses to abandon the emancipatory and progressive aspects of the modern architectural legacy.[70]

Architects like the subjects of Giamarelos' recent (2021) book, the Greek office of Atelier 66, typify Frampton's position, drawing upon the "lessons" from the architectural centres, or in this case, their emissaries, then "creolized" them by syncretically combining them with local landscapes, practices and idioms. Jameson has noted that, for all its embrace of the peripheral cultures, Critical Regionalism was linked to the Western realities of technology and modernity, as opposed to "the populist or cultural-nationalist, Third World, and anti-Western or anti-modern responses with which we are familiar". His description fits the projects we have described which, for all their ascription of local meaning to familiar global languages, appear tied to Harootunian's "ghosts of a surviving past". But the question remains, is there any element of the critical here, a critique of globalizing hegemony as Frampton might term it? Or is it a case of a self-mystifying lifeworld?

THE REGIONALIST DISCOURSE AS AN INSTANCE OF PERIPHERAL MODERNISMS

Is it possible to understand and interpret these projects as instances of peripheral modernity? For Harootunian,

---

[69] Giamarelos, 2021, 10.

[70] Kenneth Frampton, 'Critical Regionalism: Modern Architecture and Cultural Identity', ch. 5 in Frampton, *Modern Architecture: A Critical History*, London; New York: Thames and Hudson, 2007, 314–327.

> [P]eripheral modernity (...) explains the encounter between a global modernity under the aegis of capitalism, and local cultures with traditional relations, patterns and practices that continue to maintain a residual existence.[71]

In their encounter with the centres of the modern capitalist world, he argues that places within the peripheries have experienced an "intersection between the new and the residual stemming from a different time, histories, and cultural conventions" and this produced peripheral, rather than alternative and thus resistant, modernities. This is not dissimilar to certain discourses of "critical regionalism", and yet, the act of adaptation is too often misinterpreted as resistance. From the cited projects, one can adduce a characteristic regionalist discourse, a nativism, that was shaping up as the preferred establishment style of the Islamic republic.[72] We have elsewhere referred to the critique by 1970 Congress delegates Ludovico Quaroni and Georges Candilis of what they termed "false tradition": "the appearance of traditional forms, motifs and patterns of geometrical relations [deployed] as an ideological veil concealing modern programmes [that are] inconsistent with them".[73] This is consistent with Harootunian's reference to the ghosts of the past haunting the present, what he refers to, citing Ernst Bloch, as "contemporary non-contemporaneousness" (*Gleichzeitigkeit der Ungleichzeitigen*).[74]

In the intellectual climate of the Academies competition, as in the comments by Iranian architects at the 1970 Congress, one can discern what sets it apart from the discourse of Critical Regionalism—precisely a lack of critical perspective. Looking back, it is evident that none of the major and promoted Academies entries advocated or pursued what

---

[71] Ali Mozaffari and Nigel Westbrook 'The (Unfinished) Museum at Pasargadae', In *World Heritage in Iran: Perspectives on Pasargadae*, edited by Ali Mozaffari, Farnham, Surrey: Ashgate, 2014, 197–224 (220).

[72] While other Iranian scholars have observed the flourishing of different strands of regionalism in Iran, under labels such as traditionalism, *culturalisme*, or nativism, none have explored the political imperative in shaping and supporting this movement. For examples refer to: Amir Bani Masoud, *Iranian Contemporary Architecture*, Tehran Honar-e Memari Publications, 2010; and Sayyed Mohsen Habibi, *Intellectual Trends in the Contemporary Iranian Architecture and Urbanism (1979–2003)*, Tehran: Cultural Research Bureau, 2007.

[73] Mozaffari and Westbrook, 2020, 206.

[74] Harootunian, 2005, 49, 51.

could be characterized as a new worldmaking approach, or one that might engage with the world in any consciously peripheral and critical fashion.

While the outcomes appear to have been serious attempts to engage with a local cultural landscape, a regional identity, none appears to have attempted to decompose, recombine or invert Western models in the formation of a local "language" that constitutes Goodman's conception of "worldmaking".[75] In its absence there were, again the two forking paths of mimicry or repetition.

This lack of critical perspective hints at a shortage of doctrinal thinking, of schools of thought capable of engaging with the past and present, and of deciphering trends and events. It is also an indication that, perhaps, tradition as an evolving interaction between culture, society, land and history is dead. After all, criticism works within sets of doctrinal traditions, be they implicit (practically established as a matter of practice), or explicit. Indeed, as Paz notes, it is the "characteristic feature of modernity" that constantly contrasts the new with the old and in this constant contrast, the continuity of tradition is constituted.[76] The lack of criticism points at a foundational displacement—an intellectual failure. But this situation was a product of the Islamic Revolution—since the 1970s, Iranian intellectuals and ideologues had been bewildered by ineluctable modernity, and remained trapped in a peculiar position where they identified themselves as the colonized, thus appropriating, often unknowingly, anti-enlightenment Western discourses of Traditionalism in seeking an authentic position.

The competition entries presented here indicate that, despite the passage of time, and Western architecture having moved on, many Iranian architects and theorists persisted with the fetishization of traditional forms and motifs, a cultural nationalism that raised up the indigenous as authentic. This was neither a "Cultural Revolution", an act of resistance to the perceived surrender to Western values at the time of the Congresses, and at the time of the Competitions, but instead can be understood as in large part a continuation of a discourse first articulated in the Isfahan Congress of Architects in September 1970, indicating that cultural transformations have a life of their own, one which does not necessarily accord with political ruptures. The appearance in the 1970s

---

[75] Goodman, 1978, 7–17.

[76] Octavio Paz, *Alternating Currents*, New York: Arcade Publishing, 1964, 17–19.

of the Traditionalist doctrines of Seyyed Hossein Nasr and his followers has simply hinted affirmatively at their exile from the past. No matter how warmly and enthusiastically they might have been taken on board—as they were after the Revolution—the result remained lifeless. In so doing, they failed to recognize the global context of their condition, that of a peripheral form of modernity that was unavoidably imbricated in global politics, economy and culture. Thus, after several decades, architects and intellectuals were left confused about their place in the world, and thus about their sense of ownership in cultural productions such as architecture.

Meanwhile, in the place of the older generation's "anxiety of origins", in the younger generation of architects there is arguably a sense of nihilism characterized by a decline in interest in place and identity, and in the inevitable reopening to the world, a superficial and formal appropriation of foreign trends, and a loss of connection with their past, an amnesia that suggests their alienation from the local cultural context. This nihilism is yet another quintessentially modern experience.[77]

What was espoused as the true path has ultimately proved to be a voice at the margins.

Acknowledgements This chapter is part of a larger suite of research on Iranian heritage, architecture, and identity. It has been generously funded by the Australian Research Council (grant number DE170100104) and a Research Development Award (2012) funded by the University of Western Australia. The writing was carried out at the Centre for Muslim States and Societies (UWA) and the Alfred Deakin Institute for Citizenship and Globalisation (Deakin University). The authors hereby acknowledge the support of Centre for Muslim States and Societies (CMSS).

The authors are grateful to Mr. Bijan Shafei, a fellow researcher and colleague for supplying a copy of the proceedings of the Isfahan Congress and Mr. Afshin Taslimi for obtaining archival materials as well as the anonymous reviewers whose comments helped improve the work.

---

[77] This assertion is based on a small sample of field survey and interviews carried out in Iran by Ali Mozaffari with the generation of architects who were educated after the Cultural Revolution.

INDEX

A

Abadi ('Development') journal, 166, 178, 179, 181
Adeyemi periphery (semi-periphery), 22
Adorno, Theodor, 25, 26
Adriatic, 65, 69, 70
Africa, 16, 31, 33
Agamben, Giorgio, 51, 52
Alexandrov, Grigorii, 130
Alighieri, Dante, 69
Alter, Richard, 93
'amalgamation', 30
Amaral, Tarsila do, 143, 148, 149, 154
Ameel, Lieven, 78
Americas, the, 54
Amerindian(s), 158
Amir, Samir, 23
Anderson, Perry, 22
Andrade, Mário de, 143, 144, 149, 156, 159
Andrade, Oswald de, 143, 149, 150, 157

Anglo-Irish, 84, 91, 93–95, 97
Anthropophagy, 159
Anti-Alien Laws, 103
Apih, Elio, 74
Appiah, Kwame Anthony, 29
Aquapolitical Solutions, 113
Aragon, Louis, 133
Architecture, 94
Ardalan, Nader, 169–172, 174, 175, 182
Asia, 16
Australian modernism, 101, 104, 115
'Australianness', 104
Austro-Hungarian empire, 15, 21, 64, 65

B

Bahri, Deepika, 30
Bakhtin, Mikhail, 138
    Problems of Dostoyevsky's Poetics (1929), 138
Balkans/Balkanic, 65
Balzac, Honoré de, 25
Bambič, Milko, 73

© The Editor(s) (if applicable) and The Author(s), under exclusive
license to Springer Nature Switzerland AG 2024
K. Pizzi and R. Gefter Wondrich (eds.), *Rethinking Peripheral
Modernisms*, https://doi.org/10.1007/978-3-031-35546-2

194   INDEX

Barrows, Adam, 16, 17
Barthes, Roland, 52
Baudelaire, Charles, 47, 48, 50, 51, 53
Beckett, Samuel, 15
Beebe, Maurice, 43, 50
Benjamin, Walter, 48, 49, 52, 133
Berger, John, 22
    Pig Earth, 22
Berlin, 63
Berman, Jessica, 19
Berman, Marshall, 24, 85
Bhabha, Homi, 23, 68
Blake, William, 52
Blanco, Carlos, 46, 50
Bloch, Ernst, 20
Bloom, Harold, 52
Bloom, Leopold (and Molly), 78, 79, 81, 83, 86–88
Bloomusalem, 87, 88, 94, 96
Bradbury, Malcom, 62
Brathwaite, Kamau, 100
Brazil, 16, 18, 28, 53, 143, 144, 147–149, 151, 154, 156
Brazilwood, 156, 157
Brecht, Bertoldt, 32, 133
Brennan, Timothy, 27, 28, 30, 37
Briggs, Austin, 94
Bruns, Gerald, 50, 52
Buñuel, Luis, 35

C
Caeiro, Alberto, 56
Campos, Augusto de, 55, 56
Cannibalist, 158–160
Capitalism/capitalist, 21–26, 29, 31, 33–35, 46, 48, 62, 63, 68, 75
Čargo, Ivan, 73
Caribbean, 19, 27
Carmelich, Giorgio, 74
Carpentier, Alejo, 27, 28

Carter, David, 103, 104
Celtic Revival, 81, 91
Cendrars, 149
centre/periphery, 45, 46, 49, 62
Černigoj, Avgust, 73
China, 16, 18, 21
"Circe" civilization, 80, 87, 88, 96
Cleary, Joe, 16
Clifford, James, 63
Cold War, 72
colonial, 62, 63, 68
Colonialism, 48
Competition for the Iranian Academies, 179–183
Concrete (Poetry), 160
Conrad, Joseph, 17
Constructivism/constructivist, 73, 74, 121, 138
contemporary, the, 51, 52
Cooper, Melinda, 104, 111, 112, 115, 118
cosmopolitan, 45
Crane, Hart, 45, 53
Critical Regionalism, 164, 169, 184, 188–190
Croatia/croatian, 66, 67
Crusoe, Robinson, 94
Cubism, 122, 141, 150, 154
Curcio, Carlo, 72

D
D'Annunzio, Gabriele, 69, 70
Dark, Eleanor
    A Timeless Land, 111
    Prelude to Christopher, 111
    Return to Coolami, 111
    Slow Dawning, 111
    Sun Across the Sky, 111, 112, 114
    Waterway, 111–113, 115, 118
de Barros Baptista, Abel, 56
Deckard, Sharae, 29

INDEX 195

Dedalus, Stephen, 93, 97
Deleuze, Gilles, 43
Depero, Fortunato, 63
Derrida, Jacques, 47
Diba, Darab, 180, 182, 183, 185
Diba, Kamran, 175, 185
Dickens, Charles, 25, 26
Dickinson, Emily, 47, 55
Dostoevsky, Fyodor, 26
Doyle, Laura, 19, 20, 62, 100
Dublin, 78
Duchamp, Marcel, 64
Dussel, Enrique, 23
dwelling, 91, 92, 95

E

eclecticism, 94, 95
Edwards, Brent, 34
Eisenstein, Sergei, 130
   The General Line (1929), 130
Eliot, Thomas S., 19, 100, 108
Enlightenment
   post-Enlightenment, 48, 49
Entangled bank, 115
Esenin, Sergey, 131
Esty, Jed, 17, 24
ethnic, 65–67, 70, 74–76
Eurocentric, 23
Europe/European, 64, 67, 68, 72,
   73, 75
Everdell, William, 17, 18

F

Factography, 133–135
Fascism/fascist, 71
Finch, Jason, 78
'first world', 19
First World War, 64–66, 70
Florence, 67, 69, 70
Flowerville, 80, 85–89, 91, 92, 94–98
Foster, John Wilson, 80, 81

Frampton, Kenneth, 164, 184, 189
Franklin, Miles, 109
Freudian, 54
Friedman, Susan Stanford, 20
Futurism/futurists, 16, 56, 73, 74,
   121–124, 138, 141, 145, 148
   Futurist *soirée*, 70, 74

G

Gaelic, 84, 97
Gaonkar, Dilip Parameshawar, 101
Gauss, Carl Friedrich, 128
Geography, 121, 124, 125, 128–130,
   132–138
Geopolitics, 121
Germany, 16
Gibson, Andrew, 82–84, 93
Giotti, Virgilio, 70
Gleizes, 149
Glissant, Édouard, 27
globalization, 48, 75
Gough, Maria, 136, 137
Gramsci, Antonio, 22, 67, 72, 75, 76
Gris, 149

H

Habsburg Empire, 62
Haji-Qassemi, Kambiz, 186
Hallucinated, 144, 146, 148
Hallucinism, 148
Harazim, Gemma, 70
Harlem Renaissance, 16, 18, 19
Harootunian, Harry, 23, 46, 48, 57
Harris, Wilson, 27
Hayot, Eric, 17
Heath, Stephen, 30
Hechter, Michael, 80
hegemony/hegemonic, 45, 49
Hegglund, Jon, 83, 85, 98
Heseltine, H.P., 104
Heterogeneity, 142, 161

196   INDEX

Heterogeneous, 161
high modernism, 101, 111
history, 51
Hitler, Adolf, 49
Hölderlin, Friedrich, 55
Homer/homeric, 82
Honar-vaMe'mari ('Art and
    Architecture') journal, 166
Hughes, Langston, 45
Huyssen, Andreas, 20, 44, 46
hybrid/hybridize, 61, 71, 76
Hybridity, 160

I
Ibsen, Henrik, 69
Imperial/imperial archive, 83, 85
India, 18, 19
International Congress of Architects,
    Isfahan Iran, 1970, 165
Iranian Centre for Management
    Studies, 171
Ireland, 15, 16, 19, 77, 78, 80–82,
    84, 87, 93, 97, 98
Irish, 81, 84, 91, 92, 94
Islamic Revolution, 163, 165, 169,
    174, 191
Italianness/italianità, 67, 73
Italy/Italian, 64–70, 72
"Ithaca", 80–85, 88, 93, 97, 98

J
Jameson, Fredric, 22, 24, 27, 28, 34,
    62, 63, 86, 100, 138
Japan, 16, 21
'journey in', 105
'Journey out', 100, 111
Joyce, James, 15, 17, 19, 25, 65–68,
    77, 87–89, 97
Jünger, Ernst, 49

K
Kafka, Franz, 15, 25, 54, 55
Kalantari, Iraj, 183, 186, 187
Karst/Carso, 70
Kent, Buddy, 31
Kermode, Frank, 49, 62
Kern, Stephen, 63
Khlebnikov, Velimir
    Roar about the Railroads (1913),
      124, 125
    Swanland of the Future (1918),
      129
    The Teacher and the Pupil (1912),
      127
    The Trumpet of the Martians
      (1916), 128
Khomeini, Ayatollah Ruhollah, 176
Kipling, Rudyard, 17
Kohlman, Benjamin, 79, 87, 98
Konsi, 73, 74
Kosovel, Srečko, 69, 72–75
Kruchenykh, Aleksei, 123
Kupinse, William J., 89

L
Landy, Marcia, 35
Lang, Anouk, 101, 102
Lapkina, Marfa, 131
Larsen, Neil, 21
Lawrence, Nicholas, 29
Lazarus, Neil, 29
Lears, Jackson, 45
Lefevre, Liane, 164. *See also* Tzonis,
    Alexander
Léger, 149, 151, 154
Lentricchia, Frank, 45
Leopardi, Giacomo, 69
Levin, Harry, 43, 47
Lhote, 149, 154
Liminality/liminal, 75
Lisbon Liska, Vivian de, 56

INDEX

Lobachevsky, Nikolai, 128
London, 105, 106
Löwy, Michael, 26
Lubljana, 67, 73
Lukács, György, 25, 26
Lye, Colleen, 24
Lynn, Thomas J., 34

M

Machado de Assis, Joaquim, 28
  *The Posthumous Memoirs of Brás
    Cubas*, 28
Mahaffey, Vicki, 18
Maiangwa, Yusufu, 29
Malfatti, Anita, 149
Malkin, Irad, 82
Man, Paul, 51
Mao, Douglas, 18
Marin, Biagio, 70
Marinetti, Filippo Tommaso, 63, 70,
  71, 74, 122, 145
Martin, Gerald, 28
Marxist, 25, 54
materialist, 80, 82–84, 89, 92
Mazzuchelli, David, 57
McFarlane, James, 62
McLeod, John, 105, 106
Mediterranean, 65
Messier, Vartan, 34
metrocolonialism, 78
"metropolitan shuttle", 93
Mexico, 16, 53
Michelstaedter, Carlo, 70
Middle Passage, 55
migration/migratory, 61
Miletti, Vladimiro, 71
Mirijam (aka Fanica Obid), 72
Mirmiran, Seyyed Hadi, 180,
  182–184
Mishra, Vijay, 99
Mitchell, Timothy, 20

Modern Art Week, 143, 149
Modernisation, 82, 84, 141,
  143–145, 147, 154
Modernism(s)/modernist(s)/
  modernity, 15–28, 43–52, 55,
  61–65, 68, 70, 73–75, 99,
  141–143, 148, 156, 157,
  159–161
Modjeska, Drusilla, 104, 112, 115
Montgolfier brothers, 128
Moore, Marianne, 45
Moretti, Franco, 16, 30
Mulvey, Laura, 33
Murphy, David, 32
Musil, Robert, 15
Mussolini, Benito, 71

N

nation, 62, 64, 65, 68, 69, 73
National Academies competition,
  1991, 166
Nativism, 190
Négritude, 31
New York, 62, 63
Nezahualcoyotl, 53
Nicholls, Peter, 18
Nietzsche, Friedrich, 51, 52
Nolan, Emer, 84, 85
nostos/i, 82, 86

O

Odradek, 54, 55, 57
Odyssey, 82
Ogundokun, Sikiri, 34
Orientalism, 79
Osborne, Peter, 24
Osteen, Mark, 93, 96
Ouologuem, Yambo, 29
  Bound to Violence, 29

198 INDEX

P
pacific, 16
Pahlavi, Shahbanu Farah (Diba), 167
Painting(s), 149, 151, 152, 154
Pannaggi, Ivo, 63, 64
Paris, 63, 67
Parnet, Claire, 43
parody, 84, 94, 95, 98
Parrinder, Patrick, 88, 94, 97
Parry, Benita, 46, 48, 62, 68, 77
Paulicéia Desvairada, 144, 147, 148, 156
peripheral modernity, 81
Periphery/peripheral/peripherality, 46, 47, 62–65, 67–69, 72–79, 83, 142, 143, 146, 148, 160, 161
Peru, 54
Pessoa, Fernando (aka Alvaro de Campos), 16, 53, 56, 57
Petrarch, 69
Philip, NourbeSe M., 55
Philippines, 18
Picabia, Francis, 64
Picchia, Menotti del, 149
Pilon, Veno, 73
Pizzi, Katia, 64, 66, 67, 71, 72, 74
Planetary modernisms, 101
Poetry, 144, 156, 157
Pola/pula, 65
Pollard, Charles W., 100
Portugal/portuguese, 53, 56
postcolonial, 62
Post-colonialism, 99
Post-modernism, 184
Postmodernity/postmodern, 48
Pound, Eszra, 19
Prague, 78
Prampolini, Enrico, 63
Prendergast, Christopher, 30
Priestley, J.B., 16

primitivism queer, 47
Pryse, Majorie, 63

Q
Quigley, Megan, 81

R
Rabaté, Jean-Michel, 17
Ramalho-Santos, Maria-Irene, 54, 56
Realism/realist, 25, 26, 28, 29, 36
Reis, Ricardo, 56
Revenant modernism, 111
Ribeiro, António Sousa, 45, 54
Richard, Thomas, 85
Rider Haggard, Henry, 17
Rimbaud, Arthur, 50, 51
Romanticism/romantic, 70
Rooney, Brigid, 117, 118
Rosa, João Guimarães, 53

S
Samela, Markku, 78
Sanzin, Bruno Giordano, 71, 74
São Paulo, 143, 144, 146–148, 150, 151, 155
Saremi, Ali Akbar, 180, 183–185
Sarlo, Beatriz, 46
Schlegel, Friedrich, 52, 56
Schmidt, Carl, 49
Schwarz, Roberto, 28, 29
Sembène, Ousmane, 32, 33
    God's Bits of Wood, 32, 35
    Xala, 31–36
Senegal, 31
Serequeberhan, Tsenay, 23
Settler modernism, 118
Seyhoun, Houshang, 175, 180, 182
Sheikh Zeineddin, Hossein, 180
Silva, Patricia, xii, xviii

Silvestre, Osvaldo Manuel, 56
'singular modernity', 63
Slataper, Scipio, 68–70, 72, 73, 75
Slovenia/slovenian, 64, 66–69, 72–75
Soares, Bernardo, 53, 56, 57
Socialism/socialist, 73
Sorensen, Eli Park, 34
South Africa, 17
South America, 156
Soviet, 73
Spain, 16, 19
Spaini, Alberto, 70
"spatial complexity", 79, 86
Spivak, Gayatri Chakravorty, 72
Spurr, David, 95
Stalin, Josif, 121, 130
Stanford Friedman, Susan, 44, 101
Stead, Christina, 99, 104–109, 111, 116
    Seven Poor Men of Sydney, 106, 108
Stein, Gertrude, 45, 53
Stevens, Wallace, 45, 49, 53
Stoker, Bram, 17
St Petersburg, 18
'striking back', 100
Stuparich, Giani, 68–70, 72, 73
Sturm und Drang, 69, 70
Suez, 66
Svevo, Italo (aka Ettore Schmitz), 65, 67, 68
Sydney, 99, 106, 107, 109, 111, 113

T
Tatlin, Vladimir, 16
Temporality/ies, 17, 23
Thompson, Mark, 65
tradition, 45, 54
Transcultural, 142, 161
Transculturalism, 142
Transculturation, 160
transnational, 45

Tretyakov, Sergei
    operativism, 135, 136
    Through Unwiped Glasses (1928), 134
Trieste, 64–67, 69–71, 73, 74, 76
Triestinness/triestinità, 67
triestino dialect, 66
Trinko, Ivan, 72
Tropicália, 160
Trotsky, Leon, 138
Tzonis, Alexander, 164. *See also* Lefevre, Liane

U
Ulysses, 77, 79, 81, 82, 86, 93, 98
United States, 16, 18, 19, 22
Upward, Edward, 16
Urban, 79, 83, 84, 86, 88, 91–93, 95, 98
Utopianism, 79, 87, 88

V
Valente, Joseph, 78
Vallejo, César, 54, 55
Vasari, Ruggero, 63
Verhaeren, Émile, 144
Vienna, 17, 67
Virginia Woolf, 117

W
Wadia, Lily-Amber Laila, 75, 76
Walcott, Derek, 100
Walkowitz, Rebecca, 18
Wallerstein, Immanuel, 46, 47, 50
Ward, Kiron, 89
White Revolution, 165, 167
Wicht, Wolfgang, 86, 87, 91
Widdis, Emma, 122, 133
Williams, J.F., 102, 103
    Quarantined Culture, 102

200 INDEX

Williams, Raymond, 16, 46
Williams, William Carlos, 45
Winkiel, Laura, 62, 100
Wood, Paul, 18
Woolf, 17
Worldmaking, 176, 191
world-system, 16, 21, 24
Wright, Gwendolyn, 20

Y
Yeats, William Butler, 81

Z
"zaum" poetry, 123, 124